The Whole Library Handbook

Handbook

Teen Services

Edited by HEATHER BOOTH and KAREN JENSEN

D0911951

ala
editions

AN IMPRINT OF THE AMERICAN LIBRARY ASSOCIATION

CHICAGO   2014

Heather Booth is committed to serving the dynamic needs and interests of young people in a community setting. She has been a teen services librarian in the Chicago suburbs since 2002, currently at the Thomas Ford Memorial Library in Western Springs, Illinois. She is the author of *Serving Teens through Readers' Advisory* (ALA Editions, 2007) and several chapters on readers' advisory for teens in other professional works. She reviews books for youth and audiobooks for *Booklist*. Her article "RA for YA" won the feature article award from *Public Libraries* in 2006. She holds a B.A. from Kalamazoo College in southwest Michigan and her MLS from the Graduate School of Library and Information Sciences at the University of Illinois at Urbana-Champaign.

Karen Jensen has worked with teens since 1993. She holds a degree in Christian education/youth ministry from Mount Vernon College and earned her MLS from Kent State University. She is currently a teen services librarian in Grand Prairie, Texas, where she is especially focused on using the "40 Developmental Assets for Adolescents" to advocate for teens in her library and community. She is the author of several articles in *VOYA* and wrote a chapter in *Intellectual Freedom for Teens: A Practical Guide for YA and School Librarians* (ALA Editions, 2014) by Kristin Fletcher-Spear and Kelly Tyler. She is the creator and moderator of Teen Librarian Toolbox, where she blogs about pop culture, librarianship, and books (at www.teenlibrariantoolbox.com). She was named one of *Library Journal*'s 2014 Movers and Shakers.

Library of Congress Cataloging-in-Publication Data
The whole library handbook : teen services / edited by Heather Booth and Karen Jensen.
    pages   cm
    Includes bibliographical references and index.
    ISBN 978-0-8389-1224-9 (alk. paper)
    1. Young adults' libraries—Administration. 2. Young adults' libraries—United States—Administration. 3. Libraries and teenagers. 4. Young adult services librarians. I. Booth, Heather, 1978– editor of compilation. II. Jensen, Karen, 1972– editor of compilation.
Z675.5.W48 2014
025.1'97626—dc23   2014004303

Cover design by Krista Joy Johnson. Composition by Priority Publishing in the Adobe Caslon Pro, Panache Black, and Helvetica Narrow typefaces. Selected artwork from ClipArt.com.

This paper meets the requirements of ANSI/NISO Z39.48-1992 (Permanence of Paper).

Printed in the United States of America

18   17   16   15   14   5   4   3   2   1

Dedication

For Julia and Thora. You've been more patient with me than any parent should expect, and I love you more than you can imagine. Now, let's go play.

—HB

To my family. It is because of your sacrifices that I was able to write this, and I dedicate it to you with all my heart.

—KJ

Contents

7 INVOLVEMENT

8 ISSUES

APPENDICES

Acknowledgments

From Heather

This book would not exist were it not for the wonderful contributions of the librarians and authors who have shared their words and thoughts on this broad and wonderful topic. We deeply appreciate your involvement and the gift of your knowledge and wisdom that you have shared not just with us, the authors, but with the readership of the book. Every one of the contributions was crafted with care and a great understanding of the subject matter. We are so grateful that you have shared your talents with us, and it was an honor to work with each of you.

We would also like to thank YALSA—a unifying force among teen librarians. Many of the contributors to this book are YALSA members, and our appreciation for the service, leadership, and support this organization gives us is great and genuine. A portion of the royalties from the sale of this book will benefit YALSA.

I was first approached by Stef Zvirin to write and compile this book in 2008, not too long after my first book, *Serving Teens through Readers' Advisory* was published. At the time, I also had a young child, a new job, and enough YALSA committee involvement to keep me on my toes. I put it off until I finally felt ready to tackle it, and Stef patiently waited for the completed proposal until the summer of 2009. I would like to thank Stef for her confidence that I was the right person for the project, even in light of the many delays it has suffered, and for her patience and understanding as I followed this path, and to thank our current editor, Jamie Santoro, for shepherding the project through to its completion.

Life doesn't always move in the direction and timetable we anticipate, and when I found myself with this unfinished project and another new baby, Stef still believed in me and trusted my judgment in bringing Karen Jensen onto the project. When I discovered Karen's professional-development website, Teen Librarian Toolbox, I knew I'd found a kindred spirit. Karen joined *The Whole Library Handbook: Teen Services* project at my urging and to my great relief and brought with her a wealth of experience and a strong voice, which I hope readers will find to be confidence-instilling and collegial. I need to thank Karen for her outstanding contributions, friendship, support, and encouragement. This book very well may have crumbled without your enthusiasm, energy, ideas, and camaraderie, and it has been an honor to work with you. Thank you so very much.

Finally, I would also like to acknowledge the support and encouragement of my family and friends, in particular everyone who watched and entertained the girls while I wrote and edited; the patience and tolerance of my daughters, who would've much rather spent way more time at the park than I was able to give them; but most of all, my husband, Paul, who put up with more than his share of yard work, dinners, moodiness, and child care at the crunch times during the creation of this book. I couldn't do it without you, and I love you very much, even when I'm stuck on the couch with a laptop and a scowl.

From Karen

When Heather Booth first contacted me and asked me to write a book with her, I didn't realize that I wanted to write a book. It turns out, I really, really did, and I am incredibly thankful to Heather for the opportunity not only to write this book, but for the great conversations about our profession that we had along the way and for the deeply satisfying friendship we formed in the process. She put in a tremendous amount of time cleaning up my duplications, excessive use of commas, and more. Heather is a rock star to write with, and her teens are very blessed to have her as their librarian.

This book would also not exist if it were not for the contributions of all the other librarians who said yes when we contacted them and asked them to write a piece on some of the topics that we knew they were better writers on than ourselves. They graciously took the time to share their experience and passion to help make sure that we all knew and understood the topics they loved so that teens would receive the quality services that they so richly deserve and desperately need. I am thankful to each and every one of you for answering the call.

My journey as a librarian began sitting Monday mornings in an office talking with an amazing reference librarian named Mary McGavick about the TV show *The X-Files*, and sometimes about librarianship. She became my mentor, and then she became my beloved friend. Every step of the way, she has been there on my journey as a librarian, and who I am today as a librarian is thanks in no small part to her. This book would not be written today if she had not taught me everything she knew, allowed me to disagree with some of it, and answered the phone for 20 years when I had questions to ask, fun stories to share, and tears to shed.

The best part of being a teen services librarian is getting to share this journey with my fellow librarians and the teens who I have been blessed to serve. Each and every one of them have helped me do my small part to make this world a better place, to learn, to grow, and to remember not only what it is to be a teen, but how to embrace every moment—and every person—you encounter in life. I thank them all for the friendship and camaraderie. I have to give special thanks to Sam Norris and to Christie Ross Gibrich for being the best friend and the best fiend, respectively, I could ever dare to ask for.

I would also like to extend heartfelt thanks to all my friends and family who have shared this journey with me. I could not have done it without your support.

When we moved for my husband Tim's job in 2011, I desperately feared whether I would be able to find another satisfying job as a teen librarian, which I feel is my life's calling. Heather presented me with this opportunity at a time when I really needed it, and my husband and my family made tremendous sacrifices so that I had the time to research, write, and sometimes rewrite this book. There were nights when the family watched our favorite TV shows without me; when my husband took the kids to Chuck E. Cheese's (alone; the horror!) so I could have a quiet time and place to write; and when we made last-minute changes to plans so I could meet a deadline or take a call related to this project. My husband and two children are amazing in every way, and I thank them for this opportunity. I hope one day my beloved girls will look at this book and think to themselves, "My mom wrote a book, and that means I can dream big and achieve it." It is because of your sacrifices that I was able to write this, and I dedicate it to you with all my heart.

Preface

IN 1991, the first edition of *The Whole Library Handbook* was compiled by George M. Eberhart. Now, more than two decades later, this prize of librarianship has entered its fifth edition, and much has changed. One notable area that has undergone much growth is spaces, collections, and librarians for teens. We hope that *The Whole Library Handbook: Teen Services* is able to fill in some gaps, start some conversations, and ignite some interest in what we consider to be the best job, with the best clientele in the library world.

This book is divided into eight chapters. We begin in Chapter 1 by getting to know our bosses—the teens. Without a good understanding of who we are working for, our best intentions will fall short and our services will never be as successful as they could be.

In Chapter 2, we turn a similarly critical eye on ourselves. We examine the markers for ideal conduct for teen librarians, deal with special circumstances that teen librarians encounter, and discuss how to set a teen librarian up for success.

Chapters 3 and 4 discuss services and programs for teens, respectively. Although it may seem that these belong joined in one section, we explain that teen services encompass much more than after-school programs, and programs are a crucial part of any teen services plan.

Moving on to Chapter 5, we address what many think of first when they think of teen services—the collection.

Chapter 6 addresses an important topic that most of us will only learn on the job—and only then if we are lucky. Marketing services to teens is different than marketing library services to adults, and given the structure of many libraries, it is often left up to the sole discretion of the teen librarian.

In Chapter 7 we return to teens, examining what positive, productive teen involvement looks like in the library setting.

And, finally, in Chapter 8, several of the hot-button issues in teen librarianship are discussed.

In many ways, this is a book that will never be complete. Every day, another teen librarian has a brilliant idea, an innovative way of approaching teen services, a shining example of service, a clever use of new resources and technologies, or a new take on an old topic. Every day, new advancements make certain aspects of our jobs less relevant, yet many of these same advancements make aspects of our jobs more exciting and challenging. In light of these changes, we hope that the articles collected here paint a descriptive picture of teen services as they are now, with respect to the past and an eye to how things could be in the future.

Heather Booth
Western Springs, Illinois

WHO ARE TEENS?

CHAPTER ONE

Despite its title, this book begins, not with the whole library, but with the whole teen. Before we can move into the Teen Services portion, we really need to consider who we are doing all this for and how the forces acting on teens—their physiological and social development, societal position, and the culture that surrounds them—work to mold these interesting people into the library patrons that we have chosen to work for and with.

It's not uncommon for a new hire or the younger of the librarians on staff to be assigned the task of working with teens in the absence of a structured teen services department or position. But it's folly to believe that the librarian who is still wearing her jeans from college or driving the car he got after high school graduation is always the best choice to work with teens.

We are adults, all of us. We all need to work to acquaint ourselves with the teens in our community and then reacquaint ourselves with the new crop of teens every few years. A teen generation flashes by in the blink of an eye, and what you knew about teens and their culture when you were one—even if it was only a few years ago—has undoubtedly changed. This constant change is part of what makes working with teenagers so challenging—and interesting!

Defining the local teen community

by Heather Booth

IF WE ARE TEEN SERVICES LIBRARIANS, just who are the people we serve? It's not a rhetorical question—the defined group is going to vary depending on the community, and knowing the community in which we work is critical for forming strong programs and services that meet the specific needs of our young patrons. Striking a balance between local and global interests is easier once the community needs are understood. Here are some questions to consider while defining your demographic and structuring your services.

How does the school district, park district, or other community organization divide grades and ages? Knowing how a community defines *teenager* is helpful to a library as it breaks services into age groups, collects age-appropriate material together, and assigns service desks and staff in the right numbers and at the right desks. A community where elementary school ends with 5th grade may define *teen* as slightly younger than those with junior high beginning at 7th grade. One will likely see this reflected in libraries in the difference between juvenile and teen materials.

To assess this, also weigh the following: Are sports leagues splitting kids between 11 and 12, or between 12 and 13? At what age does the park district permit teens to rent a racquetball court or come to teen programs? How are teens in your community accustomed to being grouped together? Consider how this will impact the upper end of your collection as well as how you might dovetail services on the younger end with children's services at your library.

Does the community have many older teens and younger adults? It's commonly acknowledged that teens don't limit their reading to what the publishing world considers YA and that teens are eager and willing to read the right adult-market book, not to mention the burgeoning "New Adult" designation. Knowing what the older teen population is like in a community will lead to improved services, such as collecting paperbacks of adult-market books, creating displays for New Adult titles, or adding books with older YA interest to lists and pathfinders. The information needs of older teens are distinct as well. As schools are increasingly focusing on academic skills and testing, many of the courses that taught young people the basic skills of adulthood, like balancing a checkbook, writing a résumé, or cooking basic meals, have fallen away. Consider whether the public library can fill the gap in circumstances such as these.

Do the majority of graduates move away to colleges or careers outside of the community? How many older teens have dropped out and no longer have access to a school library at all? Is a community college, university, trade school, or the job market an incentive for students to stay at home after high school or for young adults to move into the community? Who is serving recent high school graduates? Although the conventional wisdom dictates that people will frequently abandon the library between school and parenthood, this need not be the case if a teen program attempts to bridge the transition to adulthood, and there are services on the other end in the adult department to catch new arrivals.

How are young people served by libraries in their schools? As school libraries and school librarians suffer in difficult economic times, the community library

1

can be an important resource if it knows the gaps it needs to fill. Additionally, the local library can be an attractive study destination for commuter students working toward degrees if the library has enough of the right resources. Although even the best-equipped public libraries are no replacement for well-stocked and well-staffed school libraries, any opportunity to help students is a good one, and a teen services department that is aware of the needs and is poised to address them will go a long way in serving its students.

What are the prevailing community sensibilities and issues involving teens and young people? Public libraries are *community* spaces. Collections and spaces are not the librarian's, nor are they the library's. They belong to the community members collectively, and, as such, the sensibilities of the community should, to a certain extent, be reflected in the services and collections. This is not to say that "majority rules," and a public library should be beholden to one viewpoint to the exclusion of others. Rather, the needs and interests of a local community must be considered and balanced with those of the global community when structuring and executing services. Are specific religious groups widely represented? Are many residents recent immigrants? What are the languages most spoken in the home? Are there many teen parents? What issues are local teens facing (parental layoffs, crime, gentrification, environmental changes, academic pressure, etc.)? What is the racial and ethnic diversity of the population? What local groups might make use of teen services at the library? Scouts? 4-H? Confirmands? Job seekers? GED test takers? Homeschoolers? Do most households have computers and internet access? At what age do local teens begin appearing with cell phones? Laptops? E-readers? Knowing who the teens are and what their needs and interests are will help direct the scope and depth of various areas of the collection and services.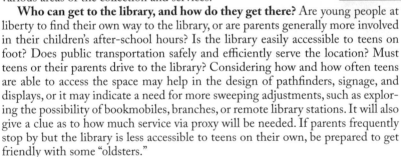

Who can get to the library, and how do they get there? Are young people at liberty to find their own way to the library, or are parents generally more involved in their children's after-school hours? Is the library easily accessible to teens on foot? Does public transportation safely and efficiently serve the location? Must teens or their parents drive to the library? Considering how and how often teens are able to access the space may help in the design of pathfinders, signage, and displays, or it may indicate a need for more sweeping adjustments, such as exploring the possibility of bookmobiles, branches, or remote library stations. It will also give a clue as to how much service via proxy will be needed. If parents frequently stop by but the library is less accessible to teens on their own, be prepared to get friendly with some "oldsters."

These questions are only some of the many that we ask while attempting to know our communities. For a librarian who was once a teen in the same hometown in which he or she works, the answers may come more quickly than for one who is a recent transplant across the country, but even if we once knew the community, we need to continually refresh our knowledge. A teen generation is a short one, and the influences that make big waves one year could leave barely a ripple five years later. As our communities change, we best serve them by being abreast of the changes—anticipating them when possible—and responding. Librarians are in the business of receiving questions and giving answers, but when it comes to knowing our teens, the tables must turn. The more questions we ask, the better we are doing our jobs.

SOURCE: Specially prepared for *The Whole Library Handbook: Teen Services* by Heather Booth, teen services librarian, Thomas Ford Memorial Library, Western Springs, Illinois.

What's hot, what's so yesterday, and how to keep up

by Heather Booth

RECENTLY I WAS DRIVING with a teenage cousin. I turned on some music I had bought a few years earlier—new music instead of the *old* stuff that I still listen to from my own teen years. I applauded myself at being a hip young role model for my cousin, still with-it enough that she could relate to me, so unlike her parents and teachers. As we sailed down the highway and the next song came on, the 15-year-old next to me laughed and exclaimed, "Oh! I love this song! I remember listening to it at my babysitter's house *when I was a kid!*" My heart sank. When she was a kid? How old was this song? How old was *I?*

Time moves faster as we age; and as we grow comfortable with our personal tastes, it's easy to forget how much new culture is being created and consumed constantly by the teens we work with. As those who have ever been assigned a collection development area they were not personally fond of can attest, you don't have to love it to do it well, but you do have to know it in the first place. If your personal taste trends more classic or retro than current, you may need to plan a pop-culture education into your week, just like you would update yourself on what this week's bestsellers are or what is happening in the news. Make a plan and a schedule for yourself, and soon the world of pop culture won't seem as daunting or foreign as it might now. Here are some resources to help teen librarians stay abreast of current trends and cultural touchpoints that are important to the teens we work with.

New Zealand pop singer Lorde performing in 2014. Photo by Annette Geneva, used CC BY-SA 3.0.

VOYA "Teen Pop Culture Quiz"

Published online (www.voyamagazine.com) bimonthly, the "Teen Pop Culture Quiz" is a quick-and-easy way to pinpoint your teen pop-culture savvy . . . or failings. It addresses contemporary issues, music, movies, and more, and even if you fail the quiz, you'll be exposed to some names, trends, and concepts that teens are talking about and that are worth knowing.

Watch some TV

You don't need to watch a lot of TV—but try to catch the CW show you overhear teens dishing about, pop over to Hulu or Netflix to see what is new instead of checking Facebook some afternoon, or use snark to your benefit and watch shows like *The Soup, Tosh.0,* or *TMZ on TV,* and get a tongue-in-cheek perspective on media; then go back and figure out what they're talking about if you don't know who any of the people are.

Weekly rags

Us Weekly, People, and *Entertainment Weekly* are just long enough to pack in a lot of useful tidbits and just short enough to breeze through on a lunch break or bus ride home. Remember: If you don't recognize the people on the cover, that's all the more reason to pick it up and find out why.

Surf

Find blogs or news aggregators with a tone you enjoy, and keep up with them, at least weekly. If it's happening anywhere, someone is talking about it online. Follow celebrities and trend makers on Twitter, Instagram, or Tumblr. Read teen-created content like *Rookie* (www.rookiemag.com); read what your teens are reading.

Apps

Load some apps on your mobile device with an eye to what is happening and what is about to happen. *Billboard, People,* MTV, *The Soup, Entertainment Weekly,* and iTunes movie trailers are all accessible via apps, and they can be browsed as a matter of your morning routine or while you're waiting for your lunch to heat up in the staff lounge. Additionally, keep attuned to new apps that teens may be using to connect with one another and that you might be able to employ in marketing or programming efforts. The YALSAblog (yalsa.ala.org/blog/) frequently posts updates on new apps and features an "App of the Week" column.

Podcasts and radio

Catch up on your commute by tuning in to pop-culture podcasts like NPR's *Pop Culture Happy Hour* or *A.V. Talk* from the *Onion*'s A.V. Club. Or tune in to top-40 radio instead of your usual station and get an earful of what your teens are singing along to this week.

Listen

You don't need to call it eavesdropping if it's for your professional edification! Listen to what the teens are talking about in programs, while lounging in your teen spaces or while waiting for a computer. This is important for two reasons. First, you'll know if they need help, aren't finding the book they need, or are involved in something that you need to intervene with. Second, you can get a straight-from-the-horse's-mouth idea of what interests local teens.

South Korean girl group After School. Photo by Kiyoung Kim used CC BY-SA 3.0.

Keeping your focus on your teens will also help hone your pop-culture education. If anime has been done to death and your local teens have moved on to something else, it's handy to know that before delving too deeply into the creation of an anime club, even if that's what it seems everyone else is talking about doing. Just like your collection will reflect local taste and interest, so should your pop-culture offerings.

It would be a well-educated librarian indeed that used all of the above tools on a daily basis, but most people will only need to find what appeals to them, set a method for regular updates, and will be on their way to feeling more connected to teens and their culture and more aware of what is happening in the pop-culture arena. Fortunately, pop culture is inclusive of so many subcultures that there will be something to appeal to nearly everyone. Find what you enjoy and learn more about it. Specializing while staying abreast of the big picture will give you an "in" with local teens who share your new passion.

SOURCE: Specially prepared for *The Whole Library Handbook: Teen Services* by Heather Booth, teen services librarian, Thomas Ford Memorial Library, Western Springs, Illinois.

Fast facts for librarians about the teenage brain

by Heather Booth

WE CANNOT EFFECTIVELY create library environments and structures to support teenagers without understanding how their brains work. The differences in teen brain function do not mean that they are deficient; rather, their needs are unique to their age. If we strive to celebrate and work with these qualities rather than trying to force teens into molds better suited to those older or younger, everyone's experience can improve. The library world is far from alone in recognizing the importance of teen brain development. Research on the subject has increased significantly in recent years, and even the Supreme Court of the United States has taken teen brain research into account on major decisions, impacting social policy and leading to a greater understanding of these people who may look like adults from the outside but are very different inside.

For example, in 2010, teen brain development was discussed during the oral arguments in two cases: *Roper v. Simmons*, which abolished the death penalty for juvenile offenders, and *Graham v. Florida*, which prohibited life imprisonment without parole for juvenile offenders, with the exception of murder convictions.

Controlling impulses and managing conflicting information in teens rely mainly on the prefrontal cortex more than the same functions do in the adult brain, which distributes the tasks throughout multiple parts of the brain. According to Laurence Steinberg in "Should the Science of Adolescent Brain Development Inform Public Policy?" *Issues in Science and Technology*, Spring 2012, this lack of distribution partially explains why the tasks are more difficult for teens.

Richard Monastersky writes that the teen brain is more positively responsive to novelty and new experiences than that of a child or an adult ("Who's Minding the Teenage Brain?" *Chronicle of Higher Education*, January 12, 2007).

Teens decipher facial expressions and interpret sarcasm in different parts of their brain than those an adult uses. Use of sarcasm in our conversations with teens or relying on facial expressions to convey our feelings can therefore lead to communication difficulties or misunderstandings. See Dave F. Brown, "The Significance of Congruent Communication in Effective Classroom Management," *Clearing House* 79 (September/October 2005): 13–14.

"Teenagers are far healthier and stronger than children in general, but the overall risk of suffering death, disease, or injury climbs 200% between childhood and late adolescence," Monastersky writes, "in large part because of dangerous behavior, such as drug abuse and unprotected sex." When approached this way, all of the teens who walk through or past the doors of the library, even the best-adjusted, best-supported, smartest, most logical teens, are part of an at-risk population.

Social and emotional functions develop earlier than cognitive and logic-based functions, which may play into the innately social nature of teens. Their group behavior is a normal developmental stage.

Between early and late adolescence, "synaptic pruning" reduces the amount of gray matter in a person's brain by eliminating connections that are unused. New research shows that if these connections are strengthened, a teen's verbal and nonverbal IQ, previously thought to be static, can increase between early and late adolescence. See Sue Ramsden, et al., "Verbal and Non-verbal Intelligence

Changes in the Teenage Brain," *Nature* 479 (2011): 113–116. When it comes to imprinting on the teen brain—with the usefulness of the library, with technological acumen, with love for words and an openness to literature, with information-seeking behavior—it is quite literally a use-it-or-lose-it situation.

Resources

Sheryl G. Feinstein. *Secrets of the Teenage Brain: Research Based Strategies for Reaching and Teaching Today's Adolescents.* Thousand Oaks, Calif.: Corwyn Press, 2nd ed., 2009.

Beth Gallaway. "Pain in the Brain: Teen Library (Mis)Behavior 101." California Library Association, 2008 Annual Conference. www.slideshare.net/informationgoddess29/pain-in-the-brain-teen-library-misbehavior-presentation.

"Inside the Teenage Brain." *Frontline*, January 31, 2002. to.pbs.org/1jJbb9u.

Valerie F. Reyna, et al. *The Adolescent Brain: Learning, Reasoning, and Decision Making.* Washington, D.C.: American Psychological Association, 2012.

SOURCE: Specially prepared for *The Whole Library Handbook: Teen Services* by Heather Booth, teen services librarian, Thomas Ford Memorial Library, Western Springs, Illinois.

Teen development:
The 40 Developmental Assets
by Karen Jensen and Heather Booth

OVER THE LAST FEW DECADES, the research on adolescent-brain development has grown tremendously. When we find ourselves asking, "What were you thinking?" we can take heart in knowing that teens really and truly do think differently than adults. But knowing the basics of adolescent development and the teenage brain are not enough. We need to be able to apply the physical-development piece to the real lives our teens are living. Fortunately, we have a great tool out there just waiting for all who serve teens to utilize: the 40 Developmental Assets (www.search-institute.org/content/40-developmental-assets-adolescents-ages-12-18). This tool enumerates specific qualities that successful teens have. Libraries that use the 40 Assets as they structure programs, services, and philosophies are employing research-based teen-development philosophies.

A brief history

The 40 Developmental Assets are a youth-development program put together and promoted by the Search Institute. Since 1990, the Search Institute, a nonprofit organization "devoted to discovering what children and adolescents need to succeed in their families, schools, and communities," has been using the findings from extensive research to help train organizations that serve youth in the assets to promote positive youth development. To date, more than 2.2 million youngsters have been studied, and the findings demonstrate time and time again that asset building is an important part of youth programming.

The concept behind the 40 Developmental Assets is simple enough. Research has shown that successful teens need to develop the 40 Assets that are outlined. These assets are qualities, both internal and external, that, when present, are more likely to lead to a supported, confident, knowledgeable, goal-oriented, successful teen, who will carry these skills over into his or her adulthood. The more assets teens have, the less likely they are to engage in risky behaviors, such as violence, unhealthy sexual activities, and drug use (though they will probably still like rock and roll). In contrast, research demonstrates that the fewer assets teens have, the more likely they will be to engage in risky behavior.

The 40 Assets distill the various elements that lead to success in adulthood into quantifiable elements that can be cultivated and nurtured during adolescence. Understanding adolescent development is key to serving teens effectively. Who are they? What makes them unique? Then we must take that information and turn it around: How do we take what we know about teens and use that information to serve them effectively?

Teens learn about media literacy at the San Jose (Calif.) Public Library. Photo by Darragh Worland.

This is where the 40 Assets are a teen librarian's best friend. For example, we know that teens tend to be very peer oriented, which means that we should give them opportunities to work together in groups. We can then refer to the assets to see that numbers 15 ("Positive Peer Influence"), and 18 ("Youth Programs") relate directly to this developmental element, and several other assets are tangentially related, such as 3 ("Other Adult Relationships") or 33 ("Interpersonal Confidence"). This means that when we put together library programs and market them, we want to make sure they have built-in opportunities for peer-group interaction and market that opportunity, and do so in the full understanding that these programs are meeting developmental needs that research-based science says will help teens succeed in life.

Assets inside and out

The assets are divided evenly into two lists of 20 assets each: internal and external assets. Internal assets are those values that come from within the teen, and external assets are those that come from the various outside forces in the lives of teens, including family, peers, and community.

Each list is divided into four subcategories that have five assets each. For example, the internal assets list is further divided into "Commitment to Learning," "Positive Values," "Social Competencies," and "Positive Identity." Then, for example, under "Positive Identity," there are more specific assets, such as "has a positive view of their future" and "has a sense of purpose." The external assets are further divided into "Support," "Empowerment," "Boundaries and Expectations," and "Constructive Use of Time." "Empowerment" includes attributes like "youth as resources," wherein teens are given valuable roles in the community, and "service to others." Elements of our teen services, such as teen advisory groups (TAGs) and teen volunteer opportunities, help teens develop these types of assets.

How to use the assets

We know that teens need to develop these 40 assets, so we should use them as a basis for planning and evaluating our teen services in our libraries. Print off the

A closer look at how libraries help teens build assets

Asset: Other Adult Relationships

Description: Young person receives support from three or more nonparent adults.
Library Connection:

- Library staff provides positive adult interaction to community teens and helps teenagers successfully navigate the library environment.
- Teens who regularly attend library programs develop a positive relationship with the teen services librarian.
- Through readers' advisory and informal book discussions, many regular teens develop a positive relationship with the teen services librarian.

Asset: Caring Neighborhood

Description: Young person experiences caring neighbors.
Library Connection:

- Library resources, especially those designed for teens, communicate that the library cares for teens in the community.

Asset: Community Values Youth

Description: Young person perceives that adults in the community value youth.
Library Connection:

- The library provides a developmentally appropriate teen program, including a special teen resource collection, that meets a variety of their needs and interests, which communicates value in the community.

Asset: Youth as Resources

Description: Young people are given useful roles in the community.
Library Connection:

- Through regular interaction with the teen services librarian, both formal and informal, teens give input into programming, services, and the collection. Teen advisory groups and teen volunteer programs are formal ways that libraries can help teens usefully interact.

Asset: Safety

Description: Young person feels safe at home, school, and in the neighborhood.
Library Connection:

- The library provides a developmentally appropriate, enjoyable environment for teens in their neighborhood.

Asset: Neighborhood Boundaries

Description: Neighbors take responsibility for monitoring young people's behavior.
Library Connection:

- The acceptable-behavior policy helps outline responsible behavior for teens in the library. When staff worry about appearing "mean" or "unfriendly" to teens for enforcing behavior policies, remember that doing so meets an asset and is one element of growing a successful adult.

Asset: Adult Role Models

Description: Parent(s) and other adults model positive, responsible behavior.
Library Connection:

- All library staff and the teen services librarian directly model positive, responsible behavior to teens in the community.

Asset: Creative Activities

Description: Young person spends three or more hours per week in lessons or practice in music, theater, or other arts.

A closer look at how libraries help teens build assets (continued)

Library Connection:
- The library's teen services programs provide a variety of opportunities for teens to be creative and engage in self-expression.

Asset: Youth Programs

Description: Young person spends three or more hours per week in sports, clubs, or organizations at school and/or in the community.
Library Connection:
- The library's teen services program offers a variety of programs that provide teens with opportunities to engage in developmentally appropriate programming.

Asset: School Engagement

Description: Young person is actively engaged in learning.
Library Connection:
- Libraries have essential resources for teens engaging in learning.

Asset: Homework

Description: Young person reports doing at least one hour of homework every school day.
Library Connection:
- Library resources are beneficial in the successful completion of homework.
- Teen spaces in libraries provide a comfortable, secure place in which to complete homework.

Asset: Reading for Pleasure

Description: Young person reads for pleasure three or more hours per week.
Library Connection:
- Library provides an extensive collection for teens' reading enjoyment.
- Library provides a variety of programs and events that encourage reading for pleasure.
- Readers' advisory services aid teens in locating reading material that they find pleasurable.
- Teen spaces provide a comfortable destination for pleasure reading.

The Asset Shortcut for Staff

In addition to the regular library programming that you do, remind staff that they can be positive adult role models to teens in the library and embody the assets:
- Smile at teens in your library.
- Learn the names of young people and greet them by name when they visit.
- Notice when teens are doing something right. Compliment them and encourage them to continue in that behavior.
- Ask teens to tell you about a good book they read recently.
- Set clear behavior expectations and enforce them consistently.
- Talk and act in ways you want teens to follow.

---

assets and keep them posted by your desk. Remind yourself of the various things that you do and how they help teens develop assets to become successful adults.

In your planning, ask yourself this very simple question: Does this program, service, thought, or idea help teens develop any of the assets? If the answer is yes, then it has value. One could argue that the more assets an idea meets, the more valuable the idea. If the answer is no, then do we really need to spend our time on the service element?

Assets can also be used in evaluating our library services and in our marketing, and that concept is discussed in those respective chapters. But the bottom line is that when you meet assets, you are succeeding because you are making a positive difference in the life of teens in your community. For access to the research, the full list of assets, and more information, visit the Search Institute website.

One of the core assets that we meet involves reading for pleasure. Developing a love of learning is a developmental asset, which doesn't surprise us, as we know the value of the written word and the power of the story to change lives. Building diversified collections that engage our teens and promote a love of reading? We have that one in the bag. But it is certainly not the only asset that libraries can help teens meet. Whether we are providing teens with a space to feel valued and a voice by participation in teen advisory groups or teen volunteer programs or providing positive adult interactions through one-on-one encounters at the reference desks, libraries are a vital part of our communities because we help teens build assets.

With an understanding of the 40 Developmental Assets and their role in the lives of teens, libraries can plan, implement, and evaluate their teen services in a different and more effective way.

Additional resources

Karen Jensen. "Mpact: An Asset Builders' Coalition: Working with Community Agencies," *VOYA* 34 (October 2011): 354.

Karen Jensen. "Asset Builders Coalition Support," Teen Librarian Toolbox, October 25, 2011. www.teenlibrariantoolbox.com/2011/10/asset-builders-coalition-support.html.

SOURCE: Specially prepared for *The Whole Library Handbook: Teen Services* by Karen Jensen, teen services librarian, Grand Prairie, Texas, and Heather Booth, teen services librarian, Thomas Ford Memorial Library, Western Springs, Illinois.

Reading in the dark: Boys, their books, and the search for answers

by Eric Devine

MANY OF MY STUDENTS, particularly boys, have an aversion to reading that is almost incomprehensible to me. Almost. Case in point: I was monitoring detention, and a freshman boy had no homework and no teachers to see for assistance. I asked him what he was reading. He did not understand the question. I called him forward and offered a pass, suggesting he go to the library so that he would not waste the hour. He said, "I don't read." I quietly queried as to whether he had difficulty. He said, "No, I just don't like to." I still sent him to the library. Ten minutes later, the boy returned with a book. I was elated. Then he sat down. It was *Twilight*. He was making a joke. But as I sat there with a dozen authors and titles in my mind—whereas he could not come up with one, or did not care to look—I was unsure who exactly was the butt of his joke.

I constantly review YA titles with a wide range of classes, and often students, boys included, will pick up the books I mention. When they do, invariably they enjoy them. Then they share with each other, and then they ask for more. Therefore, it would *seem* that all schools need in order to get boy teens to read is a voracious YA reader on staff. Good luck with that. It is increasingly difficult to find pockets within my teaching to allow for "pleasure" reading. I make them, but I cannot imagine the future trending in that direction.

It would seem then that librarians hold a greater responsibility in connecting teens with books, especially the boys. It has been well-documented that boys read less, that they skip YA and jump from middle grade to adult, while girls take the bridge offered and along the way ingrain a love of reading. I spend a great deal of time thinking about the habits of boys and their book selections, or lack thereof. I also talk to them, and their answers to my most recent questions were eye-opening but not shocking. However, there was one conclusion I drew. The summary of the challenge to create more YA boy readers and then adult male readers is this: *To convince boys that the narratives they are currently consuming (video games, YouTube, movies, social media) are not as good as books at providing the insights they need to succeed in life.*

Easy, right? You may continue reading when you have dried the tears from your laughter.

I base this belief on the responses I received from my male students to the four questions below as well as my own research and more than a decade teaching adolescents.

How many books do you read in a year? Please indicate how many fiction and how many nonfiction. The average number of books is around six, with a majority from fiction. However, that number includes boys who read 15–20 books and those who read none. It was surprising that fiction won out, as the common belief is boys need texts that teach them something they can use, and we assume this mostly comes from nonfiction. The concept may be true, but the source is not. Boys still want to learn about life, and they choose to learn from fiction.

What particular genres of fiction and nonfiction do you enjoy reading? The nonfiction selection fell into these camps: biographies, military/war stories, and historical accounts. The fiction ranged the gamut from an overwhelming demand for realistic fiction to affinities for historical fiction, fantasy, zombies, mysteries, the supernatural, and fantasy to a few graphic-novel nods. The military books bled into both genres, which is not a surprise, but the range of fiction was. Boys read all types, but what was most compelling was that in spite of the genre (with the exception of fantasy), the boys wanted realism. They wanted characters they could relate to in settings that were familiar and conflicts in which they could see themselves. Yes, this sounds a lot like how girls select books, doesn't it?

What are the roadblocks to reading in your life? I believe this to be the most illuminating question based on the answers. My school has a predominance of athletes, so "sports" eating up time made sense, but our athletes are, across the board, scholar-athletes, so this does not speak to the slanderous "dumb-jock" mentality. Rather, the demands are real, and our boys must cut somewhere, and books are typically first on the list.

Following sports came a mix of responses that all congealed under two categories: "life" and "story structure." The boys, when not busy with sports, were busy with friends—in real life or online—had an inability to sit and focus, and would rather be up and doing. Makes perfect sense to me, as being social is normal and enjoyable.

I lumped responses such as "chapter length," "book length," "time it takes to read," and "being a slow reader" under the story-structure response because these all speak to just that. Boys today enjoy quick chapters and fast-paced stories so that they can dip in and out of them and not lose the momentum or have to backtrack to remember the plot or characters. I believe any book you can pitch with having chapters that can be read in five to ten minutes is a phenomenal selling point with boys.

What, if anything, should or could be done to get you to read more? The overwhelming yet disturbing response to what could get boys to read more follows: *More books with violence and gore.* Following that, the responses all focused on shorter works with fast-paced plotlines. Overall, the boys had a gross inability to see—in spite of their social-media predilection—that a world of people discussing books exists, where if at minimum, they could at least glean titles, and at maximum, they could join the conversation.

These responses have proven to me that boys want and need to be shown how to live. They do not know how to fully function in this contemporary society. They are unsure of who they are, what they should enjoy, how they should behave, or who to emulate. They are extremely lost in a void where the information they receive is predominantly aimed at entertainment rather than education.

This brings me back to my central premise, which I believe my boys highlighted. The challenge is not simply to get them into the library; it is to get them to incorporate books as a staple to the narrative diet they are already consuming. The challenge is to demonstrate how the ridiculous YouTube clip and the culture of computer-screen passivity is addressed in YA literature—preferably in short chapters. The challenge is to show them how those tweets or the Facebook messages they send are part of a larger conversation that exists in books. That by reading, they can better inform their decisions on what to say and what not to, how to behave and how not to, because others have already walked these roads and have written about them. The challenge is to demonstrate for them the fundamental value of books, not just for books' sake, but for the sustenance they provide.

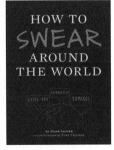

Our boys desire more. They just have no clue how to find it and then know if it's worth their while. They live in a world of unlimited selection, which is wonderful and problematic. How can they know which story is worth the undertaking, which one will help turn them into a better man? Left to their own devices, our boys will make a joke out of reading, most likely out of fear, as did the boy from detention. By doing such they will erode their ability to be more than they are today. That is a shame, and an outcome that cannot be allowed to develop. Yet it is also a situation for which the solution is attainable through a persistent attention to the shifting interests and specific needs of boy readers and potential readers, and continually working to make those vital connections.

For more information on boys and reading, see "Boys and Reading: Is There Any Hope?" by Robert Lipsyte, *New York Times,* August 19, 2011; and Guys Read, www.guysread.com.

SOURCE: Specially prepared for *The Whole Library Handbook: Teen Services* by Eric Devine, young adult fiction author of *Dare Me, Tap Out,* and *This Side of Normal.*

WHO ARE WE?

CHAPTER TWO

Now that we have established ways to know the teen populations that we work with, let's take a moment to consider who we are in association with these teens. As individuals, we are as varied as teens. We are human after all! But amid our differences, we will all face similar challenges and joys. What is the role of the teen librarian? What are we commonly called upon to do? How do we lead, even if we are not in management positions? And how can we best relate to teens as friends and allies while maintaining an appropriate professional distance?

What does it mean to be a teen services librarian?

by Karen Jensen

YOUNG ADULT LIBRARIAN, teen services librarian, youth services librarian, teen specialists . . . We go by many names but have one important goal: to serve teens in the library through collections, programs, and services. But what that means, and how we do that, will vary depending on the library that we work in. All positions are not created equal, though all are important.

More and more, libraries are embracing the idea of serving teens and creating positions, sometimes even departments, dedicated to serving teens. If you are lucky, you will find yourself working as a specialist at one of these libraries. Here, your time will be solely dedicated to serving teens.

In many libraries, however, you will find yourself tucked into either the youth services or adult services department. What this means for you is that though teen services may be your primary area of focus, you will also find yourself called upon to help in other areas of library service. Although you may work a 40-hour work week, not all of those 40 hours will be spent doing teen services.

A look at the life of a teen services career

Together, coauthor Heather Booth and I have worked at seven different libraries, all with an emphasis on teen services, each position different.

Karen's job 1: Young adult services assistant. In my first position, I was a young adult services assistant, tucked into the Youth Services Department. I did all things YA, but I also was called upon to assist with youth services in general. I was pulled in to sub at storytimes and to help plan and present programs for all ages, and although we had a teen summer reading club, I was also very involved in the children's reading club.

Karen's job 2: Teen services team leader. At my second job, I worked at a slightly larger library and was responsible for a small team that served in two buildings. Here I coordinated teen services between myself and two other individuals. And yet, we were still not entirely dedicated to teen services alone. We worked the children's

Karen Jensen

desk a few hours every day, and we were also heavily involved in the planning and presentation of children's programming.

Karen's job 3: Teen services librarian. In my third position, I was at a medium-sized library, and I was the sole librarian working to serve teens. This position involved all that you would think it involved, but I also maintained the entire adult fiction collection, worked the reference desk, and did the library's marketing.

Karen's job 4: Youth services librarian. In my fourth position, I served as a youth services librarian, serving children and teens grades 3 through 12. In addition to doing the collection development and programming for these age groups, I work the reference desk half of my scheduled hours.

Heather's job 1: Teen librarian. My first position was new to the library. Where one librarian had previously served the teen population in two libraries, this new position was created to give each library its own dedicated teen services librarian. But we were both under the umbrella of adult services, and my facility had no dedicated teen desk, so most of my desk time was spent on adult reference. Additionally, I was charged with creating a graphic-novel collection for both buildings.

Heather's job 2: Young adult and readers' advisory librarian. My second library's young adult services were housed within the adult Readers' Advisory Department. In addition to serving the teens through the collection and running the teen advisory board (TAB), I spent roughly half of my time at the adult readers' advisory desk, and over my years there, I selected half of the adult fiction collection, a large portion of the music collection, and the Dewey 800s in addition to the YA materials. I also participated in technology, community-wide (adult) reading, and web-design committees.

Heather's job 3: Teen services librarian. In my third library, I am again under the umbrella of adult services. Here, part time, I manage the teen collection, plan and execute teen programs, network with the schools, manage teen-focused social media, and also do adult reference work and some adult programming in addition to serving on library-wide policy and procedural committees.

There are larger library systems that have departments dedicated to serving teens with a small staff that specializes in collection development, programming, and more. Larger library systems may have one person in the system, usually at the main branch, who coordinates teen services among multiple branches, and random staff at each branch are pulled into duty (unfortunately, sometimes reluctantly).

However the teen services department is arranged, there must be a public-service element to the position (for example, a reference desk of some sort). Teens need to see you and have a face at the library that they know. The teen librarian needs to spend time interacting with teens so he or she knows what questions they are asking, what services they are needing, and what topics are hot and would make a good program at the moment. You can't effectively serve an audience with whom you don't interact.

Heather Booth

Being a teen services librarian does not mean the same thing to all libraries. There are important variables that come into play, such as library size and budgets. But, regardless of the library, all teens deserve, and need, quality library services because communities need empowered, educated teens. Whatever the job position you are hired into, you become an advocate for teens in your library system; you become the voice representing a generation asking for access to services and materials to enhance their quality of life.

Why do we work with teens?

When you tell people you work with teens, they often get a look on their faces and will give you a "bless-you" pat on the back, thinking you are making some noble sacrifice to the greater good because you work with a generation that is not often highly regarded by society. But the truth is, teens are wise, witty, intelligent, passionate, and so much more. You can sit down and have a serious conversation with

Teen Area, Fullerton (Calif.) Public Library. Photo by Shirley Ku, used CC BY-SA 3.0.

a teen one minute and then turn around and play games with them in the next. There are very few dull moments when working with teens. Yes, they have unique developmental needs, as do humans in all stages of life. And yes, some of them can be challenging. But working with teens can be so very rewarding because you know that you are making a difference in someone's life at a critical, formative time period.

Why it matters

Here's a little secret: When you are the teen services librarian, no matter what happens in the library, when it involves a teen, other staff in the library will call you to deal with it. Although sometimes frustrating, especially when you are pulled away from a task to deal with an issue that many other staff members could have managed, this is not always a bad thing. It gives you the chance to turn a potentially bad situation into a positive one. Take, for example, Anthony.

My first meeting with Anthony did not begin in the most pleasant of ways. I was working in my office at my desk when the phone rang: "There are some teens outside writing on the building. We need you to go take care of it." So I went, and of course the group members ran away in different directions.

But for some reason, Anthony stayed. So there Anthony sat outside the director's office as we discussed what we were going to do. Call the police and report the vandalism? The vandalism was written in pencil, so we decided to have Anthony come back the following day and clean up the graffiti.

To our surprise, he actually showed up the next day, and I sat out there and talked to Anthony as he scrubbed the wall. No lectures, no threats—a simple get-to-know-you conversation.

Anthony soon began to come to my Tuesday after-school programs. That summer, he came to every single meeting of my summer reading program. Although we had good program attendance during the school year, summer program attendance always plummeted to the abyss. So Anthony would show up sometimes to an empty room, where he would pull out his cell phone and text his friends, who would come if they could.

For years, Anthony and I hung out together at the library. I watched him fall in and out of love. I watched him struggle when a friend died. I watched him become a young man who is now in college, working hard to make a different life for himself. I am not going to lie; Anthony never became a reader. I am pretty sure he never checked out a book. But he came and did his homework. He came to library programs. He became a library user and supporter.

Throughout the course of your career, you will have many Anthonys. Each story will be different, but you will meet teens who will touch your life as you are touching theirs. You will help teens wrestle with their faith, their sexuality, their home lives, and their relationships. Most of the time, you will help them without ever knowing that you help them; you will do it by putting the right book in their hands at just the right moment. Or by hosting a program that makes something click for them and opens up some new world. Or by giving them a genuinely warm smile on their very worst day.

Sometimes you will have the readers' advisory moment in the stacks, and the book you give them changes them, changes their heart. Sometimes you will give them a good laugh, a good memory, at a time when they are facing unspeakable pain. But the biggest way you will make a difference is because the teens in your community will know that there are adults in the community who care.

SOURCE: Specially prepared for *The Whole Library Handbook: Teen Services* by Karen Jensen, teen services librarian, Grand Prairie, Texas.

Same pattern, different cloth:
School and public librarians

by Naomi Bates

I'M A LIBRARIAN; so what does that mean? For teens, it all depends on which librarian you're referring to. If it's the school librarian, then the definition may center around research, current young adult books, and homework assignments. If it's a public librarian, the definition would be slightly different, with a focus on young adult reading, teen programming, weekends open, and computer use. School librarians and public librarians are very often the same type of people but cut from different cloth when it comes to their jobs.

As a school librarian, I am working every day with 2,500 young adults between the ages of 14 and 20. Eight hours, five days a week, from 8:00 a.m. to 4:00 p.m., I get to see them come and go into the library for a variety of reasons, and I only have that amount of time to make a difference in the way libraries and what we do are conceptualized in their minds. Planning teaching, working with other district librarians, meeting students, dealing with administra-tion, meeting teachers' needs, and creating presen-tations for workshops are just some of the things a good school librarian does. Top that off with ordering and processing books, creating lists for classroom and pleasure reading, and maintaining and ordering tech-nology for the campus, and you have a cocktail strong enough for a dauntless school librarian.

In the town I live in and its surrounding areas, there are public libraries, but not many children's/ young adult librarians on staff. One public library has an outstanding teen librarian, but our paths don't cross

Library Club teens participate in Read Across America programming..

often. It's not that we don't like each other. In fact, I admire the work she does with teens. The question that begs to be answered is, "Why don't you meet with her then?" Collaboration should be a key component. So what are those barriers?

Timing seems to be the biggest opponent in collaboration. On most calendars for the public libraries, teen programming happens in the evenings, while school programs happen during the day. Oftentimes programming can be very similar, but the timing makes it difficult. Pit that against after-school meetings or extra-curricular activities and even extended library hours, and it makes it difficult to synchronize programs and activities.

Another issue with time that comes into play is the testing calendar the state sets forth for schools. Libraries are often shut down and librarians are proctor-ing, moderating, or helping with other test duties. Believe it or not, testing takes up a lot of days. This year, for example, there are more than 54 testing days, not including Advanced Placement testing, which is an additional 10 days. For school librarians, the days before and after the tests are vital. It's the narrow window when we can step out of the library and into the classroom and ensure we are educational partners, not separate entities. This then leads into relationships.

As school librarians, we want relationships with the teens, exactly like public librarians do. But the relationships with the teachers in the building are also very important. Why? Because teachers ultimately decide whether the library and I are worth "pursuing." Building a reputable program, both academic and for teens, can be a two-headed dragon. All the time spent in the building doing presentations, assisting with teacher in-service, teaching lessons, booktalking, and anything else to enhance curriculum, including planning all of these things, becomes a focus on self, leaving collaborating with a public librarian, unfortunately, on the back burner.

Those public and school librarians who collaborate have created strong bonds. We must keep in mind, though, that bonds can also be forged without face-to-face collaboration. What one library doesn't have, the other will. What one library can't offer, perhaps the other can. Reminding students that there is another library out there to help is also a signal of collaboration, albeit one built on reputation and a fellow-library-esque kinship. There should never ever be an "us-against-them" mentality but a relationship that can be forged on professionalism, virtual means, and relying on each other.

There are other factors I don't know or haven't encountered on the public librarian end, but I'm sure they exist. There is no reason not to collaborate with a public librarian—all it takes is an invitation. Which makes me realize I need to make a call right now to my favorite teen librarian at the public library—time to start tag-teaming!

SOURCE: Specially prepared for *The Whole Library Handbook: Teen Services* by Naomi Bates.

What does customer service to teens look like?

by Karen Jensen

NON-TEEN-SERVICES STAFF MEMBERS seem to think that teens are some mythical creatures for whom they never got the instruction manual, so I find myself frequently answering the question: What should customer service to teens look like? Although there are some distinct developmental needs of teens that we need to be aware of and address, the truth is this: customer service to teens should look the same as customer service to any other library patron. *Every* library patron who walks through the library door should get the same high-quality and friendly service, regardless of race, gender, disability, and—yes—age.

Your library should have only one approach to customer service, and it should apply to everyone evenly. Anything less than consistent, quality customer service to all patrons is both discriminatory and bad for business.

Hopefully, your library has a strong emphasis on customer service and provides routine training. If it doesn't, discuss putting some training in place with your administration. And, as your library's teen services representative, make sure you are a part of the planning and decision making in your library to ensure that teen interests are represented in the discussion. Some library policies, like obtaining library cards and internet use, can be more complicated with the teen audience. You want to make sure that the unique challenges of teenagers are at least considered in the discussion.

So, what should good customer service to teens look like?

It should be friendly and approachable. Every teen wants to feel welcomed and valued. Staff should be friendly and approachable. Smile. Interact with teens in a professional and courteous manner. As part of your training, have staff think about their positive and negative customer-services experiences as teenagers. Ask them what made those experiences stand out in their minds. As you discuss and outline these experiences, you will come up with both positive and negative examples. When staff members reflect on their own experiences, it helps them realize the hallmarks of good customer service. The golden rule of life applies to customer service: Treat others as you would want to be treated.

Remind staff of the importance of good customer service to a healthy organization. Patrons are much more likely to go out and share their negative experiences than their positive experiences. This type of negative public relations is very hard to counteract, and your best defense is a good offense; make sure patrons walk out of your library with nothing but good experiences to share. Today it is easier then ever to share one's experiences. Many teens have Facebook or Twitter accounts, and all it takes is for a teen to get online and share with his or her 200-plus friends that "Generic Public Library *hates* teens." But we can also use social media to our advantage by giving them reasons to share their positive library experiences with their friends.

It should be consistent. A good starting point for customer service is to make sure your library has policies and procedures in place letting staff know how to handle a wide variety of patron interactions and ensure high-quality, consistent services to all patrons. The consistent implementation of policies and procedures helps both staff and patrons understand expectations. Understanding expectations decreases the hostility that can arise from miscommunication.

Consistent policies and procedures also help ensure that all patrons' experiences will be the same regardless of what staff member they are interacting with; for example, when they come in on Friday and see staff member A, they will get the same experience as when they see staff member B on Tuesday. In addition, they will see other patrons being given the same high-quality service and being asked to meet the same patron responsibilities. The fastest way to create negative experiences is for teens to see other patrons being given service that they are not. Patrons—including teen patrons—like to have clearly defined expectations, from general behavior in the library to internet use and everything in between. Consistency and a clear adherence to guidelines across the board also keeps behavior management less personal. If a staff member has to enforce a rule with a teen, knowing that the same rule would be enforced with someone else goes a long way to smoothing the interaction.

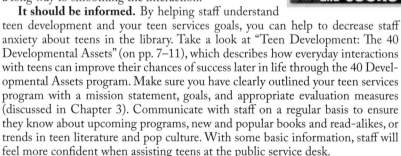

It should be informed. By helping staff understand teen development and your teen services goals, you can help to decrease staff anxiety about teens in the library. Take a look at "Teen Development: The 40 Developmental Assets" (on pp. 7–11), which describes how everyday interactions with teens can improve their chances of success later in life through the 40 Developmental Assets program. Make sure you have clearly outlined your teen services program with a mission statement, goals, and appropriate evaluation measures (discussed in Chapter 3). Communicate with staff on a regular basis to ensure they know about upcoming programs, new and popular books and read-alikes, or trends in teen literature and pop culture. With some basic information, staff will feel more confident when assisting teens at the public service desk.

YALSA has put together a helpful presentation titled *Guidelines for Library Services to Teens Ages 12–18* (yalsa.ala.org/guidelines/referenceguidelines.pdf).

Consult it as you help put together your library's customer-service model and training packet.

Reshaping our experiences

So often when we walk away from a patron service desk, we walk into a back office and begin sharing a story about the horrible customer interaction that we just had, forgetting that there were many other completely routine ones. But those negative interactions stay with us, and we need to process them, to process the stress of it and state our case. There is a catharsis in getting it out and sharing. But what if, after we discussed our negative experience, we made it our goal to always follow the negative with a positive. Making sure, for ourselves and others, that we share our positive interactions will remind us that they are more often good than bad. Although we respect the needs of our staff to talk about the negative aspects that can, and do, come with having teens in the library, we need to keep an emphasis on positive experiences between teens and the library. Report statistics, positive feedback, and those stories when a teen came back to tell you that he or she loved the book you recommended. We need to be reminded of why we do what we do and how we are being successful at it.

Reshaping our view of teens

With a better understanding of teen development, we can more easily understand why teens do the things they do. Brain research shows that they literally do not have the biological mechanisms in place to make the same types of decisions that adults do (see "Fast Facts for Librarians about the Teenage Brain," pp. 6–7). When we understand behavior, it is easier to deal with it. Making yourself and staff familiar with the 40 Developmental Assets will also assist you as you help develop your library's role in ensuring teens obtain assets and grow in healthy ways. By reshaping the way we see teens and our services to teens, staff can be more comfortable when the clock strikes 3:00 and you get the after-school rush.

Reshaping our staff

As we share our knowledge of teens and teen services, we invite coworkers to be a part of our teen services program, to be a part of the team. Team building is important because as staff becomes a part of the team, they become vested partners in providing quality customer service to teens. It's no longer you providing customer services to teens but the library providing quality service to teens.

You often hear teen librarians making a case for teen services by saying that "teens are our future." The truth is, teens are also our here and now. Teens are members of our community with information, education, and recreation needs. They are making important decisions about who they are and who they want to become. They are forming foundational opinions about the library and its role in their lives. They are deciding whether they will be library users and supporters. If teens walk away from the library today, it will be hard to get them back later. Today, more than ever, there is a lot of competition in programming, services, and informational needs. If we fail to capture and keep our teen patrons today, it is unlikely that we will be able to do so later; make sure your teens feel welcomed and served by every staff member in your building. And use the powerful force of social media by creating loyal teen customers who will spread positive words about your library.

SOURCE: Specially prepared for *The Whole Library Handbook: Teen Services* by Karen Jensen, teen services librarian, Grand Prairie, Texas.

Friend, advisor, enforcer, professional: Relating to teens as a YA librarian

2

by Maggie Hommel Thomann

IF YOU'VE CHOSEN TO GO INTO young adult librarianship or to work with teens in general, you probably already have a love for the age group and a good idea of the rewards and frustrations that come with it. As a new librarian fresh out of graduate school, I had worked with teens of different ages, was armed with knowledge about adolescent development and readers' advisory, and had a dedication to and a soft spot for teens. Although I felt that building relationships was extremely important in successfully serving teens, I hadn't realized exactly how many roles I would be playing as the sole teen librarian in my library. It quickly became clear that much of my after-school on-desk time would be dedicated to serving as a disciplinarian—or, more accurately, ringleader of a three-ring circus. As teens came streaming up the stairs to the young adult area, my ideas of relationship building quickly went out of the window, and instead I went into survival mode. That discipline would be such a major component of librarianship came as a total surprise to me, and unlike beginning teachers, I had never had any instruction on how to approach classroom–YA room management. And to top it off, how was I supposed to build relationships and be an accessible and friendly advisor at the same time as I was shushing them and confiscating their contraband food?

On the other end of the spectrum was a complication that came into play as I connected and built relationships with teens. I was in my late twenties, probably looked even younger than that, and found that keeping professional distance and control over the room in the YA space and at programs and events was something that took some practice. I was pleased that I was building connections with teens but uncomfortable when they asked for my friendship on Facebook, my personal email address, or even my cell-phone number. Several kids would pull a chair up to the service desk when they came in and want to have an ongoing conversation with me, even when I was trying to help other patrons; and once while I was dining at a restaurant, teens knocked on the window and then joined me at my table uninvited. I was happy to be building these important relationships, but where does one draw the line?

If you work with teens, you've probably had similar experiences. Teens are social by nature and build relationships quickly—many teens seek approval and connection with positive adults. I have a colleague who has had his car toilet-papered (in a loving way) by regular teen library patrons, and another colleague unwittingly left her cell phone out at a program and then started receiving texts from teens who had copied down her number. Some of this comes with the territory, but there are also strategies and approaches that can make handling all of these different interactions a bit easier.

The importance of positive relationships between teens and adults cannot be overstated. Research has shown that it is important developmentally for teens to have positive role models outside of their parents. Further, teens with positive adult role models tend to demonstrate decreased risk factors, higher self-esteem, and better communication and leadership skills. As librarians who serve teens, we have an obligation to be accessible and friendly to our patrons but also to make sure we are being responsible and professional.

You can be friendly with your teens but still set boundaries; in fact, you really have to in order to be successful. First and foremost, a strict no-touch rule should be enacted—even when an appreciative teen wants to give you a hug or a pat on the back. Another good boundary line is centering interactions with teens around the library. I say no to teens who want to be my friend on social media, but they can "like" the library's social-media presences and stay in touch that way. Same with emails, phone numbers, and instant messaging. They are more than welcome to have my professional contact info, and my accessibility is during my work hours. Situations such as toilet papering or interactions out in the community may have to be dealt with on a case-by-case basis, but building a solid groundwork of limits helps to set the right tone.

Although chatting and personal interactions have their place, it's also good to remind teen patrons that you are working and that work is your first priority. If a teen wants to get book suggestions, then pulling up a chair at the desk is OK, but chatting has to be on a very limited basis. Connecting on a personal basis is not all bad, however—some connection is needed for teens to be comfortable coming to you when they need library-related help. One piece of advice I got early on that has helped me immensely is to take nothing with teens personally. Try not to get too offended or angry when a teen is misbehaving or being disrespectful (they are just wired that way), but also don't get too flattered or emotionally involved when teens are being complimentary or seeking attention. Maintaining that balance can be tricky, but using your instincts and keeping things from getting too personal can help. There is a great side benefit to keeping the focus work-related and professional—it helps teens to see you not just as a friend but as an authority in readers' advisory, research, and homework help. They are more likely to think of you first and come to you with questions when you have framed your interactions in this way.

Many teens are looking for social interaction when they approach you, but some may need help that goes beyond the everyday. The book *Extreme Teens: Library Services to Nontraditional Young Adults* (Libraries Unlimited, 2005) by Sheila B. Anderson, offers some good advice for serving teens who have outside-the-mainstream needs, such as homeless and at-risk teens, incarcerated teens, and pregnant and parenting teens. It's a good idea to compile a list of community resources to keep at the desk or post on the library's website in case a teen comes to you for help in a time of crisis. Remember that you are not a trained counselor or social worker, and you need to abide by teens' right to privacy. Though laws may vary by state, most public librarians are not mandatory reporters and can't act in loco parentis. What librarians can provide for teens in need, however, is a supportive ear and a link to resources and ways to contact professionals who are trained and ready to help them. For more on this topic, see "Teen Development: The 40 Developmental Assets," pp. 7–11.

Serving teens in a public library setting is challenging in part because of the many hats that a teen librarian must wear. You must be friendly, accessible, and open to young adults; get to know them and interact with them in fun ways at programs and in the teen space; and also, at times, be a disciplinarian, enforcing the rules of the library and keeping other users and library staff members happy. And even though it is important to be a friend to the teens, it's just as important to be professional. When you strike a good balance you will have the respect of your teens and be best able to serve them.

Resources

Some helpful online resources touch on this topic:
Teen Librarian. teenlibrarian.co.uk/category/advice/.
Teen Librarian Toolbox. www.teenlibrariantoolbox.com.
Sarah Thompson. "So You Want to Be a Teen Librarian?" GreenBeanTeen-Queen, July 26, 2010. www.greenbeanteenqueen.com.
Young Adult Library Services Association (ALA). *Guidelines for Library Services to Teens.* yalsa.ala.org/guidelines/referenceguidelines.pdf.

SOURCE: Specially prepared for *The Whole Library Handbook: Teen Services* by Maggie Hommel Thomann, reader services manager, Park Ridge (Ill.) Public Library.

Where's the handbook for that?

by Karen Jensen

SHE WAS 14 YEARS OLD. There was a haunted look in her eyes, and I knew before she spoke the words: "I'm pregnant. I don't want to keep the baby." No matter how many professional books you read, some situations are difficult to know how to handle. They require an honesty and a special sensitivity, but they also require a certain amount of professional caution on our part. We are not social workers. We are not counselors. We are not spiritual advisors.

When you work with teens, they will open doors and invite you in. They will share their lives with you. But there is a certain amount of caution that you must engage in to protect yourself and to protect your library. Even the most innocent interactions can sometimes be misconstrued. And sometimes, situations arise that we just aren't prepared to deal with. So what do you do?

Setting boundaries

Working with the public, especially minors, is a delicate dance. Know your employer's limits and respect them. I advise keeping all communications professional. Don't accept friendships on your personal Facebook page. Don't give out your personal cell-phone number or email address. Don't put yourself in a situation that can be misconstrued: For example, never drive a teen home from the library, and observe guidelines about teen-to-staff ratios.

The trickier boundaries to set involve our daily communications with teens. They will ask you what you think about things, how you feel about things, what you were like as a teenager. "I'm grounded," one teen volunteer told me as we sat cutting out craft supplies. "I've been hanging out with this guy; he's 24." Then she said, "My parents are really upset about it, but you're cool; you wouldn't care, right?" To which I replied, "I'm not your parents, and I certainly can't speak for them. But if my daughter was your age and hanging out with a man that age, I would chain her to me, and I would tell her, 'You're young; you have your whole life to be a grown-up. Enjoy being where you are at right now in life.'"

I have been asked about my religious beliefs, my political beliefs, and so much more. And yes, I get asked my opinion a lot. I try and find ways to answer questions from my teens honestly and respectfully while making sure to remember that, in those moments, I represent the library. I don't want them to go home and say, "Well, the library lady said x, y, and z" only to have an irate parent come in to see me the next day. Those boundaries are different for every person, but you don't want to be the librarian on the nightly news with a series of questionable text messages with a teen, and you don't want teens misconstruing what you say and deciding that you told them it was OK to have sex with their significant others or to stage a protest and skip their senior finals.

Know when and who to refer

As information specialists, it's our job to know who does what in the community. When a teen reveals to you that he or she is hurting, you can subtly pass along the information to people in the community who may be able to help. Make sure you know the warning signs of things like domestic violence, abusive relationships, drug and alcohol abuse, self-harm behaviors, mental health issues, suicide, and so forth.

Ask for help

If you find yourself in a situation where you aren't sure what to do, step back and ask for help. Ask for clarification about the library's policy from your library director. Contact respected peers, and ask them what they think would be appropriate ways to handle a situation.

Don't take chances

If you have any suspicions, you can call and anonymously talk to the people who specialize in these issues. Hotlines for local social-service agencies are accustomed to receiving what-if phone calls from people like yourself who need to know from an expert if what they observed merits reporting to authorities. If you are concerned that there is an immediate threat, you can call the local police or children's services. As a police officer once told me, "You are not trained for this. Call us. We are the ones who are trained for this." Don't take any chances, with either the well-being of a teen or your own professional safety.

At one point in my career, I was working the reference desk when an agitated patron came up to the desk. She had seen a young girl who staff knew to be about 14 and developmentally challenged kissing a man outside. We knew this man to be in his early to middle twenties. I walked over to see what was happening, and when I saw the two of them leave the library premises together, I didn't hesitate. I called the police. This was a crime in progress because in my municipality, a 14-year-old girl cannot legally consent to any type of relationship with a man of this age. When the police came, they asked if we knew who the man was and how and where to contact him. Despite libraries' strongly and rightfully held views on patron confidentiality, this was a whole new scenario, and we gave the police the information immediately. (The ALA Office of Intellectual Freedom maintains a page detailing state privacy laws regarding library records, at ala.org/offices/oif/ifgroups/stateifcchairs/stateifcinaction/stateprivacy.)

You will be surprised at the types of situations that you encounter for which there is no handbook, and when faced with a difficult incident, you will have to hold on to what you know, trust what you believe is right, and then wing it.

As for my 14-year-old friend at the beginning of this story, I listened to her when she needed to talk until the point when she made her decision. The last I saw her, she was doing pretty well. We never talked about what happened. I respected her boundaries as we said our brief hellos. She was not the first and she will not be the last of the troubled teens I have the opportunity to walk with on their journey for a brief period of time. As a teen services librarian, you too will be invited to walk with teens on many of your own journeys. Tread knowledgeably but cautiously.

SOURCE: Specially prepared for *The Whole Library Handbook: Teen Services* by Karen Jensen, teen services librarian, Grand Prairie, Texas.

The importance of networking in the life of a teen librarian
by Heather Booth and Karen Jensen

A LOT IS WRITTEN and discussed about why and how we can better connect with teens. But why and how should we connect with other library professionals? Many teen librarians do their jobs in isolation. It can be a lonely job. Many are the only teen librarian in a location. We plan programs on our own or with the hopefully enthusiastic but sometimes grudging or misguided assistance of a teen advisory board (TAB). We order and read books that we might not be able to gush about with anyone else we work with. We serve a population with distinct needs, and we're on our own deciphering what those needs are and how to address them through our service. Depending on when we are on-desk and what population that desk serves, we may go days without having a really engaging conversation with a teen patron, let alone another colleague who shares our passion and focus. The Illinois library system, for example, has recently morphed from a regional system to one that encompasses half the state. What was once fairly local networking meetings are no longer as convenient—or possible—to attend. The irony of this isolation is that the job of a public service librarian is all about making connections with people, and connecting those people to what they need.

Connection

Just like attending a professional conference can give you new ideas and energy, having regular, informal meetings with other teen librarians can do the same. Why is this important? Our performance and attitude are positively impacted after conferences. We might offer new programs, order books we just heard about, try new approaches in booktalking or readers' advisory, change signage, and explore new websites or technology. Meeting the librarian down the street or three towns over for a sandwich or cup of coffee isn't the same as attending the YALSA

YA Literature Symposium or PLA, but it serves a similar purpose. It breaks us out of our own way of doing things and allows us to share our knowledge and ideas with each other. It reminds *all* of us that although we're doing this alone, we're not really out there all on our own.

Working with teens takes energy. Some days, it takes lots of energy. Some days, it takes *all* of our energy. Despite this, it is a labor of love. And for every night we fall onto the couch at the end of the day with our coats on and the keys still in our hand, there are going to be other nights we drive home with the windows down, singing at the top of our lungs because the day, the patron, the interaction, or the thank-you note we just got was exhilarating beyond belief. Not everybody understands that dynamic, but having someone who does, having someone with whom we can share these moments, pulls us up when we're down, and we can use the positive momentum to push our programs or services in new and exciting directions. Who else understands the frustrations and rewards of being an unofficial department of one like someone else who is an unofficial department of one?

We need to meet each other, and not just to vent and pat each other on the back. We must seek out the kind of camaraderie and information sharing that our colleagues in other situations come by naturally. If there are five people in the Adult Services Department, they have each other with whom they can bounce ideas, get a second opinion on a resource, share interesting articles, teach new technologies, and try new services. Working in a bubble will eventually lead to problems with our service. This will show through providing stale programs, missing new trends in publishing, and changing the dates and then reusing the same poster session after session. It's poor service, and our patrons will pick up on it.

Collaboration

Some projects are just bigger than you, bigger than one library, and bigger than one TAB. Consider what could have been accomplished if there were two of you, twice as many teens, twice as many locations (and dare we hope twice the budget?), and twice as much energy for the last great program you hosted. If you've

---

Networking start-ups

If collaborating on a major project is an overwhelming thought right now, start smaller. You could collaborate and share information on . . .
- Book-display ideas
- Slogans and activities for your teen advisory board
- A joint book drive
- Thematic book lists
- Volunteer responsibilities and guidelines (it's nice when there are consistent expectations across an area)
- Excess craft supply or leftover prize swaps
- What to do about all of these darn series?!
- Best times for programs
- Summer reading themes
- What's hot for teens in your neighborhood
- Cross-promoting programs

seen programs or services offered elsewhere that seemed impossible because of the limitations of your own situation, think about striking up a partnership with another nearby library to make it happen.

Start by thinking about the areas of service that are difficult for you. We all have strengths and weaknesses, areas we love, and tasks we only do because it's part of the job. Pick a part of your job that you wish you had a better system for, a better eye for, or a better understanding of; look around at what other libraries are doing in those areas; and make improving that aspect your goal.

2

In-library networking

The easiest and most important place to find a partnership is in your own library. Yes, you may be the only teen librarian, but think about the overlap that you have with children's or adult services. Perhaps you could recruit someone from each of those departments to create a Teen Services Committee, much like you might have a staff development, technology, or customer service committee drawn from all areas of the library. Teens are a service population that demands more than one person can provide in any community unless the teen librarian is staffing the desk every hour the library is open.

Even if that is the case, it doesn't mean that the teen librarian *should* be the only one tasked with their service. It would be a horrible breach of service for someone to tell an octogenarian, "Oh, the senior-citizen librarian isn't here today, but here's her card" or "Um, I don't really work much with old people; let me go get Joe." Help create in your library a culture of teen friendliness by finding staff who are willing to have a monthly discussion with you about how your library can do things better for teens, how new policies are working out for them, which services from each person's respective department are underutilized by teens, and how to promote them. Chances are you'll uncover a secret YA reader in there somewhere.

Branching out

Though in-library networking is essential, broadening your network is still critical. Begin by thinking about your commute—do you pass any libraries before

---

Virtual networking

For teen librarians in rural locations or regions with a dearth of teen librarians, the meetings may need to take a different form. Reach out virtually to those librarians who are nearest you or who share your interest. Send them an email, and see what they have to say about your idea or predicament. Is there someone whose posts on an electronic discussion list really jive with how you see the library landscape? Or maybe someone who seems completely different than you? Send a note. Open a conversation. If you don't see resources or conversations around the issues most critical to your service or challenges, start that conversation yourself.

- Start a Google Hangout.
- Host a Skype chat.
- Start or join a Twitter chat or begin conversations around hot-topic hashtags.
- Follow a teen librarian on Twitter.
- Subscribe to blogs and electronic discussion lists.
- Use Pinterest, Tumblr, Instagram, nings—wherever people are connecting, they can connect about teens and library issues.

The self-assessment quiz

- Are you signed up for the YALSA-BK electronic discussion list?
- Are you signed up for a state or regional electronic discussion list?
- Do you follow librarians, publishers, and authors on a social media site?
- Do you go to professional conferences at least once a year on the state or national level?
- Do you participate in a couple of webinars a year?
- Are you engaged in any local or regional groups that meet regularly, even if informally, like meeting the teen services librarian in another library for lunch once a month?
- If you have a concern about a teen issue, are on the fence about a book purchase, or have a teen librarian–specific vent to get off your chest, do you have someone to call?

---

you get to work? Leave half an hour early for your 1:00 p.m. shift some day, stop in, and see if you can meet a teen librarian. You can also pick up the phone and make a call, but remember that you're trying to forge a friendship and partnership here, not sell yourself to the board or get your foot in the door as a booktalker at the school down the street. This is a peer relationship you are initiating, and you don't need to enter into it trying to accomplish any more than a meeting, an idea exchange, and a little commiseration.

Regional networking

If patrons that frequent your library are also within a comfortable-enough driving distance to other libraries that they are willing to pick items up at those locations, know if those libraries have a teen librarian, and know that person's name. Organize a meeting with this librarian. As the organizer, you don't need to be on a board or have a position in any kind of regional organization to call a meeting. Anyone can send out a broadcast email to the teen librarians within a short drive, suggest a central location, or offer his or her own meeting room, and get a meeting together. It really can be that easy. You don't need an organization or a system or an acronym to be the one to get a bunch of librarians together; you just need a few chairs. A good first meeting can be just that—meet one another, exchange contact information, go around the room and ask what everyone is reading, have some cookies, and make a plan to meet again soon. Likely, more than a few people will have a question or an idea that will generate enough conversation to fill at least an hour.

Running a local or regional networking group

- Determine your focus: book reviews, programming, all areas.
- Pick a regular meeting time to avoid confusion: the second Monday of each month, every third month.
- Have a coordinator: This person will collect email addresses and create a distribution list, create an agenda, and send out reminders prior to the meeting and recap notes following the meeting.
- Rotation is key: Rotate libraries so that the same people aren't always driving, you are visiting new library to get new ideas, and you are sharing the burden of setting up, providing food, and cleaning up.
- Have food: Everyone likes food, not just teens.
- Keep it light and informal, but set some ground rules: confidentiality, no gossip, honest but positively focused.

Keep in mind, networking is good. And it doesn't just have to be with librarians who work in your type of library or librarians at all. There is benefit in networking with anyone who works with teens. You can share your knowledge of adolescent development; you can share your knowledge of the local teen culture; and you can learn from each other's strengths, weaknesses, and experiences. You can also network with the organizations in your area who work with teens to learn more about local programs and services, share local insights, swap success stories, and train each others in areas of expertise. There is tremendous value in knowing the people from your local boys and girls clubs as well as your fellow teen librarians. You can also participate in local or regional teen book-review groups that meet regularly and share book reviews.

Resources

Karen Jensen. "Mpact: An Asset Builders' Coalition: Working with Community Agencies," *VOYA* 34 (October 2011): 354.

Karen Jensen. "Asset Builders Coalition Support," Teen Librarian Toolbox, October 25, 2011. www.teenlibrariantoolbox.com/2011/10/asset-builders-coalition-support.html.

Tasha Squires. *Library Partnerships: Making Connections between School and Public Libraries.* Medford, N.J.: Information Today, 2009.

SOURCE: Specially prepared for *The Whole Library Handbook: Teen Services* by Heather Booth, teen services librarian, Thomas Ford Memorial Library, Western Springs, Illinois, and Karen Jensen, teen services librarian, Grand Prairie, Texas.

What's in your files? What to ditch, what to keep, and for how long

by Heather Booth

ON THE FIRST DAY OF MY FIRST JOB as a teen services librarian, I packed my tote bag with my "Librarian Avengers" mug, my frozen dinner, a few good pens, and my treasured files from library school. Surely they would come in handy, these in-depth articles about bibliotherapy, storytelling, and the justification of graphic novels in a library. And even if I only drew on those now and then, the reading lists from my YA services courses, the book lists my classmates created for practice booktalks, and the reference worksheets that enumerated the vast resources to draw upon when answering a reference question would be things I'd use every day. Although there may still be some real gems in those files—I can't tell you for sure—I haven't opened them up in the past decade. But what I do use on a daily basis are the nuts and bolts that are not addressed in most library school programs but are essential for the practicing teen services librarian.

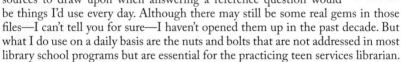

Whether they're digital or paper resources, every teen services librarian has a lot of information to organize to keep the teen library year running smoothly. But just like weeding the collection helps relevant material better circulate, weeding our own files will help us be more effective and efficient at our jobs. Recently, a representative of the state library visited our building to counsel us on document-retention regulations. She promised that, by following her instructions, we could reduce our storage space by roughly half. She followed this up by pointing out that phone messages must be retained for one year, at which point I balked—no way would I be reducing my storage by half if I had to start retaining that kind of minutia. Then I returned to my desk, peeked into my file drawer, and noticed a file full of teen advisory board (TAB) applications for people who must be juniors in college by now. What is a better use of the space? Outdated contact information or recent messages from people with whom relationships are developing?

What's in, or should be in, your files? If you've just moved into your position, should you start fresh, or keep your predecessor's records? Do you need to keep any of it? These details are going to vary from place to place and person to person, but there are some topics that we all need to monitor.

Book lists and reviews

It only makes sense that we would collect and keep lists of books since so much of the work of a teen librarian revolves around books. But with the easily accessible lists found online, the need to keep a file is waning. That said, there are some reasons to keep paper records of book lists and reviews:

- You are actively working on similar lists and refer to what you have in doing so.
- The lists contain collections that are not readily available elsewhere, as in lists of local authors or books frequently used in local assignments. If so, consider moving this out of the personal files and into a publicly accessible format.
- You pull and share these lists with patrons or store them in a way that gives patrons or staff easy access for use in readers' advisory interactions.
- You use these lists to pull books for displays on a regular basis.

The commonality is that the lists are in active use. Saving nice lists for an unspecified future project is unnecessary.

On old files. Use the same criteria for evaluating old files. Is the information available elsewhere? Is the information something that *should* be accessible elsewhere and ought to be digitized and made available? Is the information being used, or will it be used in the future? If not, disposing of the old files is practical.

Budgeting

Do you have a collections budget? A programming budget? An outreach or incidentals budget? A library credit card or charge accounts at vendors or local businesses? What about professional development funds allotted to you? You will need a way to organize and monitor your budget, your expenses, and any bills for which you or your department are responsible. Some will find using an online spreadsheet suits their needs best, while others will only need to keep simple paper records of receipts and reimbursements. Be sure to keep notes of payments requested and reimbursed from grants, Friends, or other funding sources. Date everything that comes to you without a date, and create a system for tracking the progress of payment or repayment.

On old files. Scan through what has been left, pull out any year-end summaries, and make notes of general trends, but you will likely be able to safely recycle or shred most of what is more than a year or two old, depending on document-retention regulations specific to your area.

Challenges

Now and then you'll order a book that you know, for one reason or another, will elicit some negative attention despite its merits in your collection. Now and then a patron may challenge, formally or informally, an item you have on your shelf. Documentation relating to potential or active challenges is vital to retain so that you can quickly, calmly, and effectively respond. Keeping reviews or links to reviews from both professional and popular outlets is one way to do this.

On old files. Keep any record of past challenges and the resolution at least as long as your tenure at the library. Your successors will also benefit from knowing this piece of institutional history.

2

Outreach

You know you got a summer reading list from someone at the high school last year. Carol, was it? No—Cathy? Was it the English Department head who sends it or the librarian? Who was it now who wanted emailed assignment alerts at the public library, children's or reference? These are questions that every teen librarian will need answers to, and the best way to save yourself time and energy is to keep a file with contacts in your teens' community.

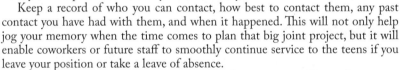

Teachers you've booktalked for, librarians you might collaborate with, park district or after-school program coordinators, the National Honor Society faculty advisor, the school newspaper contact, school liaison officers at the local police department, and youth group advisors at local religious institutions or civic organizations are some of the contacts that you can (and will) draw upon to create and nurture your library program and make the library a third place for teens in your community.

Keep a record of who you can contact, how best to contact them, any past contact you have had with them, and when it happened. This will not only help jog your memory when the time comes to plan that big joint project, but it will enable coworkers or future staff to smoothly continue service to the teens if you leave your position or take a leave of absence.

Save, digitally or on paper, any piece of information you plan to draw on in the future. Look at the organization of school websites to determine whether the information you use is taken down and replaced year after year or whether it is archived. Keep in mind that things like summer reading lists are popular go-to spots for many people to draw reading suggestions year-round and are still useful after the initial assignment has culminated.

On old files. Hopefully you will find a file like this. Consider it your welcome-to-the-community packet, and study up! Recycle any contact information that is outdated; make notes of past or ongoing programs or collaborations. Don't rely solely on your email for storing contacts.

Statistics

In this time of dwindling resources and assessments based on quantifiable metrics, you will, at some point, need to draw on the numbers to justify your budget, your services, or even your job. Statistics can also help in planning better programs, displays, and events, as they enable us to track trends and objectively evaluate the success. Whether it is through elaborate graphs and spreadsheets or simple numbers, keep track of your circulation, door count or space usage, program attendance, readers'-advisory or reference interactions, and summer reading club numbers.

Some libraries have a formalized system for collecting and distributing statistics, and others do not. Seek out the information you need to collect the statistics that will help you. If this means getting trained in database functions outside of your normal duties, do it! Find the database wizard at your institution and learn everything you can about how to find the numbers and what they mean. This is one file to definitely save if it's there as you move into a new position, though you may want to cull it to a reasonable number of years.

On old files. Keep anything relating to the current and past year and year-end summaries for the past three to five years. Vary this time span depending on the volatility of the library's current budget, the term length of your library board,

and local ordinances regarding document retention. Consider taking the time to evaluate general trends before recycling older statistics. Create an ongoing document that tracks major statistics that give a snapshot view of the health of the service: circulation, collection size, reference and readers' advisory interactions, computer use, program attendance, summer reading program participation. Inquire about where else archived statistics may be kept to avoid duplicating efforts or wasting storage space on duplicate records.

Other

Like in the junk drawer at your house, you will no doubt come across material you feel the need to save that doesn't fit in the above categories.

Procedures

Before taking a three-month leave of absence several years ago, I methodically typed up detailed procedures for each task I was responsible for during that time so that the coworkers who filled in for me would know what to do. Step-by-step processes, websites, log-ins and passwords, tips and tricks, and overall philosophy and evaluative criteria were all included in these documents. When I moved to a different library, how I yearned for such a guidebook! Keeping a record of how you do what you do may seem redundant, but the unexpected happens. You could be called away for a family emergency or personal illness. Duties may be reassigned. You might win the lottery and jet off to Fiji. You might find your dream job in the next county over. And, sadly, sometimes our jobs disappear despite the need for our services remaining unchanged. Creating and saving procedures is ultimately a service to our teen patrons. They help ensure consistent service in our absence. Additionally, creating procedures for *yourself* will save you time with tasks that happen only rarely or on a yearly cycle. Who hasn't wished they had written down a list of every step to get the summer reading club up and running or all of the settings in a rarely used technology?

On old files. As long as the task is still being done and the procedure is still correct, retain the document. Ideally, these documents should be created, reviewed, and updated frequently. Procedures that are no longer in use can and should be discarded to keep this file a sleek and practical guide that is easy for others to find in a time of crisis.

In general, a good rule of thumb is to apply basic collection-management concepts to your own files. Is it in demand? Is it current? Is it correct? Is it taking up space that is needed for other, more correct, current, or in-demand material? Retain what is legally required, what is necessary to preserve an institutional memory, what will serve you well in your current practice and future planning, and remove what is in the way so that you will find what you need more quickly and easily.

SOURCE: Specially prepared for *The Whole Library Handbook: Teen Services* by Heather Booth, teen services librarian, Thomas Ford Memorial Library, Western Springs, Illinois.

2

Get your reading habits organized
by Allison Tran

SO LET'S TALK ABOUT organizing our reading. As Julie Bartel wrote in YALSA's The Hub, we all organize our books in different ways. But how do we approach our reading habits? With so many great titles out there to catch our attention, how does one decide what to read next?

Personally, I couldn't survive without my to-read list on Goodreads. I also read award-prediction blogs like "Someday My Printz Will Come" and "Heavy Medal" and try to read at least a portion of the titles under discussion. After the ALA Youth Media Awards are announced in late January, I typically pick up whatever winning or recommended titles I missed. This usually keeps me busy for a few months. And to squeeze in as much reading as possible at all times, I'm usually juggling print, digital, and audio formats.

Here's how some of my fellow Hub bloggers organize their reading:

Kris Hickey: "I check out a ton of stuff from the library and I read it in the order it is due. If I can keep renewing it, I usually end up reading it later."

Michelle Blank: "I don't read from a list, though I usually have some ideas of upcoming release dates. Most of my reading is simply from browsing. I read whatever strikes me at the time or is available."

Jennifer Rummel: "I have a Goodreads to-read list. I choose books to read based on the cover (who *doesn't* do this?), the title, the author, and the summary. I have must-read authors, but I'm not opposed to trying out new authors. I'll read books that I've heard about on Twitter or read about on blogs. I find books looking through library journals or the *Ingram Advance* magazine. I challenge myself to 365 books a year. I like to read across genres because I want to know what's going on in the book world, outside of YA lit. I'll choose picture books based on reviews (mostly from *Publishers Weekly*). I mostly read YA books: I adore teen romances, historical fiction, books with strong female characters, high fantasy, contemporary, action/adventure/thrillers, and some science fiction. For adult books I devour cozy mysteries, Regency romances, and contemporary fiction. I review books for *VOYA*, which exposes me to books I wouldn't always pick up. I cohost a 4th- and 5th-grade book club, where again I read books I wouldn't always choose to read."

Erin Daly: "I am totally disorganized about reading! I start lots of books and generally only finish them if I am interested in them or if I feel the need to have an opinion about them (for readers' advisory or The Hub's Morris/Nonfiction Reading Challenge, for example). A great professor I had in library school told us to read widely and deeply, meaning to become an expert on the things you love and try to read a little bit of everything else. I try to follow this idea. I like speculative fiction best, sci-fi, fantasy, anything that's a little weird or magical, but I will read anything if it captures my attention. Maybe this post will help me organize my own reading habits!"

Jessica Pryde: "I'm what Jen Doll on The Wire would call the Multi-Tasker (or maybe the All-the-Timer/Compulsive/Voracious/Anything Goes Reader). I'm reading all the time, with whatever I've got in my hands. I'll read one thing on my phone while I'm waiting for the Metro and a completely different thing on my couch or on my lunch break. I've got a Goodreads to-read list, which I will add to frequently, but I could stray from that list if a trusted reader-friend tells me I should read something not yet on it. My Goodreads to-read list currently consists

of 2,222 books (I'm trying to keep it on that number as long as possible!) with 46 subcategories, which include genre and other ways to categorize (for instance, I have 'borrowed from library' and 'abandoned or on hiatus' alongside 'sci-fi' and 'history-biography'). Keeping them organized in such a way helps me to see what I've read, what I'd like to read, and what I probably shouldn't pick up. For the most part, these are books I will end up reading for fun, even if it's the painful type!"

Diane Colson: "My priority reading is books assigned by committee work or for review. If that's caught up, I try to read the books my teens like or ones that are recommended by other youth librarians. My real pleasure 'reading' is audiobooks. My work commute is one hour each way, so that's when I can listen to adult books!"

Sarah Debraski: "I use Goodreads to keep track of my to-read list, but I confess that although it grows enormously, I only occasionally remember to look at it (mostly because if I hear of something new that I must read, I get it right away). I do jot titles down on paper, or email them to myself, depending on where I am when I hear about a book I want to read. I feel like I am constantly hearing about good books, so I do need to keep track of what I want to read. I try not to be such a slave to my lists that I don't allow for just finding a good book on the new-book shelf at the library or an old good one in the stacks. Often, these unexpected treasures are the best and open the door to a new-to-me author."

Maria Kramer: "I try to read as many books on the lists of nominees for various YALSA lists and awards as I can. Typically, I lose steam after about two months and read Star Trek novels and Lovecraft until a new list is released, when the process begins again."

Becky O'Neil: "Oh, I feel that my reading is very disorganized. I do keep a Goodreads list and it is *huge*—so impossibly huge that it's more a record of books that I've had to let go or want to remember or tag somehow and that I would read if I had a thousand lives, but not an actual list that I'm methodically working my way down. I get distracted from everything easily, always reading several books at once and switching between them depending on how I feel, or which is newest and coolest, or which has the most reserves and has to be returned to the library, or which I am reading in order to review (deadlines are great priority-makers!). I am also in a book club, and that sets another deadline, so I often find myself with 'assigned' reading. I like most of the assigned reading, because it gives me something to stick with and fight off my 'reader's attention deficit,' and it also brings me to books that I would never pick up on my own. On the whole, though, I wish I could feel more organized about my approach to reading!"

Jessica Miller: "Before I became a librarian, I used to read pretty exclusively within the fantasy/sci-fi genres. I will admit, even now, that those are my go-to book choices. Now, however, I try to continuously remind myself to read across all the genres because readers' advisory is such a huge part of my job. I find that the professional reviewing I do helps me in this aspect, as I'm constantly assigned books that I might never have picked up myself without prompting. Some of those books have even become my absolute favorite reads! In the past two years, on top of my regular reviewing, I've also been part of a book-award selection committee. This has greatly improved my knowledge of books geared for a middle-school audience, but it also means that I have very little time right now for my 'just-for-fun' reads. When my current term on the committee ends, I have visions of being able to just wander the bookshelves and pick out books at random to read."

Dena Little: "I have good intentions when it comes to organizing my reading! I really do. I keep a Goodreads list; I write down titles I come across that sound great; I even take digital notes when I am out and about and want to remember a suggestion from a friend. But . . . when it comes down to action, I always end up perusing the shelves here at the library or asking my coworkers and the patrons for something new to read!"

Annie Schute: "I have too many books to count. So I downloaded an amazing $18 computer program called Bookpedia that creates a personal catalog for you of all your books. You can scan in all your books to the catalog with a webcam, and then search and sort through your books using the program, rate them if you want, and even check them out to friends. It's the perfect program for an organized book geek."

Carla Land: "I am forever and a day being distracted from my list of things to read—there are titles on my Goodreads list from 2009 that I still have not read. I do a lot of reading for a selection committee, so I tend to read those in the order I check them out and intersperse them with titles that I choose myself to avoid burnout. I read more than one book at once, and I find that I'm most successful doing this with nonfiction titles or with only one fiction and a nonfiction. I used to be able to read two or three fiction titles at a time, but I guess I'm just not the multitasker I was when I was in my twenties!"

There you have it: reading-organization tips and tricks from a well-read group of librarians. Sounds like a lot of librarians use Goodreads to keep track of it all, and preferred genres seem to be fantasy and science fiction. How do *you* decide what to read next?

Resources

American Library Association Youth Media Awards. www.ala.org/awards-grants/awards/browse/yma?showfilter=no.

Julie Bartel. "What Your Bookshelves Say About You." YALSA The Hub, January 21, 2013. www.yalsa.ala.org/thehub/2013/01/21/what-your-bookshelves-say-about-you/.

Bruji. Bookpedia. www.bruji.com/bookpedia/.

Jen Doll. "What Kind of Book Reader Are You? A Diagnostics Guide." The Wire, August 29, 2012. www.thewire.com/entertainment/2012/08/what-kind-book-reader-are-you-diagnostics-guide/56337/.

"Heavy Medal: A Mock Newbery Blog." School Library Journal. blogs.slj.com/heavymedal/.

Karyn Silverman and Sarah Couri. "Someday My Printz Will Come," blog, School Library Journal. blogs.slj.com/printzblog/.

Allison Tran. "YALSA's 2014 Hub Reading Challenge Begins!" YALSA The Hub, February 3, 2014. www.yalsa.ala.org/thehub/2014/02/03/yalsas-2014-hub-reading-challenge-begins/.

SOURCE: Allison Tran, "Get Your Reading Habits Organized," YALSA The Hub, January 28, 2013, yalsa.ala.org/thehub/2013/01/28/get-your-reading-habits-organized/.

Growing a young adult librarian
by Margaret Redrup-May

STAFF ARE THE MOST EXPENSIVE ASSET in any organization—this is true in the public library environment as in any workplace. Staff costs mainly derive from the time that recruitment and selection consumes. Once the new person is hired the costs continue, whether you have made the right decision or not. The time it takes to make the new hire a contributing member of your team depends on the clear understanding of what support he or she will need. The manager must provide several mentors—a professional mentor, organizational mentor, and a service mentor—although sometimes this can be the same person.

If your selection is wrong, then the costs will continue in low performance, a slowdown in achieving your strategic plan, and the costs of going through the hiring process again.

Recruitment

The recruitment process is about identifying the best candidate for the job. First, the library must undertake a review of its own need for a youth services position: How and where does it fit? What are the needs of the community at large and the targeted youth community? What are the expected outcomes? What resources does the position require?

Second, review the job description. Determine the skills, knowledge, and other requirements for the position. What personal characteristics will make this position work best with youth, with the community, and within the library? This review will help you recognize a match rather than reach for something that's not there.

What are the skills you should look for? In 2009, Stephen Abram identified five skills that all librarians should have—leadership, advocacy, interpretation, empathy, and imaginative entrepreneurial skills. Leadership skills are those that influence society in a positive way. To be blunt, we might have the best library services in the world, but if our community is unaware of them and does not make full use of them, then our doors are blocking the community and we lack leadership. We need to be advocates and show that we understand our community and the issues it is facing. We should be making the library a place where people can come to see how technology fits into their lives. We must recognize that the world is changing and that doing things the way we always have is not a model for success. Abram issued a challenge: "It is up to us to create the changes and future we want to see."

What are the attitudes, skills and knowledge that we are looking for in young adult librarians? First, acknowledge that skills and knowledge can be developed in the right candidate. Attitude defines the person and the success of the organization. The reputation of all libraries lives and dies on the attitude of the frontline staff.

The ALA Young Adult Library Services Association publishes *Competencies for Librarians Serving Youth* (ala.org/yalsa/guidelines/yacompetencies2010), which states: "Individuals who demonstrate the knowledge and skills laid out in this document will be able to provide quality library service for and with teenagers." It lists seven competency areas:

- leadership and professionalism
- knowledge of client group
- communication, marketing, and outreach
- administration
- knowledge of materials
- access to information
- services

Job descriptions for young adult librarians need to include these competencies. However, it is sometimes difficult to define the attitudes you want for the job. The best candidate is not only the one with the skills and attitudes but who is a natural youth advocate.

Recently, we advertised for a young adult librarian. In the interview we asked, "How would you decide on what services we should offer to young adults?" The successful candidate said that she would ask young adults what they want and ask the local youth agencies and the library staff what needs they have identified. This candidate recognized the need to consult. These are skills, but the attitude that she demonstrated was a willingness to go beyond expectations and consider the opinions and perspectives of a broad group of relevant people.

Here is a list of attitudes. Some are essential and some are highly desirable to make life easier as the manager:

- flexibility
- sense of humor
- ability to read people
- ability to follow instruction or ask questions for clarification
- willingness to undertake continuous learning
- willingness to take the initiative
- creativity
- motivation to take the job further
- ability to adapt to change
- integrity
- willingness to work and work hard for what they are committed to
- teamwork and an information sharer

The two most important areas to assess attitude are the candidate's commitment to youth and to customer service. It surprises me that people would even apply for a youth job without having these, but life is full of surprises. The attitude will come out in the examples they use to show they have the required skills and knowledge. Do they actually refer to youth in their answers at all? When they do, what does their body language tell you? Are they smiling when they talk about young adults? Do they love customer service? Do they look to other life experiences to review their service?

Selection

You must have people on your interview panel who clearly demonstrate an understanding of the position you are interviewing for and who will devote their valuable time to reviewing applications and conducting interviews to find the perfect candidate. The panel should be involved in developing interview questions, reviewing candidates, and selecting interviewees.

Résumés and application letters are a lovely mixture of reality and fantasy. Applications must be judged against the selection criteria that were carefully established in the job description and not by the mere look of the résumé. Are the skills the candidate has highlighted in the résumé and letter transferable to your situation? Is their experience legitimate or is it too good to believe?

The interview process takes a considerable amount of time, so you need to look after the physical and psychological comfort of the panelists and candidates. Make sure that the interview room is comfortably warm, with enough water to drink. Give them enough breaks so they can refresh themselves. Provide the panelists with pens and pencils, a sufficient supply of writing paper, and adequate time to discuss and rate each candidate.

The interview questions will be the most important tool you have in selecting the best candidate. Questions should be open-ended, giving candidates the opportunity to show that they have the attitudes, skills, and knowledge that you require. Present the candidate with hypotheticals and situationally targeted questions. Ask them some questions as they walk into the interview room to see how quickly they think on their feet.

In a recent interview for a young adult librarian, we developed an array of questions to test several things—their ability to think quickly, their commitment to prepare, their knowledge of technology, and their ability to make a presentation to young adults. Naturally, we did the "tell us about yourself" questions, but we also sent them two questions one week prior to the interview that involved demonstrating a website and explaining library services to a young adult audience. These two questions revealed the superior candidate. This person had clearly prepared, researched our resources, and even developed a flyer for the young adult audience on what the library could do for them.

Do not be influenced by a candidate's one strength—look at the whole picture—and do not be tempted to hire the best of a bad lot.

Interview panels must ensure that it is the candidate who does most of the talking. Impose the 20/80 rule: The panel talks 20% of the time and the candidate talks 80% of the time. Sometimes a candidate can impress the panel based on one particular question. The risk exists that the panel might ignore the other deficits that other questions turned up.

A tired interview panel might decide to hire the best available rather than look at how the top candidate fits into the job requirements. The best in the candidate pool might not be what the library needs, so any decision to compromise will result in a bad selection decision.

Finally, be certain you are reflecting the best of your organization. Yes, you are looking for the best candidate, but the candidates are looking at the library and how they have been treated. They are not waiting for the last question—"Is there anything you want to ask?"—to formulate their opinions. Give the candidate every opportunity to form a favorable opinion. How long has it been since they applied? How did you communicate with them about the interview? How were they welcomed as they arrived for the interview? How comfortable did you make them feel in the interview?

Retention

Retention consists of the elements in your workplace that encourage the new hire to become a long-term, value-adding employee. The library must make a commitment to develop their skills and knowledge to ensure that their work is done in the best and most efficient way. Selecting the right people is the first step; making sure they have the resources they need to do their job is an ongoing responsibility.

Give new employees time to experience the wide range of services the library offers to help them see where they fit and network with other supportive people. Allow them the opportunity to take additional training. Let them read professional journals to keep up to date with new ideas and innovations that can be incorporated into your library services.

Young adult librarians need to be active partners with other local youth-oriented organizations. They should be introduced to staff at high schools, community youth workers, and public and private organizations that assist young adults and their families. This network will assist them in marketing their services and enable them to keep up to date on youth issues.

Supervisors of young adult librarians must offer support as guides, mentors, sounding boards, and experts on library services and the profession. They need to be there for the occasional complaint and as backup when the worst happens. Virginia A. Walters, author of *Twenty-First-Century Kids, Twenty-First-Century Librarians*, writes: "I found that nurturing the people who worked for me always paid off. . . . Remember, good employees make you look good as well."

The candidate's role

The candidate has an important role to play in this equation. It is important for a candidate not to be swayed by the advertisement's persuasive words, which are truly a marketing ploy. Peruse the job description and reflect on the organization's needs and determine whether they match your desires for your goals and future. Before the interview, review the job description and develop questions that show you have the requisite skills and knowledge. Research the library by looking at its website and physically walking through it. This should ideally happen before you apply, or at least before your interview.

The interview can be a nerve-racking experience, and it is important to remember that the people on the other side of the table have already invested time in you—relate to them and show them you are worth it. This can be done by showing that you prepared. Tell them that you looked at the website; tell them you looked at the young adult space. Demonstrate your enthusiasm, and they will reflect it, making the experience better for everyone.

Conclusion

Finding the best young adult librarian for your community is a huge investment in recruitment, selection, and retention. Ultimately, the prize for all this investment is the best public library service for young adults, giving them a welcoming space where they can find inspiration, information, and the means to be the very best they can be.

SOURCE: Margaret Redrup-May, "Growing a Young Adult Librarian: Recruitment, Selection, and Retention of an Important Asset for Your Community," *Australasian Public Libraries and Information Services* 23 (June 2010): 74–79. Reprinted with permission.

TEEN SERVICES

CHAPTER THREE

Many teen services librarians are a department unto ourselves. But just because we may work alone does not mean that we are exempt from the types of structure and self-examination to which our coworkers in larger departments are accustomed. Part of what will legitimize teen services in your specific library and in the larger library world is subjecting ourselves and our own plans to the same scrutiny as the longer-established departments.

This chapter functions as a template for strategic planning for your teen services. Included are steps to take to become a leader in your library that others can turn to, as well as ways to distribute the responsibility and ownership of serving teens to others in the library so that you can eat dinner at home now and then, safe in the knowledge that the teens at your library are being well cared for.

An introduction to the teen services plan

by Karen Jensen

TEEN SERVICES IS A COLLECTION of multiple parts, including collection development and programming. There are other elements that affect teens and service to teens but are definitely outside of teen services in general. For example, a library will have a variety of general policies and procedures in place that affect teens but are in no way exclusive to teens. Some of these elements include library card acquisition policies, policies regarding AV materials, and internet use policies. When thinking about teen services, consider those elements exclusive to teens and then consider how general library policies, procedures, and services impact teens as well. All of these elements come together when discussing a teen services plan. See Appendix A, "A Sample Teen Services Plan," pp. 187–190.

Your teen services plan: Multiple parts, one whole

First, these basic elements must be in place:

1. A customer-service plan (See "What Does Customer Service to Teens Look Like?" on pp. 20–23)
2. A document that describes adolescent development
3. An acceptable-behavior policy
4. The components of your teen services plan
5. A marketing plan to get the word out to your teens—and the community—about teen services

Basic element 1: A customer service plan. It is essential that libraries have customer service plans and training in place. Customer service is the heart of what libraries do, so libraries should do it thoughtfully and purposefully. The customer-service plan should not be unique to teens, but staff should be reminded that it does extend to teens. It is important to remind staff that every patron who walks through your doors gets the same quality of customer service regardless of their race, gender—and yes, their age. This should come from the top down and be a regular part of all your customer-service discussions. Every patron should be greeted in a friendly manner, every question should be given the same quality answer, and every person who walks through your library doors should walk out

feeling satisfied with his or her library experience. Teens are not just future library supporters; they are library supporters *right now,* and it is their experiences in the library that will continue, or restrict, their support of the library.

Basic element 2: Adolescent development. A basic fact sheet on adolescent development will help staff understand why teens act the way they do. Why do they always walk through the doors in large, noisy groups? Well, teens are peer oriented and have just spent eight hours trying to sit still, quietly, in school—but their bodies are not really designed to do this. Do some staff-training exercises to get them thinking about what they were like when they were teens. What music did they like? How much time did they spend with their friends? How did they feel about adults and authority figures? Keep it simple, no more than a page of bullet points. If you have a college or university in your town, or nearby, you can also ask a psychology professor to come in and give a brief presentation on the topic; this can be an important part of staff-training exercises.

Virginia Cooperative Extension has created a good document addressing this topic at pubs.ext.vt.edu/350/350-850/350-850.html. It can be adapted for use in library staff training.

Basic element 3: An acceptable-behavior policy. If the library doesn't already have one, work with administrators to develop a good, solid acceptable-behavior policy. This should be a brief policy that outlines the overall mission of the library and touches on behaviors that would be a hindrance to others using the library. The policy should also outline what actions library staff will take in the event of behavior issues. All staff should be trained on how to handle difficult patron situations, when they should call the police, how to diffuse potential problem situations, when to get other staff members involved, and so on. It is important for staff to understand that the acceptable-behavior policy applies to all patrons across the board; it is not a tool to tame teenagers—it is a tool to help staff achieve quality patron service and maintain a comfortable and safe library environment. Again, this is something that should be included as part of staff training. Have staff engage in role-playing activities and learn how to interact with teens in a wide variety of situations. Better yet, get a panel of teens together and have them discuss with staff the positive and negative experiences they have had—in your library or in any business—to help them understand what quality customer service looks like to a teenager. Use the behavior policies of the Sharon (Mass.) Public Library and the Boston Public Library as examples. They can be found at www.sharonpubliclibrary.org/Policies/LibraryBehaviorPolicy.html and www.bpl.org/general/policies/acceptableuse.htm.

Remember, teens actually want and need limits, and they respect consistency. It is important that every staff member deals with problem situations fairly, consistently, and immediately. Remind staff that for every problem patron they have, whether teen or not, there are hundreds of other patrons that will never cause a problem.

Basic element 4: Components of a teen services plan. The previous three documents will make creation of a basic teen services plan much simpler. This document outlines the department's mission statement for teen services and demonstrates how it fulfills the overall library's mission. It should touch upon YALSA *Competencies for Librarians Serving Youth* (ala.org/yalsa/guidelines/ya-competencies2010) and the Search Institute's 40 Developmental Assets (www.search-institute.org/content/40-developmental-assets-adolescents-ages-12-18). These tools provide a good framework for evaluating your overall service goals and for communicating the benefit of teen services to staff, the board, and the greater community. Basic teen services plan components include:

1. A mission statement, which should support the overall library mission while respecting the developmental needs and individuality of teens.
2. Goals: what teen services are trying to achieve and why achieving them is important.
3. An enumeration of the specific ways in which the library will reach those goals:
    * Programming
    * Collections
    * Services

- Outreach
- Networking with community agencies and schools
- Marketing

Basic element 5: A marketing plan. See Chapter 6 for information on marketing plans.

A special note about collections: The library should have a collection-development plan and a materials-challenge policy in place. The latter need not be—and is preferably not—a teen-specific document; rather, it will describe the way collections are handled library-wide. All staff need to understand the scope and breadth of a teen collection and be given the tools to address any challenges that may come up.

Putting it together

When you have these components in place, you now have the tools you need to communicate with staff, to train any newly hired staff, and to put together a solid marketing plan. In fact, all new-staff training needs to involve basic teen services training. Also, whether or not the library has a dedicated teen services department, discuss with administrators the need to have a teen services representative at all management meetings to help ensure that any new policies and procedures consider the potential impact on this section of the population; children and adults are often well represented on management teams, but there is often a disconnect when it comes to teen services and management. Internet policies, obtaining library-card policies, and the use of AV materials are just some of the areas that can be challenging to teen services.

Consider the ways a teen services plan would work in your community or would benefit from additions or changes based upon the specific needs of your library program.

SOURCE: Specially prepared for The Whole Library Handbook: Teen Services *by Karen Jensen, teen services librarian, Grand Prairie, Texas.*

Teens on the platform: YALSA's National Teen Space Guidelines

by Katherine Trouern-Trend

YALSA'S GUIDELINES FOR PUBLIC LIBRARIES Task Force convened in 2011 to develop a set of guidelines for teen spaces in public libraries. The goal was to provide the library community with a foundational document that advises on what constitutes an effective library space for teen patrons.

According to the *2012 Public Library Data Service Statistical Report* (Public Library Association, 2012), only 33% of public libraries currently have at least one full-time staff member dedicated to teen services. The guidelines were therefore created as a tool for all staff working with teens. They are also a response to changing dynamics of teen culture and standards of 21st-century life.

Teens have new expectations for interaction with information as creators, leaders, and collaborators using varied interactive platforms. There is a clear convergence of social and learning platforms where teens are knowledgeable leaders in online environments. This includes gaming environments where teens serve as strategists and team members with peers and adults rather than solely as consumers of adult-created content and adult-led experiences. Teens use social media to harvest, create, and share information for entertainment and educational purposes. Schools are transforming how they relate and share information with students with the implementation of educational-technology initiatives such as the Games, Learning, and Assessment Lab (GLASS), in which popular video games are modified to create new videos that teach and help to evaluate student learning skills.

Gaming space at Aarhus Public Library, Denmark.

The GLASS Lab is based on the premise that video games are designed to measure progress, as learning is captured via a gaming experience and youths' proclivity toward digital media makes this a workable option. With an understanding of teens' high level of engagement in this type of environment, it makes sense that libraries would model a similar experience for teens. Teens expect to participate, collaborate, create, and consume.

With this thinking in mind, the National Guidelines Task Force set out to develop a set of standards that are relevant to libraries serving teens in 2012 and are aligned with the reinvention of how knowledge is created and disseminated today. Just as schools are transforming their teaching models to address new expectations for a participatory learning experience, libraries must consider this changing media ecology in shaping physical and virtual teen spaces to stay relevant with our teen customers.

Teen ownership

An important concept running through the *National Teen Space Guidelines* is the idea of teen ownership in defining and maintaining both physical and virtual spaces. If teens are able to create content using many popular digital platforms, it makes sense that teens would expect to do the same in their library space, and it makes sense for libraries to pay attention to this.

Teens expect to be able to interact with digital content and share ownership of information relevant to them. The way teens interact with content in popular virtual environments should help define the way in which a library structures its online presence with teens. Simply feeding information through librarian-created content is no longer an effective means of reaching teens and engaging them in the library. Giving teens leadership in creating library content gives them ownership of their library's virtual and physical space. There is a range of possibilities for teens to create content for libraries: online book reviews, music reviews and playlists, game reviews, website reviews, Facebook pages, Twitter posts about library events or programs, how-to videos on creating Facebook cover photos, mixing beats online, or learning dance steps. The key is knowing what information is relevant to your teens, what kind of content they want to create or learn to create, and how your library can facilitate that to give them ownership of the content and what happens in their space.

Our role as librarians has changed for many of our patrons, especially our teen patrons. We, of course, hold specialized knowledge, but we

Teen space, Dunedin Public Library, New Zealand. Flickr photo used CC BY-SA 3.0.

must present information in a new way that validates teens as knowledge creators and collaborators. Our role is as a guide, collaborator, and supporter of teen interests and needs. Our teens use our libraries for varied purposes. We may serve teens who use the library solely for online entertainment or as a source of recreational reading; that is how they define the library. We may have teens who use the library solely to study; that is how they define the library. We may have teens who use the library as a hangout; that is how they define the library. A library's purpose is to serve all customers based on the community's need. This is true for teens and for adults. YALSA's *National Teen Space Guidelines* recognizes this need to serve the ways teens define the library.

Where's the money?

When most librarians think of teens, they think technology. The next thought often is about money and how technology means spending money. Yes, hardware costs money, but there are many creative ways to build a high-impact teen space that does not require thousands of dollars. It's great if you get funding, but if you don't have the funding for Mac labs or iPads, you can still build a vibrant teen space. You work with what you have. A way to think about this is "How do I increase access and engagement within the space that we have?" instead of "We don't have enough stuff or money for the stuff we need." For example, teens bring their own mobile technology into the library space, and the guidelines therefore recommend having adequate outlets to accommodate this technology (cell phones, MP3 players, tablets, laptops) for teens to plug in their many devices for use in the library.

With a few extra tables from the downtown library, we created a Teen Zone in our branch library. In the Teen Zone, teens can bring in their laptops, listen to music, and watch videos. On Fridays, we have snacks for teens. Our policy: no earphones required. Conversation easily flows from world news, to school drama, to celebrity gossip, to personal triumphs and fears. Youth share and create media with peers using their own technology brought into the space. All staff interact with teens naturally and easily, giving value to their presence, interests, and needs within the library. Teens check out magazines, urban lit, YA novels, and graphic novels, and we allow the teens to navigate their own experience.

Allowing teens to navigate and lead peers in the library environment gives teens a platform for engagement and learning. Let teens define their service model and space needs. Teens expect to have ownership of information that is relevant to them, as evidenced by their behavior as creators, collaborators, strategists, consumers, and leaders in their online entities. Teens are citizen reporters and content creators in online leisure communities as well as propagators of information in national events. Eyewitness accounts of the movie-theater shooting in Aurora, Colorado, on July 20, 2012, came first through text, photo, and videos on Twitter by young people. Youth across the Middle East precipitated the Arab Spring, which began on December 18, 2010, using social media to provide real-time reports on military crackdowns and citizen unrest in their communities. Online and social forums have given teens the voice and power to affect local, community, national, and global movements of empower-

Teen area, Schaumburg Township (Ill.) District Library. Photo by Mariusz Mizera.

ment and change. This is their natural environment, and they are the leaders. Teens expect to have a voice in their information environments.

Teen space guidelines

YALSA's *National Teen Space Guidelines* are divided into six areas related to shaping physical teen spaces and three areas focused on shaping virtual teen spaces. Each is further defined with key considerations and recommendations for implementing components of the guidelines.

The Physical Guidelines

1. Solicit teen feedback and input in the design and creation of the teen space.
2. Provide a library environment that encourages emotional, social, and intellectual development of teens.
3. Provide a library space for teens that reflects the community in which they live.
4. Provide and promote materials that support the educational and leisure needs of teens.
5. Ensure the teen space has appropriate acceptable-use and age policies to make teens feel welcome and safe.
6. Provide furniture and technology that are practical yet adaptive.

The Virtual Guidelines

7. Ensure content, access, and use are flexible and adaptive.
8. Ensure the virtual space reflects 21st-century learning standards.
9. Provide digital resources for teens that meet their unique and specific needs.

These guidelines are meant to be a starting point for defining high-impact teen spaces and a measurement tool for libraries to gauge their level of success in meeting the needs and expectations of 21st-century youth. The guidelines are available for free at ala.org/yalsa/guidelines/teenspaces.

SOURCE: Katherine Trauern-Trend, "Teens on the Platform: YALSA's National Teen Space Guidelines," *Young Adult Youth Services* 11, no. 1 (Fall 2012): 4–6.

Evaluation: Is where you begin where you end?

by Karen Jensen and Heather Booth

IT IS IMPORTANT as teen services librarians that we spend time evaluating our work. We want to make sure that we accomplish what we set out to accomplish. Although most librarians keep track of statistics and can rattle off a numerical account of the year, we all know that the numbers don't tell the whole story. Additionally, it isn't just librarians who need to learn from these evaluations. Our boards of trustees, directors, and department heads will use our program evaluations when determining funding, staffing, and overall importance of the library's teen services. For this reason, we recommend looking beyond simple statistics and really evaluating what you are doing in terms of your teen programming.

First, let's clarify some terminology. A teen program is a single event, say a Zombie Prom or a craft event. Some librarians encourage event attendees to complete individual program evaluations, which is not an ideal situation. The theory behind traditional program evaluation involves the desire for immediate feedback and asks teen patrons to fill out an evaluation sheet at the end of a program. We don't invite guests into our homes for a peek and ask them to fill out an evaluation sheet, and we shouldn't be doing it at a teen program either. Filling out evaluation sheets is too reminiscent of school, and it can dull the program experience by putting the official paperwork stamp on it. Although it is a good idea to have goals for your specific programming events, whether or not those individual program goals were met can be determined by self-assessment. Instead, offer teens a once-yearly evaluation form to complete.

Why do evaluations?

Evaluations are important because they help us determine if we are meeting the goals we have set out for ourselves as teen librarians. This means you have to have goals, which is, in fact, the perfect place to start. But goals themselves are not enough. Evaluations are necessary tools that give us feedback on our progress toward meeting those goals, and they indicate whether we need to adjust our methods to better or more quickly meet our goals. Evaluations, then, are the rudders that help you steer the ship.

Youth Services Librarian Darla L'Allier with zombie at the 2012 Tulsa City-County (Okla.) Library Zombie Prom.
Flickr photo used CC BY-SA 3.0.

Thoughtful and well-developed evaluations also provide talking points to discuss the success of your teen services plan with administrators, community influencers, and the community at large. The findings of evaluations can become your selling points. Statistics help clarify what you are doing to the public; they are one form of raw data for reporting. More thorough evaluations go beyond the simple reporting of numbers and provide context and meaning. It's easy to say you circulated X number of books and held Y number of programs attended by Z number of teens, but good evaluations provide feedback that goes beyond numbers. For example, on an evaluation, ask for feedback statements, and use those statements in yearly reports and publicity statements. If a teen responds on an evaluation form that "I really like the summer reading program; it gives me something to do and helped me learn to love reading," this actual survey-response statement can become a selling point to include in yearly reports to your administration and community. These type of statements show benefit and enjoyment outside of numerical statistics; they put value on library efforts.

Goals: The end starts at the beginning

Evaluations help us determine whether we are on the right track. They ensure that we are accomplishing the things that we want to accomplish. To evaluate our performance, we have to have some starting goals. Your goals can be quantitative (to have at least one program a month) or qualitative (to enhance the lives of teens in your community by providing access to a diverse collection of recreational reading materials). Quantitative goals are easier to evaluate, because they come with a built-in measuring stick. Qualitative goals are less easy to evaluate but still an important part of the planning process.

The beginning of a new year is a great place and time to set goals for teen programs (see the section on teen services plans, pp. 44–46, for more information). First, outline the various components of the library that you are responsible for and both directly and indirectly serve teens. Those areas include collection development, programming, the teen area, policy development, networking, and outreach to schools. Next, outline specific goals that you and your library would like to accomplish in those various areas during the next year. For example, under outreach to schools, you can set several goals: Do four school visits, create an email database of teachers, send them a monthly update of upcoming teen activities, and participate in the yearly open house nights. At the end of the year, it is simply a matter of going through your service plan and indicating if, and how, you met the goals.

If you didn't meet your goals, it is important to ask yourself why. For example, going back to our outreach to schools, perhaps you will note a resistance on the part of the schools, which sometimes happens. Maybe what you are offering is not what they need so they didn't embrace it, and you need to adjust what you are offering. Maybe there are past bad relationships that you need to work on fixing. Whatever the issues may be, evaluating your yearly goals will help you identify them and address them. In the same vein, identifying your successes helps you know which elements to keep.

When discussing evaluations, think of everything you do—from collection development, to your teen space design and layout, to your individual program events—as your overall teen services plan. Every library should have an overall mission statement, some vision statements, and a yearly (or long-term) plan, and teen librarians can set up a subset of plans for the teen services department. Having an overall teen services plan makes it easier for teen librarians to evaluate the impact of the various services they offer. Instead of looking at individual programs and events, evaluate your teen services as a whole. Look at the big picture. There are three frameworks that you can use to do this:

- the YALSA competencies, as an evaluation framework
- the 40 Developmental Assets, as an evaluation framework
- input from teens in a yearly evaluation form

Think of it as a triangle that provides a stable foundation for a successful teen services program, and ideally a good evaluation practice involves using some form of all three.

YALSA best practices

When developing a yearly plan that will be the basis for evaluation, consult the YALSA *Competencies for Librarians Serving Youth* (ala.org/yalsa/guidelines/yacompetencies2010). Here, a group of YA librarians have put together a comprehensive list of elements that are essential to teen services; these provide both a good basis for planning and a good framework for both self- and teen services evaluation. Many of the elements of this book are designed to help equip teen services librarians to be successful in the various areas listed in the *Competencies*.

It should be a yearly practice to evaluate oneself and the library's teen services program to determine how well you are meeting the above listed competencies. Under each subheading, you should be able to state specific examples of how you or the library's teen services program demonstrates a level of competency. These also serve as good talking points when discussing teen services with administrators, community leaders, and others.

40 Developmental Assets

The 40 Developmental Assets are an important tool because they help us plan and evaluate what we are doing in our youth services departments. As discussed on pp. 7–11, when planning programs and services, meeting one or more of the 40 Developmental Assets adds value to libraries. When evaluating and communicating about your library's teen services, the assets provide a stable, proven framework that helps those working with teens ensure that they are, in fact, meeting the needs of teens and are therefore successful.

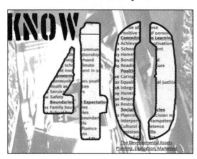

Take, for example, a traditional library public-relations tool: the yearly director's report. A library can put out a report that says items in the teen collection circulated *X* number of times. ("But what does that mean? Compared to what? I don't know; is that good or bad?") In comparison, you can say: "Through a variety of programs and services such as [specific examples], the [Sample Public Library] helped teens in the [Sample community] reach 27 of the 40 Developmental Assets." Again, give specific examples, such as providing teens with opportunities to have leadership roles and giving teens a voice through your teen advisory board, providing teens with opportunities to serve their community through your teen volunteer program, and supporting a teen's commitment to learning by providing quality library collections, opportunities to engage in literature-based programming and discussions, and homework-support materials.

By using the 40 Developmental Assets as a planning, evaluation, and communication tool, you help underline the value of libraries in your community, and you do so in a way that puts the library's success into a specific, understandable, measurable framework.

Surveys

The final evaluation component of our evaluation triangle involves getting teen feedback. It is true: Libraries can't serve teens successfully unless librarians care about them, know them, and value them. If teen librarians are really good at their jobs, they will empower teens and help give teens a voice. One of the best ways to do that is to get teen input. This can be done on an ongoing basis with teen advisory boards (TABs) and teen advisory groups (TAGs), but there is tremendous value in doing a yearly, large-scale survey to get a wider breadth of feedback.

TABs and TAGs cannot take the place of yearly surveys. The truth is, TAGs attract a certain type of teen, and they tend to be limited in scope because you

Sample survey

Teen Summer Reading Club

Did you participate in this year's Teen Summer Reading Club?   □ Yes   □ No
If yes, what is your overall grade for the club?   (Excellent) A B C D F (Poor)
How do you prefer to keep track of your reading?
    Number of Books Read   Amount of Time Spent Reading   Other _____
What types of activities would you like to see included in future Teen Summer Reading Clubs?

What did you think of the prizes?   (Excellent) A B C D F (Poor)
What types of prizes would you like to see in the future?
General comments about the Teen Summer Reading Club:

Teen Programs

Did you attend any of the teen programs in the last year?   □ Yes   □ No
If yes, what did you think of the programs?   (Excellent) A B C D F (Poor)
What type of library programs are you interested in? (circle all that apply)
    Crafts, Trivia, Games, Speakers, Book Discussion, None, Other _____
Suggestions for future programs:

What is the best day of the week for you to attend programs? (circle all that apply)
    Monday Tuesday Wednesday Thursday Friday
What is the best time of day for you to attend programs? (circle all that apply)
    3:00–4:00 p.m.   4:00–5:00 p.m.   5:00–6:00 p.m.   6:00–7:00 p.m.   7:00–8:00 p.m.
How do you hear about our programs? (circle all that apply)
    Website, Newspaper, School, Friends in Library, Other _____

Teen Contests

Did you participate in any of the teen contests in the last year?   □ Yes   □ No
If yes, what did you think of the contests?   (Excellent) A B C D F (Poor)
What was your favorite contest from the past year (and why)?

Suggestions for future contests:

The Teen Area

What is your overall grade for the teen area?   (Excellent) A B C D F (Poor)
What parts of the teen collection do you use?
    Nonfiction   Never Monthly Weekly Other _____
    General Fiction   Never Monthly Weekly Other _____
    Graphic Novels   Never Monthly Weekly Other _____
    Inspirational Fiction   Never Monthly Weekly Other _____
    Audiobooks   Never Monthly Weekly Other _____
    Teen Magazines   Never Monthly Weekly Other _____
What are your favorite genres? (Circle all that apply)
    Realistic Fiction, Historical Fiction, Science Fiction, Inspirational Fiction, Horror,
    Mysteries, Humorous Fiction, Fantasy, TV/Movie Tie-ins, Graphic Novels, Nonfiction
General suggestions for improving the teen area:

have to limit their numbers for them to function effectively. With TAGs, libraries don't always get the diverse feedback that comes from reaching out to outliers. So at the end of every summer or the beginning of the school year, put together a large-scale survey.

A yearly survey is not a perfect tool, but any tool is better than no tool. Surveys are limited in their usefulness for a few reasons. They require opt-in participation, which will skew your sample. Also, since surveys work best when they are anonymous—to ensure more honest feedback—there are few direct incentives that can be used to encourage participation. Because of the limitations of surveys, a best-case scenario uses a variety of tools to develop a more fully formed picture of a library's teen services program. Ideally, you would have a TAG, engage your teens on a daily basis, do mini surveys on your social-media sites, and so forth, but don't underestimate the value of a large-scale survey, which can have these benefits:

- Providing large-scale feedback from a wider sample of your target demographic
- Providing feedback upon which to make decisions and discuss the decisions in terms that make sense to administrators (remember, numbers matter to administration)
- Providing feedback to share with your community and community agencies that work with teens
- Providing valuable teen quotes to share in all your various PR forums
- Giving your teens a voice and empower them

So, how do you do a survey?

1. Outline the type of feedback that you need to have a successful, comprehensive teen services program that includes collection development; programming, including types, hours, days, etc.; summer reading programs, including prizes and format; and more.
2. Formulate a template (an example is provided on p. 53). Make sure the survey has a way to get both statistical data and verbal feedback. Ask open-ended questions as well as empirical data questions.
3. Find a way that works well to distribute the survey. If you have a good relationship with your schools, you can ask the schools to help distribute it. Put copies in your teen area and share them through your various online resources.
4. Set a specific but reasonable time window for survey completion. Make sure instructions for completing and returning the survey are clear.
5. Remember that anonymity helps ensure more honest feedback.
6. Compile the data and run with it.

When getting feedback, pay particular attention not only to the empirical data, but to any verbal feedback that teens leave. For example, give room for teens to discuss what they like and don't like about the library's teen space, the types

of programs presented, the materials in the collection. Sometimes, teens provide gold-nugget quotations, such as "The Summer Reading Club gave me something fun to do over the summer and I found a lot of books I loved." These types of quotes can be utilized in marketing materials and provide quality sound bites that go beyond statistics and library employee opinions.

Like marketing, planning requires intentionality. Intentionality helps a library determine what it wants and needs to do to serve its teens, and evaluations help libraries make sure that they are reaching those goals. If yearly evaluations prove that we aren't meeting those goals, they provide information that can help libraries readjust and get back on the right course. A three-sided triangle approach helps us make sure we are meeting professional competencies, known youth assets, and the wants of our teens as voiced by the teens themselves. This type of input is invaluable and leads to greater success.

Focus groups

Though a large-scale yearly survey will likely yield a more diverse body of responses than just polling your TAG, such surveys are not always the right tool for your community. How else to gather lots of responses from a wide variety of teens?

A focus group will yield fewer responses than a survey, but an effort can be made to make sure that these responses are diverse by prescreening interested teens. Placing an ad in the school newspaper, requesting that teachers share the invitation with teens, or asking other local youth organizations—such as sports teams, religious-fellowship groups, scouts, choirs, or park-district groups—to recommend participants can achieve a similar diversity to the group that might complete a survey. Offering a small thank-you gift (such as a nominal iTunes or coffee card) and feeding the group will sweeten the opportunity. If desired, once enough teens have expressed interest, these teens could be further screened to make sure that the group is representative of a wide enough group of ages, library users and nonusers, and genders.

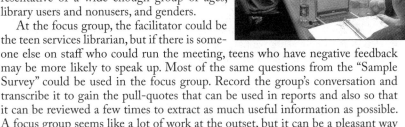

At the focus group, the facilitator could be the teen services librarian, but if there is someone else on staff who could run the meeting, teens who have negative feedback may be more likely to speak up. Most of the same questions from the "Sample Survey" could be used in the focus group. Record the group's conversation and transcribe it to gain the pull-quotes that can be used in reports and also so that it can be reviewed a few times to extract as much useful information as possible. A focus group seems like a lot of work at the outset, but it can be a pleasant way to get a good amount of information in a short amount of time and is likely less time-intensive than tabulating piles of paper surveys.

The evaluation report

Once all of the three legs of the evaluation triangle have been completed, you can compile a report of your teen services evaluation. As should be clear now, all three will complement one another. For example, YALSA Competency 4 from "Area II," "Knowledge of Client Group," is "Identify and meet the needs of patrons with special needs." In the evaluation report, you might give evidence of meeting this competency by illustrating new titles that feature teens with special needs, describing the annual meeting you have with special-needs educators at the local high school, and discussing how the library is handling new developments in ebooks and e-readers with regards to special-needs teens. The report could include a teen comment from the survey; for example, "I'm glad there are more audiobooks now because it helps me understand what I'm reading better if I can hear the books too." Then point out that the additions to the collection support Developmental Asset number 27, "Equality and Social Justice," and several of the assets in the "Commitment to Learning" section. All three pieces of the evaluation triangle work together to create a thoroughly supported, holistic look at the success of the teen program.

SOURCE: Specially prepared for *The Whole Library Handbook: Teen Services* by Karen Jensen, teen services librarian, Grand Prairie, Texas, and Heather Booth, teen services librarian, Thomas Ford Memorial Library, Western Springs, Illinois.

Teen Librarian Advocacy 101

by Karen Jensen

ADVOCACY IS THE ACT of making your library's presence in the community known, understood, and valued. The teen librarian needs to make sure the community knows what the library is doing for teens in the community and why it matters. Basic literacy, education support, lifelong learning, helping teens gain the tools they need to succeed, and more—every member of your community needs to know. Publishers talk about "impressions": Each time a book cover is seen, it makes an impression; their goal is to get enough impressions that their book can't be ignored. Your job is to get your library—your teen services programming—enough impressions that it too can't be ignored. As your message is repeated and ingrained in the community culture, your community members themselves become your best advocates. The question is, how do you do that?

As teen services librarians, we find ourselves doing multilevel advocacy: We advocate to our coworkers, our administrations, our communities. We want support and resources; we want our frontline staff to be our voice; we want our administrators to make sure we have the time, space and money we need to effectively serve our teens. That is why we must advocate.

Phase 1

Make your presence known in the community at large and with your administrators and staff.

Goals: Move your patrons and community members from thinking of it as "the library" to thinking of it as "my library." Creating a sense of pride and ownership on the behalf of the community means less advocacy work for you as they now become your greatest advocates.

Areas of focus: Developing relational librarianship, customer service, social media, and presence.

Relational librarianship. When members of the community feel that they know and are known by their library staff members—at all levels—we enter into a relational partnership. Some of this can be accomplished through the library's effective use of social media. Blogs can be your

Staff picks, Harris County (Tex.) Public Library. Flickr photo, used CC BY-SA 3.0.

friend. At my last two library positions, I created staff-picks displays (like all good librarians, I borrowed the idea from elsewhere). At my current library position, staff picks are continually put out with a staff name and face to go with them. Over time, patrons find the staff members with whom they have common reading interests and seek them out for personalized readers' advisory services.

Customer service. Good businesses know that quality customer service is key. It helps build relationships one-on-one. The simple act of calling someone by name can make all the difference. Continual staff training and communication is key to good customer service. A satisfied teen is your best advocate. Create the best library policies to create consistent, quality services and train your staff not only how to implement them, but why. Key talking points help staff keep messages on point and keep your patrons satisfied. Some examples:

"Why do we have public computer limits?" To help make sure that the greatest number of teens get to use the computers in ways that are satisfying to them all.

"Why do we have check-out due dates?" So that the greatest number of patrons can get their hands on the materials they need in a timely matter.

Social media. Facebook, Twitter, Pinterest, and more—social media is an important tool in today's culture. It helps you build relationships with your teens and community members and increases your presence. Different types of groups use different types of social media in their own ways, and the library really needs to be using them all to reach as many teens as possible. Twitter works well for brief blasts, fun contests, chats, and more. Pinterest, one of the fastest-growing social-media tools, has several advantages: (1) it is visual, (2) it is more easily organized and accessed, and (3) it can be used in such a diverse number of ways. You can use Pinterest to share booklists, staff favorites, programming information, and more. You can also invite your community to create their own additions, which helps generate buy-in. (See the Bookfessions Tumblr, bookfessions.tumblr.com, for a fun example of community involvement.) Share teen-created artwork. And don't forget to blog!

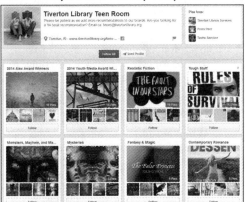

Pinterest board for Tiverton (R.I.) Library Services Teen Room.

Presence. Get your name in the press as often as possible. Contact the local newspaper and ask if you can write a regularly occurring guest column. Attend community planning and development groups. If they don't exist, start your own. Have regularly occurring programming events that keep your library's name on the tips of patrons' tongues. These events should range in variety and audience but generate buzz.

Phase 2

Network with your community leaders.

Goals: Build partnerships with your community leaders and maintain relationships that keep your library moving forward and viable.

Areas of focus: Meet and greet, extend an invitation, and social media.

The meet and greet. Want to know your community leaders and advocate for your library? Go out there and meet them. Or invite them to a meeting. Better yet, do both. Visit the leaders in your community; drop them off a welcoming gift and your business card. Make sure you have a tip sheet (consider using infographics for an extra punch) that highlight the who, what, where, when, and why of your library and teen services programming to leave behind. Then, invite them all to the library for an open house with tours, highlights, and, yes, food. Don't just seek to meet your community leaders; seek to be one. Remember, show your community leaders how you are helping meet the 40 Developmental Assets of teens; more assets means fewer risky behaviors, and all communities agree that is a good goal.

Extend an invitation. Find out where your community leaders are active—Rotary Club, Key Club, community foundations, etc.—and offer to be a part. Regularly attend meetings and contribute meaningfully to the dialogue and goals. If you see, or hear expressed, a need in your community, create an organization to help meet that need, and invite others into partnership with the library. Let your leaders know that the library is available to help provide information research, meeting rooms, or staff to do programming.

Social media. Create unique social-media pages to dialogue with your community leaders. If you have a business-oriented blog, consider a teen services blog open to community organizations that serve teens. Create a community wiki where organizations are invited to share information, such as hours and contact information as well as upcoming calendar dates. This keeps everyone in the dialogue and has the bonus feature of allowing staff members to know where to send patrons for assistance when questions arise, in addition to positioning the library as the information center of the community.

Phase 3

Who does this? On some level, you—the teen services librarian—have primary responsibility. But every staff member has unique talents and interests, and these can be tapped. Phases 1 and 2 are concurrent and ongoing. Advocacy is a process, and your goal is to do it effectively and continually. One voice in the wilderness is hard to hear, but a chorus of angels cannot be ignored.

Advocating for teens internally. It is easy to assume that everyone who works in the library is passionate about libraries and embraces the idea of teen services. Unfortunately, this is not always the case. When working with teens, you will

run across other library staff members who don't necessarily jump on board with teen services. Sometimes, this may even be your administration. But there are things you can do to help them understand teens and why library services to teens are important.

First, make sure you have these four basic elements in place:

- A basic customer service plan
- A document describing the basics of adolescent development
- A basic acceptable behavior policy
- The teen services plan (see "An Introduction to the Teen Services Plan," pp. 44–46, and Appendix A, "A Sample Teen Services Plan," pp. 187–190)

With a plan in place, you'll want to make sure you have regular communication with library staff. This ongoing communication should keep staff updated on current trends, popular titles, the latest research on teen development, and upcoming library events. There are several "BE-attitudes" that can help you be successful in your communications with staff.

"BE–attitudes" of communicating with staff

When you have these components in place, you now have the tools you need to communicate with staff and to train any newly hired staff. In fact, talk to your administrators and make sure that a part of any new-hire training involves sitting down with you and discussing teen services. Also, discuss with administrators the need to have a teen services representative at all management meetings to help ensure that any new policies and procedures that are being discussed are considering the potential impact on this section of the population; children and adults are often well-represented on management teams, but there is often a disconnect when it comes to teen services and management. Managing internet policies, obtaining library card policies, and using AV materials are just some of the areas that are interesting areas for teen services librarians.

The best way to get all staff on board with teen services is to make sure they understand why you do what you do. To help communicate with staff, follow these basic "BE-attitudes," core customer-service tenets that help quell negativity, equip your coworkers with knowledge, and position yourself as a strong internal advocate for your teen patrons.

BE informative. We love to share information with our teens. Book lists, cool links, upcoming movie news, program promotion, updates on newly added titles—if you are sharing any of this with your teens, make sure you are sharing it with your staff, too. You, the teen service librarian, will likely not be at the library and available every minute the library is open, so you need to share your information with the rest of the staff. This way, when teens ask about what they saw online or on display, staff will have the answer.

- Make sure staff know about new and popular materials.
- Make sure staff know how to address inquiries into current trends: vampire fiction, paranormal reads, what to read if you like *The Hunger Games.* Try and share one readers' advisory tool made by you or an online site weekly. Make sure there is a folder of teen links bookmarked on the library's favorites so staff know where to find them when RA questions arise and you are not around.
- Anytime you give a book talk or distribute a book list, be sure staff has access to a copy of the list so the night after the school visit, when teens come to the library only remembering a few details of the book you described, staff can refer the student to the list to jog their memory.
- Let staff know about events in popular teen culture: what books are being made into a

The six BE-attitudes, in Latin.

movie, new music, and more. Highlight popular people and stories covered in your magazine collection, music collection, movie collection, and online.

- Share campaigns aimed at teens, like the "It Gets Better" project or "[Delete] Digital Drama."
- Share the latest research in adolescent development, technology use, and trends, etc.
- And, of course, make sure staff know about upcoming events, new resources and services, teen services campaigns, and so on.
- For events like a summer reading club or a Read Off Your Fines event or a special contest, develop specific FAQs outlining what they need to know, including dates and prizes. Save your flyer as a JPEG, and put it in your FAQ so staff see what the patrons will be seeing.
- Find creative ways to share what you're reading and your reviews with staff, too.

BE proactive. As information and technology gurus, it is our job to lead the way. We don't want to be reactive; we want to be proactive. We want to know about new trends, services, sites, and more so that we have answers when our teens have questions.

- Keep up to date and share tools often and regularly. By skimming a variety of outlets, you can help staff stay ahead of the information and technology curve, truly showing your teens that the library is *the* place for information. Get together a list of resources that meet your needs and then visit them frequently. Sign up for RSS feeds, newsletters, and Facebook updates. Keep your list visible by your computer as a reminder to check them out. Cover a wide variety of topics: teen literature, teen development, teen culture, music, movies, technology. Also, be sure that a couple of marketing sites are in your rotation (and use sites that are good *at* marketing).
- Try to anticipate needs, trends, and questions before they come up; it is a horrible feeling for staff to think they are the last to know something.

BE inspiring. Pass on positive feedback from teens, inspiring stories—those moments when a teen raves about the library.

Keep staff in the know about statistics—book circulation, program attendance. It helps to see growth and positive outcomes. Show staff that the library is meeting the goals that you set.

BE honest. Sometimes a situation occurs; acknowledge it. Use it as a training moment to refer back to policy and indicate what staff should do in the event that it happens again. Then, because we want to be inspiring, remind staff that a majority of the teens who come into the library are positive, as are a majority of staff interactions with teens.

BE consistent. Develop a regular format and schedule. A simple weekly email works, or if it's more your style or better suits your organization, develop a paper newsletter or utilize a staff communication notebook or post tidbits on the staff fridge each Friday. Whatever method you choose, brand your communication in a way that is consistent with both your library and your overall teen services scheme. Give it a title: "Teen News Today," "The Teen Services Must List" (yes, I am an *Entertainment Weekly* fan—great communication vehicle!), "Teen Services Top 10." Staff should come to anticipate and appreciate your weekly newsletter feed and find that it is a helpful tool.

BE fun. Occasionally, have a fun staff contest. Ask staff to share their favorite teen reads. See if they can complete the latest contest sheet that your teens are doing. See how they do at the *VOYA* Pop Culture quiz. See if they can find the title. You can modify the same activities you do with your teens and make it a fun mini moment with staff for team building, communication, and, again, buy-in.

By communicating regularly and frequently with staff, you lessen the need to have those big moments where you have to defend staffing and budgeting issues for a teen services program. Staff will already know what you are doing and that you are doing it successfully. In addition, staff feel valued and empowered by the sharing of information, and it creates that sense of buy-in; they are more likely to promote, promote, promote without thinking twice because it is second nature.

The end and the beginning of the year

At the end of each year, put together a year-end visual report (think data visualization), and share it with staff and administration. Discuss statistics, goals met, and highlights.

At the beginning of each year, put together an outline of known programming and events: "Teen Tech Week," "National Library Week," "Teen Read Week," "Summer Reading Club," etc. And put some goals for the year on paper. This helps put the year in focus, is a great tool to share with administrators and boards, and provides a general outline for the staff. Then, whenever anyone asks—a parent, community member, or a teen—staff can provide positive answers that highlight what an awesome teen program your library has!

Advocacy resources

ALA Office for Library Advocacy (ala.org/offices/ola).

ALA Public Library Association, Turning the Page Online (ala.org/pla/education/turningthepage).

SOURCE: Specially prepared for *The Whole Library Handbook: Teen Services* by Karen Jensen, teen services librarian, Grand Prairie, Texas.

PROGRAMMING

CHAPTER FOUR

Libraries are dynamic institutions that adapt and grow to meet the changing needs of the communities they serve. As part of this growth, contemporary libraries, thriving libraries, seek to become not temples of knowledge, but active spaces of learning, community partnership, group discussion, and hands-on experience. Libraries do this by engaging in programming. There are many types of programming that libraries can provide to teens in their communities, depending on the library's specific goals, space, staff, and budget. Here we will discuss what programming is, why we do it, and how we do it.

An introduction to teen programming

by Karen Jensen

PROGRAMMING IS ONE OF THE CORE SERVICES that libraries offer to teens in their communities. It can also be one of the most challenging services that we offer. Getting teens to attend programs can seem like an uphill battle at times; it is hard to find the right program and the right time to help maximize your program attendance. There are so many competing factors: extracurricular activities, jobs, other community organizations, etc. And programming can be expensive; you usually have to purchase materials, hire presenters and performers, and calculate the staff time spent researching, planning, marketing, setting up, and cleaning up for programs. When you have those moments where few teens show up for a program, it can be easy to forget exactly why teen programming is such an essential and vital part of teen services. And sometimes, we have to remind our coworkers and administrators why it is necessary for us to have budgets, time, and the tools necessary to be successful in our programming. So the question we must ask ourselves is, why bother?

Why program for teens?

Programming keeps your library visible in the community. Each program you have makes your presence known in the community and communicates the message that your library is a viable part of the community's educational and recreational needs. It also communicates the message that you understand, value, and respect the teens in your community and are actively providing a way to meet their needs.

Programming helps bring in new library patrons and encourages return business. Each program is an opportunity for a new teenager to become a regular library user. It is a way to demonstrate to your teens various ways that they can use the library that they didn't realize. Almost all programming can be tied in to our collections and services, so they remind patrons of the various resources and services we offer. Yes, even while you are playing *Survivor* with teens, you are also demonstrating to new teens the various ways that the library is accessible to them. Each program, especially those in a series like clubs or "Teen Coffeehouse," helps bring in repeat business.

Programming helps libraries build community partnerships. Programs are opportunities to work with various community resources and build partnerships—which most libraries have as one of their primary goals. You can partner with local businesses and agencies for prizes, share time and financial resources (as well as wisdom and experiences), and piggyback with larger agencies to gain greater visibility. For example, your local Big Brothers Big Sisters has developed programs that can be done in your library, thus saving you the time of developing a new program; these programs involve financial education, health issues, and more that are based on researched standards and well developed. The Red Cross offers several programs of interest to teens, such as courses on babysitting, first aid, and so forth.

Programming increases circulation, promotes your collection, and promotes literacy. As you develop a core teen patron base, your circulation will increase. In addition, you will have opportunities to better know your teen patrons and learn their reading interests so that you can purchase and place targeted books in their hands. Since teens are so peer oriented, they will often become your best publicity. The greatest thing that will ever happen is to stumble across a book that teens love enough that they tell all their friends that they have to read this book. Each program is also an opportunity to highlight parts of your collection that relate to the topic of the program or simply display new teen titles.

Programming helps fulfill your library's mission statement. Your library should have a well-developed mission statement, and it should include a reference to programming. Even if it doesn't, programming helps meet the educational goals, recreational goals, and life-long learning goals that are all a part of most library mission statements. Each program is an opportunity to market your methods of meeting these goals. A craft program will meet the needs of one part of your audience and focus on some parts of your mission statement, while a gaming program will meet the needs of a different part of your audience and mission. They demonstrate that "wow" factor: Here is an exciting event for teens to participate in. Because it is easier to market an individual program than to market the all-inclusive but abstract value of the library, programs can be an effective tool in conveying your methods of taking action on your mission statement.

4

Foundations of teen programming

So now that we understand why we need to do programming, where do we start? Well, like all life endeavors, we need to have some good foundations in place for teen programming.

At the very core of teen programs are the teens themselves. Before you begin planning programs, it is essential that you understand and respect the teenage years and developmental process. Additionally, you must understand the teen brain, and the distinct needs of teens in your community. Not only must you, as a teen librarian, have this knowledge, but you must actively and continually share it with all library staff. See Chapters 1, 2, and 5 in this book for more detailed information on understanding teens, their development, your local community, and how to train staff, respectively.

Considerations in teen programming

Next, you need to think about what type of teen programming you want to do. Not all library programming is created equal; different types of programs take different amounts of time and money, and they produce different results. In addition, they can reach different audiences. As you consider the types of programming to undertake, consider not just your audience, but your budget, your time, and your organizational support.

Structured versus unstructured. A structured program is one with a fairly comprehensive setup and a clear path the teens will take to see the activity through to the end. In an unstructured program, the librarian's responsibility will be to create an environment and setup in which the teens can essentially lead themselves through an activity or task. There should ultimately be a variety of degree in structure. Not all programs should be highly structured, nor should they all be without structure. Variety is indeed the spice of life, and finding the right balance in program structure goes a long way to its success. As an example, our library hosts an annual gingerbread-house program. The years we have provided each participant with a prepared kit for a house and the option to add on, versus the years when all of the supplies are on a central table, result in dramatic differences. The more structured setup yields a room full of very similar houses. The unstructured years are the ones in which our zombie Christmas– and Mies van der Rohe–inspired ecofriendly homes emerged.

Passive versus active. Passive programs allow teens to work in their own space at their own pace. These can include contests, scavenger hunts, and submission-based activities. Active programs have the benefits of being completed in a finite amount of time, bringing teens together with their peers, and having that "wow" factor that demonstrates that the library is a fun, exciting place to be. Some programs will naturally lend themselves to one type over another, but it never hurts to push the expected boundaries. If your in-person teen book group isn't picking up a following, try it as a passive online program, or create a conversation around books using sticky notes on the wall in your teen area.

Consider your audience. Middle-school teens are often a library's primary audience because they come with the least amount of competition. High school students are more engaged in extracurricular activities, relationships, and jobs. This means that you have to work harder to draw in high school students, but it is essential that all libraries do their best. The conventional wisdom is that middle school students are more likely to come to library programs to socialize and have fun, and high school students may be more attracted by programs that offer them something concrete that they need: study help, volunteer opportunities, college-essay workshops, or other skill-building activities.

Type of program. One of the best aspects of the teen librarian profession is the group of vastly creative individuals who are constantly devising new and engaging program possibilities. Here are some of the more popular standbys.

Gaming can include video games or traditional board games. Or get creative and do large-scale versions of popular games, such as a murder mystery (live *Clue*) or a human chess tournament à la Harry Potter.

Scavenger hunts can be fun and engaging ways to bring teens into the library, and they help teens learn rudimentary library skills as they race from task to task.

Cafés, from drop-in study nights to poetry cafés and open-mic nights, require the least amount of prep and planning and allow teens to be in peer-group settings.

Hands-on activities can be inexpensive or costly, and though each craft may have a limited target area, our contemporary maker culture provides an opportunity for teens to gain a sense of satisfaction as they walk out with something they have made, and they can also promote the library collection.

Speakers will demand teens to sit and remind them of school—but provide them with important information and very likely to reinforce library services or collection areas. Speakers can be free to the library or very costly, depending on the topic and presenter. The local public-safety police officer will likely give a brief, free presentation on babysitter safety, but an author event could run up quite a bill for the library. Either program will give teens a meaningful experience.

Promotion for the 10 to 1 Book Club.
Photo by Heather Booth.

Book clubs may be the most predictable type of program for a library to host, but they need not be traditional! Graphic-novel book clubs have grown in popularity, as have clubs oriented around state and local "best" lists, Mock Printz groups, mother-daughter book clubs, "Guys Read" clubs, or "Book Buddies" programs. All have books as a base but can be molded to the needs and interests of your community.

Teen advisory boards (TABs) give teens input on library matters. Because of their popularity and ubiquity, more on TABs will be discussed in Chapter 6.

Nontraditional programming. A lengthy discussion of nontraditional programs can be found later in this chapter.

The before and after of program planning

Before organizing a program, determine what your specific goals are: audience, attendance, expenditures—both staff time and money, and what you want the teens to accomplish.

Have a mechanism in place after a program so that you can determine if you have met your goals and how you can further meet them in the future.

Marketing your teen programs

Once you have your program in place, you'll need to start getting the word out. Although librarians are not trained in marketing, it is essential to market our programs if our significant investment of time, funds, and energy are to pay off in the form of a room full of teens. A lengthy discussion of marketing can be found in Chapter 6, but the basics of marketing programs are simple. When promoting your teen programs, consider the following.

Use the schools. Take or send flyers to be posted in classrooms or the library, or write brief PSAs to be read on the announcements. Here you have a captive audience, and it could be the beginning of a mutually beneficial partnership.

Don't forget local businesses. Where do the teens go after school but before doing homework? Where is the place to be after the choir concert or football game? Local ice-cream parlors, snack shops, bookstores, bowling alleys, and youth clubs are all great places to hang flyers and get to know the staff. They may even throw in for prizes down the road!

Word of mouth is your best publicity. Teens will go where their friends go and will take their friends' advice over the most enticing flyer or cleverly worded PSA. As you develop teen followers, they will spread the news for you, and it only takes one teen to get the ball rolling.

Let your fingers do the marketing. If you have the means, collect email addresses and send notices; get a Facebook page, and use the event function to invite teens to events; or post reminders in your status feed. If your teens aren't on Facebook, find out what their preferred online social network is and use it.

Make it a habit. Develop routines so that teens can better predict programming. If they know that there will be something great for them every Tuesday, the first Saturday of the month, or at 10:00 in the morning on days off from school, your programs will work their way into their plans and be easier to remember. This eliminates some of the guesswork for your patrons.

These basic elements will be useful in any type of program planning for your teen patrons. As you read through the more detailed thematic programs that follow, consider the purposes they fill, the considerations that are weighed, and the marketing strategies that make these programs successful. That said, even if you do everything right, there will be times when a program that you were sure would book weeks in advance just falls flat. Teens can be mysterious and fickle . . . and you never know when someone just happens to be planning the party of the year on the same day as a much-requested gaming program. It is discouraging, but don't give up. If they know that the library is a dependable, reliable place to find an activity, you will come out ahead in the long run.

SOURCE: Specially prepared for *The Whole Library Handbook: Teen Services* by Karen Jensen, teen services librarian, Grand Prairie, Texas.

Technology programming and teens
by Stacy Vandever Wells

TEENS ARE MORE CONNECTED THAN EVER, to their phones, gaming systems, and more. From social media to the latest apps, teens have an aptitude and ever-increasing appetite for technology. As advocates for teens, teen librarians must recognize the teens' thirst for technology and how their desire can be used as a platform in teen programming. It's not surprising that teens view learning as it fits in with, as Marc Prensky writes, "stuff they know from all their connections to the world and its people—from television, YouTube, the internet, IM, chat, social networking—and then lets them follow their own interests, learning things only as they become useful, sharing their views with each other along the way." Understanding how today's teens learn, as well as adopting a more studentcentric, collaborative learning approach, presents a wonderful opportunity for teen librarians to help foster this new learning paradigm by creating technology programs of interest and value.

To create programming that incorporates technology, there must be some understanding of current technology trends, and that can be daunting. In a world with new information, gadgets, and technology pouring in daily, it can become overwhelming. Sifting through the countless websites, magazines, and social-media sites to uncover the gem that will work with teens and your technology programming can be exhaustive.

Young Adult Library
Services Association
www.ala.org/yalsa

One important source to tap is the Young Adult Library Services Association (YALSA). YALSA has a host of resources available to stay connected and current with the ever-changing landscape of technology, from electronic discussion lists to the YALSAblog to YALSA national

---

Tech Squad search tips

How will you find the teens who will inform and even lead your programs?
1. **Observe.**
Take note of who and what is around you. Are you beginning to recognize faces? Are you seeing the same types of devices appearing in teens' hands?
2. **Engage.**
Introduce yourself. Ask questions. Pay attention to what teens are saying and doing.
3. **Listen.**
Once you have asked your questions, really hear the answers and do what you can to make sure that teens know that they have been heard.
4. **Recruit.**
If your location doesn't drop a Tech Squad into your lap, post signs, advertise in local school papers, reach out online, offer contests, or post flyers in local teen hangouts to recruit a group.
5. **Repeat.**
Just because you have a great group doesn't mean you're done. Once these teens graduate, you don't want to start from scratch. Continually run through these steps to keep yourself and your Tech Squad fresh and vital.

---

programming such as "Teen Tech Week." The amount of information that can be gleaned from YALSA and its members is enormous and applicable to your needs and your teens' needs.

Another viable source are the teens themselves. David Loertscher says to "surround ourselves with a Geek squad of young techies," and he's absolutely right. To get teens involved in technology-based programming at your library, you need to work with the teens who have an aptitude for technology. Finding these teens may take some time, but through keen observation and meaningful conversations, they can be found (see box above).

Once you have found your Tech Squad members, get them to give you ideas on programming, how to run the programming, and maybe even have them help set up or run the program or have them act as cohosts.

Additional sources of information include accessing the internet and actively using social media, from Twitter to Facebook and more. Visit Apple's website weekly and check out the new apps available and play around with them. Check out the *Publishers Weekly* online "Digital" section. For other technology advancements, read the technology sections of online news sources like *USA Today* or CNN.

Make sure to follow teen librarians you admire on Twitter, and learn by watching what they do and say. Follow techie people, and follow your friends. A lot can be learned by observation and interaction. The same is true for Facebook. "Like" things that teens would like and follow conversations— see what they're doing, what type of technology they're using. The key point here is observation.

For more specific and detailed programming ideas, there are two wonderful resources available that provide an abundance of information on understanding technology programming for teens and creating those programs. A great starting place is YALSA's "Teen Tech Week." This annual event focuses on teens and technology and provides numerous examples of programming that will get teens involved in the library.

The other is more specific and detailed: *Technology and Literacy: 21st Century Library Programming for Children and Teens* (ALA Editions, 2012), by Jennifer Nelson and Keith Braafladt. This book goes into detail about gaining staff support, program planning, growing an audience, and using the free online program Scratch (more about Scratch follows).

Quick-start programming ideas

Texting wars. In this round-robin tournament using the teens' phones, have them text preprinted scripts that you provide. Start off with simple scripts and have them get progressively harder.

One-minute movie contest. In groups, using a small and simple video camera, have teens film their movie and then have them edit their films using movie-editing software on a designated computer. Small video cameras can be purchased for under $100, and good editing software can be purchased for under $50.

How-to podcast workshops. Once a topic for discussion is decided upon, using a designated computer(s), use the free recording and editing software Audacity to create a podcast, in groups of two to three. Several online sources can help with the more technological aspects of this type of program. External microphones can be purchased for under $10.

Avatar workshop. Several free avatar websites are available online. The idea is to spark creativity.

Twitter scavenger hunt. Determine several "objects" to find on Twitter, some specific and others general. For example, you might ask teens to find a picture of a balloon or ask them to find out what Misha Collins had for lunch on Thursday. Make sure teens keep screen captures of items found. Twitter accounts are needed for this program.

Scratch workshops. Scratch (scratch.mit.edu/about/) is a free online website that teens can use to create "interactive stories, animations, games, music and art." Scratch accounts are required.

When conducting a technology-based program, it's always best to be familiar with each element and have a good understanding of how each piece works.

Getting teens to a library program can be a challenge. Marketing that works for adults isn't necessarily going to work for teens. Teens are less likely to read the local newspaper ad you placed or notice all the flyers located at checkout. So where do you start? A great place to begin is with the teens who do frequent your library. Talk to them. Ask them questions. In *Technology and Literacy: 21st Century Library Programming for Children and Teens,* the authors heavily suggest hand selling to teens individually with a small flyer in the library.

Take it to the next level by working with local gaming centers, movie theaters, teen clothing stores, and other places that teens frequent. Talk to the shop owners about placing flyers on their community bulletin boards or at their checkout stands and possibly hosting a teen technology event in their stores. Also, let the teens know it's okay to bring their friends, because word of mouth is the best marketing tool available.

In a world where teens and technology go hand in hand,

Texting WAR.
Are YOU up for the challenge?

When: January 23, 2012 at 2p.m.
Where: Arlington County Library, in the Teen Zone
Bring: Your game face and your favorite texting device

it's more important than ever that teen services librarians embrace this new paradigm. With the incorporation of technology into teen programming not only are teen services librarians creating programs of value, but also of interest to teens. With time and dedication, it is possible to create technological programming for teens that is relevant and entertaining.

Resources

Andrew Churches. "Comparing 20th and 21st Century Educational Paradigms." Educational Origami. October 2, 2010. edorigami.edublogs. org/2010/10/02/comparing-20th-and-21st-century-educational-paradigms/.

Megan Fink. *Teen Read Week and Teen Tech Week: Tips and Resources for YALSA's Initiatives.* Chicago: ALA Young Adult Library Services Association, 2011.

David Loertscher. "The State and Future of Educational Technologies." *Teacher Librarian* 38, no. 4 (April 2011): 40–41.

Jennifer Nelson and Keith Braafladt. *Technology and Literacy: 21st Century Library Programming for Children and Teens.* Chicago: American Library Association, 2012.

Marc Prensky. "Changing Paradigms." *Educational Technology* 47, no. 4 (July–August 2007): 64.

SOURCE: Specially prepared for *The Whole Library Handbook: Teen Services* by Stacy Vandever Wells, who earned her MLS from the University of North Texas in 2006 with an emphasis in youth services.

4

Making / Art: A flexible model for teen services

by Erinn Batykefer

"The future belongs to young people with an education and the imagination to create." *–President Barack Obama*

AT THE LIBRARY AS INCUBATOR PROJECT (www.libraryasincubator project.org), we define *art* broadly and include not only traditional fine arts like painting and printmaking, but also writing, music, performance, craft, and other creative pursuits. But why make creativity a cornerstone of your practice as a teen librarian? Why spend time and effort and money—sometimes big money—finding ways for teens to learn art, craft, and making techniques?

Why?

On the whole, teen services strive to provide emotional, educational, cognitive, and developmental support to teen patrons. This is a big job!

Just think of some of the huge changes teens go through:

- Tweens and younger teens' brains develop, streamlining how they process information and allowing for greater problem-solving skills and reasoning.

- As part of the general cognitive shift, teens have a hard time differentiating between what others think and their own preoccupations (usually, they assume others will judge them as harshly as they judge themselves).
- Teens' limbic systems—which control emotion, behavior, and motivation—are also in flux, creating a need for new ideas, experiences, and even risks.
- Teens who are early or late bloomers can suffer socially from an out-of-step transition and feel isolated.

At the Library as Incubator Project, we spend a lot of time talking with librarians, artists, and creative types all over the country (and the world) about creativity: how to nurture and incubate it in the library, and why it's important—especially for teens. Here's what we've learned:

- Creativity doesn't just happen; it needs to be encouraged. Right now, our educational system is doing a lot to discourage creativity, to our detriment.
- Creativity isn't exclusive to artists. Everyone can be creative and apply that skill to what they're interested in, whether that's writing poems or writing code.
- Creativity is a process, and it can be learned.
- Creativity needs space. If you provide the right circumstances, opportunity, and attitude, creativity can happen.

Providing opportunities for teens to learn and develop their own creative process at the library can do more than fill educational gaps in school curricula with standardized tests on heavy rotation. Art, craft, and making programs can also help to level the playing field for teens at all different stages of adolescence, giving them the chance to develop their new cognitive abilities, engage in social interactions that are process—not product—oriented, learn new ideas, and take creative risks.

How

"The ideas that underpin makerspaces such as cooperation, resource and information sharing, self-directed education, and a diversity of views are concepts that are central to our profession's ethos. And in these economically difficult times, a movement that offers an alternative to consumer culture and a return to DIY independence is timely indeed."—*Fiacre O'Duinn (right), librarian, writer, maker, and self-described cyborg*

One obvious way to integrate creativity into the library for teens is to create a "makerspace"—a process that is much less about actual physical *space* than it is about copping a creativity-friendly attitude and making some connections. Yes, some makerspaces are expensive, tech-heavy "hackspaces" with 3D printers or digital learning labs with pricey software and equipment. Chicago Public Library's YouMedia Lab (youmediachicago.org) is a good example, and Fayetteville (N.Y.) Free Library's Fab Lab (fflib.org/fablab) has been successful. But the *template* for a successful makerspace is simply a collaborative "skillshare" (that is, an event where people come together to share their skills with each other without asking for anything in return); the materials used and the stuff made could be *anything*—and it doesn't have to be expensive.

So here's how we define "makerspaces" for libraries:

Makerspaces, *n. pl.* Workshops where people come together to share materials and a collaborative learning environment in order to learn a new skill.

The skillshare template is perfect for teen services at the library because it is so flexible: It can accommodate both traditional art

Teens enjoy the FabLab at Fayetteville (N.Y.) Free Library. Used with permission.

forms and less formal crafting and building, and it relies on community knowledge and shared materials to spark creativity. Outreach and partnerships are the key here; the makerspace itself and the programs that are a part of it serve as a way to organize "community knowledge" and provide access to it. In a way, it's just like collection development.

The self-directed, educational model of makerspaces is also flexible enough to accommodate the broad range of adolescence and to support the specific educational and developmental needs of teen patrons:

- Makerspaces can provide a safe space where teens can not only develop and hone their new cognitive and learning abilities, but also be exposed to new skills, new people, and new ideas on a constant basis.
- The DIY method of "try it and see if it works" can also provide enough risk to satisfy some teens' thrill-seeking behavior.
- Maker clubs or meetings can support early or late bloomers by creating a community where physical development is not as important as their willingness to try something new, their ability to acquire and apply new skill, and the tendency to get obsessed with a new project.
- The collaborative environment of a makerspace also allows for nonjudgmental interaction.

You can set the tone for creative learning and information sharing for the teens in your library by tapping into DIY culture—which values very different skills than those held up in other contexts—by creating a makerspace, DIY station, or skillshare series directed by your Teen Advisory Board's interests.

Make it happen

Maybe you're a person who is not terribly artistic. That does not mean your teen services will be the same. You're a librarian! Even if you don't know the answer, you know how to find it; even if you're not a person who makes art, you can still provide opportunities for art making and creativity in your library.

The wealth of easy, accessible, and free DIY templates for all kinds of projects online makes brainstorming

MAKER AT WORK

programming ideas easy—you can set up your RSS feed, Twitter, or Pinterest account to comb the internet for DIY tutorials on YouTube, through maker publications like *Make* magazine, and from artists and crafters who share their ideas on blogs.

But this is only just scratching the surface. A more sustainable option—one that builds community while it fills up your programming calendar—is to tap into your area's "library" of skills. If you live in a city or an area with an amazing arts and crafts scene, you won't have trouble finding community partners to share printmaking, sewing, robot-building, knitting, or woodcarving skills with your teens. But no matter where you live, there are partnerships to be made.

All of these maker ideas—from expensive high-tech programs to the slashed-budget no-tech programs—rely on building partnerships with the artists, crafters, and makers in your community. Consider partnership-based programming a kind of collection development: Pulling together creative teen programs should be community-driven. Just because a program is free doesn't mean it serves your community. If you've got a raft of teens who want to draw and write their own manga, you're on the lookout for an illustrator, comic, or writer (or all three!); don't waste your time on a program about embroidery.

Creative writing. Get in touch with local writing professors or instructors in your area and ask them to judge a creative-writing contest for the teens at your library (select the top five before sending to your judge). Host an open-mic event featuring the winner and runners-up. If your judge has a book, get a signed copy for the winner (and your library).

Kick it up a notch. Use your connections to local writers to host a series of writing workshops in the months leading up to the contest so teens can learn new writing techniques from an expert and polish their entries.

Community content. Collect all entries into an anthology. Catalog and shelve it in a special section, and use it to advertise the event each year. Combine it with a drawing contest to create an illustrated tome.

Example. "Ralph Munn Creative Writing Contest at the Carnegie Library of Pittsburgh." www.libraryasincubatorproject.org/?p=4012.

Poster for National Poetry Month 2014. From poets.org.

Poetry. Tap into the great resources, activities, and contests associated with National Poetry Month (April) and give teens the option to engage with and share poetry in a variety of creative ways (not just writing!). Host a *kukai* haiku contest to introduce teens to other cultures' writing traditions, or make poetry visual by challenging teens to illustrate a favorite poem (or their own original work) with photographs or by using Glogster to create interactive posters.

Community content. Create a Flickr page for your teens' Glogster posters and poetry photographs and have it stream on the teen web page or the library's home page. Consider printing out some photographs to display in the teen section of the library (with permission, of course).

Resources. Check out the Free Verse Project's Flickr page, where participants submit photos of poetic lines (you can engage with the online community or create your own). www.flickr.com/groups/freeverse/.

Learn about the tradition of haiku and social poetry circles in Japan, and host a fun, low-pressure *kukai* of your own. www.libraryasincubatorproject.org/?p=4134.

Fan art. Tap into teens' excitement over the worlds they read about in their favorite books, and challenge them to create a piece of art that illustrates or reimagines the story. This can be as simple as redesigning book covers or as complex as filming a book trailer or recording a song for your website or YouTube channel (depending on your budget and resources). Host a program or a series of programs with a designer, filmmaker, or other artist so teens can learn about interpretive art and techniques for communicating mood and narrative in a medium that isn't written. Display finished pieces around the teen section or online, and hold a contest to determine the best art.

Geralt of Rivia and Kristina. Fan art by Saturne based on The Witcher, from DeviantArt. Used CC BY-SA 3.0.

Learn more. Not sure what fan art is or why it's important? Check out this essay by Katie Behrens: "Why You Should Pay Attention to Fandoms." www.libraryasincubatorproject.org/?p=7618.

Kick it up a notch. For a twist on fan art and book design idea, choose some great books from your collection with *terrible* covers. Recover them with plain paper and challenge teens to read them and redesign the cover to be as awesome as the story inside.

Example. "It Came from a Book! Teen Read Week Art Contest." www.library asincubatorproject.org/?p=5113.

Filmmaking and animation. If you have access to computers, iPads, or other handheld filmmaking equipment, you have what you need to plan a filmmaking event. But even if you only have a few computers, you can still access some great *free* stop-motion animation programs online that you can use to create short films that bring stories and books to life. Create book trailers as a way for teens to recommend their favorite books on your website, or host stop-motion animation workshops for teens more interested in drawing, collage, and animations.

Partner ideas. Partner with local screenwriters, animators, or actors in a drama company to plan the DIY aspect of your program or series. Screenwriters and filmmakers might share storyboarding techniques for planning an effective film, and actors can help teens stage their scripts. Animators can be great resources for creating a lively stop-motion workshop.

Kick it up a notch. Hold a film festival and project teens' finished videos on a screen. Provide popcorn and other movie-theater refreshments and then ask viewers to be the "Academy" and vote on their favorite films in a variety of categories (you can set the rules so that each film wins a prize).

Examples. "Flip Filmmakers Kit." www.libraryasincubatorproject.org/?p=2131.

"Carnegie Library of Pittsburgh Stop Motion Animation." www.libraryasin cubatorproject.org/?p=6186.

"Carnegie Library of Pittsburgh QuickFlix Workshops and Contest." www.libraryasincubatorproject.org/?p=5975.

Crafts. Crafters—professional and amateur—can be found in every town, so teaming up with a local expert who can share printmaking, collage, knitting, woodworking, or other skills at your library will be easy to do—get in touch by haunting gift shops that stock the work of local makers. A great model originally created for the twenties and thirties crowd is Handmade Crafternoons, at the

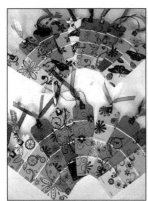

Paint-chip bookmarks by sgbalone.

New York Public Library. The "Handmade Librarian," Jessica Pigza, created the Crafternoons, which are free, and each event has a few common elements: "a visiting special guest artist or maker, a hands-on project, and an intriguing selection of books and magazines from the library's collection" to both inspire participants and show off the range of materials available at the library. A great way to promote your collection!

Examples. "Creative Class at the District of Columbia Public Library." www.libraryasincubatorproject.org/?p=1716.

"Handmade Crafternoons at the New York Public Library." www.libraryasincubatorproject.org/?p=2699.

Drawing, painting, and other fine arts. Get in touch with local art professors or instructors in your area and ask them about hosting creative workshops (or series!) about fundamental art techniques or their medium of expertise. It might seem expensive to fund a workshop on painting, for example, but consider how other community partners can help here, too: There are lots of organizations, like Re-Art Swap, that collect art materials for teachers, librarians, and artists to use or trade for free.

Community content. Take a page out of the Public Library for New London's crafty book and have teens illustrate their impressions of their hometown; see "I Draw New London." www.libraryasincubatorproject.org/?p=7723.

Example. YA Art Programs at the Acton Public Library. www.libraryasincubatorproject.org/?p=5911.

Resources. "Literacy through the Arts," an essay about materials sharing for art education in Madison, Wisconsin. www.libraryasincubatorproject.org/?p=1385.

Photography. Like many other partnership ideas, this one would benefit from an expert—you can find them teaching at community colleges, high schools, and universities or showing their work in galleries and small shops around town. Our teen librarian was an accomplished amateur photographer himself, and he leveraged his knowledge into a great program. Don't forget to include yourself in your "library" of community makers! If you have a skill, think about how you can share it in your library.

Library kit. "Teaching Teens the Art of Light Photography," by Michael Cherry, teen programming specialist at the Evansville (Ind.) Vanderburgh Public Library. www.libraryasincubatorproject.org/?p=1785.

More resources

Free Tech for Teachers. www.freetech4teachers.com. (There are some great links to free animation programs mentioned above.)

Handmade Librarian. handmadelibrarian.com.

The Library as Incubator Project. www.libraryasincubatorproject.org.

Library Makers Project. www.libraryasincubatorproject.org/?p=6298.

Make magazine. makezine.com.

Poets.org. www.poets.org/page.php/prmID/394. Poetry resources for teens.

SOURCE: Specially prepared for *The Whole Library Handbook: Teen Services* by Erinn Batykefer, co-founder and managing editor of The Library as Incubator Project.

Author visits

by Kristin Treviño and Allison Jenkins

A VISIT TO YOUR LIBRARY from a popular teen author is the crème de la crème of teen events. Giving teens the chance to brush elbows and exchange words with their literary idols is the kind of program that can change a teen's life in one evening. The amount of work and variety of tasks involved in executing a successful author visit may seem daunting at first, but remember that the work is spread out through several months and, if you keep organized and follow the different steps described in this article, easily manageable.

Author visits provide these one-of-a-kind opportunities for teens to connect and put a face with the names on their favorite books while offering an added dimension to the reading experience with direct interaction with an author. This article provides detailed steps to organizing such an event, serving as a guide for hosting a successful author visit.

Know your budget

First, determine how much your dream author visit will cost; next, establish what you can realistically spend. Before proceeding with inquiries to authors, always get approval and confirmation of funds from your library administration, Friends group, or alternate funding source.

4

Author visit sample expense worksheet				
Items purchased	Cost	Quantity	Total cost	Purchased from
Single event				
Honorarium			$$	Ms./Mr. Author
Author hotel			$174.92	NYLO hotels
Author flight			$339.20	Southwest Airlines
Tablecloths	$1.99 per pack	3	$5.97	Party City
9 oz. cups	$2.99 per 20 ct.	5	$14.95	Party City
Napkins	$2.49 per 50 ct.	1	$2.49	Party City
Cupcakes	$13.58 per 30 ct.	4	$54.32	Sam's Club
Simply Lemonade	$3.88 per 2 ct.	5	$19.40	Sam's Club
Total			**$611.25+**	
Two-part visit: Teen party and formal evening event				
Honorarium			$$	Ms./Mr. Author
Author hotel			$174.92	NYLO hotels
Author flight			$339.20	Southwest Airlines
Tablecloths	$1.99 per pack	3	$5.97	Party City
9 oz. cups	$2.99 per 20 ct.	5	$14.95	Party City
Napkins	$2.49 per 50 ct.	1	$2.49	Party City
Cupcakes	$13.58 per 30 ct.	4	$54.32	Sam's Club
Simply Lemonade	$3.88 per 2 ct.	5	$19.40	Sam's Club
Iron-on paper	$19.99 per 10 ct.	2	$39.98	Joann's Fabrics
T-shirts small	$2.50 per shirt	14	$35.00	Joann's Fabrics
T-shirts medium	$8.47 per 3 ct.	5	$42.35	Walmart
T-shirts large	$8.47 per 3 ct.	3	$25.41	Walmart
Total			**$753.99+**	

Sample contact email

Hello, Ms./Mr. Author/Publicist,

I hope you are doing well! We at the Anytown Public Library are big fans of Ms./Mr. Author, our teens love Ms./Mr.'s work, and we are eagerly awaiting the next book. As part of our teen summer reading club, we are currently planning a young adult author event and would love to invite Ms./Mr. Author. Is this something she/he would be interested in?

Our teen council would also like to host a teen-exclusive party in the afternoon, with Ms./Mr. Author as the guest of honor. This event, open to teens only, is very laid-back, with crafts and refreshments, lasting only a little more than an hour.

We would be honored if Ms./Mr. Author could join us in City, State!

Quick breakdown of the events:

- Date and time: mm/dd/yy or mm/dd/yy, 2:00 p.m. teen party, 7:00 p.m. evening author event
- Summary: (1) teen-exclusive party (2) and evening author presentation and Q&A, followed by book sales and signing
- Budget: $$ to cover honorarium and travel expenses

If you would like more information on our library, please visit our TeenScene page: www.mylibraryteenpage.com.

Hope to hear from you soon!

Your Name | Your Title
Anytown Public Library

When presenting your case for the necessary expenses, give a detailed list of expenditures for the type of author visit or programs planned. These can include refreshments and decorations for an evening speaking event, craft supplies for a teen exclusive or book-release party, and—most important—your speaker's honorarium and travel expenses. The bulk of your budget will go toward author fees and travel costs.

Even with a detailed budget, allow wiggle room for unforeseen incidentals. You may need to order additional copies of the visiting author's book, or airfare and hotel expenses may increase between the planning and actual booking stages. If there is a gap between what you are able to spend and the event's costs, readjust your budget, pursue additional funding from outside grants, or solicit donations from local businesses.

Ideally, set your budget a year ahead of your event date. However, since most cities' budgets operate within a fiscal year, you are often limited to nine months or less if you are planning a summer reading club event and a shorter time period if you are coordinating within the school year. This is where having outside funding is beneficial. Most grants are awarded farther in advance, and donations can be obtained at any time for future use.

Make contact

Compile a list of potential authors with multiple options in case of scheduling conflicts or budget restrictions. If you are setting up the visit as part of a larger event, such as summer reading club, you may want to consider inviting authors whose books fit with your theme.

Always get input from your teens. If you have a teen council, consult them for suggestions; or get feedback from your teen patrons. Getting teens involved and excited about the upcoming author visit will also help to promote the event. Looking at circulation statistics can also help you ascertain in-demand authors or popular genres among your young adult readers.

Once you have your budget set, start initiating contact. The earlier you inquire, the better chance you have of booking your desired author. Contact your potential author a minimum of six months in advance but preferably 9 to 12 months ahead of time. Authors' event schedules quickly fill up with annual conferences, book festivals, and tours.

Your first stop should be the author's website. Many authors will have a contact listed for appearances. Depending on the authors, they may want you to contact them directly. Others may redirect you to their publisher or publicist. It is best to have a specific contact person rather than a general publicity email address or form. Also, check the author's website for future event listings to avoid scheduling conflicts.

When composing an invitation email, you will want to be brief, enthusiastic, and professional. Include a quick breakdown of the event, with the date, time, program summary, and budget. You may have a desired date, but be open to additional dates. Flexibility makes it easier to fit into an author's availability.

After confirming an author event, send a follow-up email reiterating the date, time, and program summary. Provide an invoice if the author or publisher does not supply one. You can include any administrative details, such as requesting tax forms, publicity photos, and finalizing travel arrangements.

Keep all your contacts, especially different publicists or library-visit coordinators at the various publishers. These will come in handy when booking future visits with authors from the same publishing house.

Create publicity

Start promoting your event at least two months in advance. Publicize internally with book displays, bookmarks, flyers, and posters. Involve your library's teen

---

Publicity checklist

- Plan and set up a book display
- Create bookmarks
- Design and distribute flyers
- Make posters
- Distribute promotional buttons for all library staff to wear
- Post event on library's website, online calendar, and all e-newsletters
- Send press release to local news media
- Email event info to all the library's electronic discussion lists
- Email local school librarians and teachers
- Make sure author receives all info and graphics to post on website and/or blog
- Create a Facebook event page and share with online contacts
- Initiate a Twitter campaign (involve the authors, library teens, and local book bloggers)
- Post on Tumblr

Week of checklist

Administrative details
- Make sure all forms (W-9s, invoices, receipts, etc.) are submitted to administration/ accounting department.
- Make sure honorarium check is ready or scheduled to be cut by day of event.

Verify all travel arrangements.
Email author to confirm visit details and travel arrangements.
Coordinate teen volunteers for day of visit.
Order and purchase all decorations, craft supplies, and refreshments.
Final publicity campaign push
- Email event information to all library electronic discussion lists.
- Promote event on Facebook, Twitter, and Tumblr; here the author, library teens, and local bloggers are key to spreading the word.

Event-day checklist

Auditorium setup
- Display decorations, posters, bookmarks, etc.
- Set up tables for crafts (if having a teen party prior to evening event), refreshments, and book sales and signing.
- Set up all chairs.
- Auditorium setup should be completed relatively early in the day, at least an hour before the event begins. Teen volunteer help will prove crucial in this stage of the event; they provide much-needed manual help and, more important, build enthusiasm and momentum for the author visit.

Provide timely transportation for author to and from airport, hotel, and library.
Have honorarium check ready for author.
Introduce author, and the fruition of months of work begins.

---

council by distributing flyers and spreading details through word of mouth. Place flyers in books on the hold shelf, and have staff hand out information to patrons checking out young adult materials. Design buttons for employees to wear.

Send out an official press release to all local news outlets. Make sure to include the event information in electronic promotional materials such as the library's event calendar, website, and newsletters. Sign up your library's teens for email program reminders.

Involve your community's schools. Send out emails to school librarians and English teachers. Attend outreach opportunities at local middle and high schools. If possible, tie in your author visits with school book clubs through book selection or by handing out flyers.

Give the visiting author current-event details to post on his or her website or blog. Teen authors are great at keeping readers informed about any speaking opportunities and make great advocates for library events. Don't be afraid to ask them for help in spreading the word.

Involve your book community in promotion by sending out details to local young adult authors and bloggers. Social media is vital in drawing in attendees. Focus on what outlets work best for your library. This may include tweeting promotional pictures on Twitter, creating a Facebook event, or posting on Tumblr.

"Good evening everyone! We at the Irving Public Library are excited and exceedingly honored to have with us tonight the critically acclaimed and bestselling author . . . So please give a warm welcome to . . ." This short and simple introduction is a sharp contrast to the level of complexity and coordination involved in the preparations leading up to an author visit, from securing budgets to juggling emails and running detailed publicity campaigns. The end results, though, make all the months of planning, organizing, and working worth it; few things equal teenagers' reactions to meeting one of their favorite authors in person, dreaming beyond words on the pages.

SOURCE: Specially prepared for *The Whole Library Handbook: Teen Services* by Kristin Treviño and Allison Jenkins, teen services librarians, Irving (Tex.) Public Library.

Gaming in libraries
by Justin Hoenke

THERE'S A HORRIBLE STEREOTYPE out there that all that gamers want to do is sit in front of their TVs and play games all day. There's also the one that describes gamers as not the most social people in the world. These stereotypes couldn't be further from the truth. Game designer Jane McGonigal sums it up best, stating that games "consistently fulfill genuine human needs that the real world fails to satisfy. More than that, they may prove to be a key resource for solving some of our most pressing real-world problems" ("Be a Gamer, Save the World," *Wall Street Journal*, January 11, 2011).

Gaming in the library creates community. Whether it is four players crowded around a table and playing the board game *Settlers of Catan* or a group of soccer enthusiasts enjoying the most recent FIFA video game, the end product of game programs is a group of teens enjoying an experience in a library together. In his article "Why Gaming?" *Digitale Bibliotheek* 1, no. 1 (2007): 17, Scott Nicholson states that gaming programs in public libraries offer a place "where users can come together and engage in gaming experiences." Gamers are social people. The rise in online video gaming and tabletop gaming (such as *Magic: The Gathering*) shows that we want to be connected to one another. Why not give this audience a place to play games in public?

Gaming = good

You may run into questions from your administration as to why libraries should offer gaming and also the good ol' "just how much is this gonna cost?" Gaming doesn't come cheap, that's for sure. Instead of taking this angle, why not try directly acknowledging it: "Yes, though the initial investment is high, the return is priceless." Emphasize how your library will be reaching out to a new population of users and how through this program those users will be more likely to attend other library events and use the library for their media needs. If you plan on running gaming programs, compare the cost of the console and games to the cost of hiring performers, and you will find that after one or two game programs, the cost will be the same or less than the cost of hiring outside performers for programs.

It's going to take time to get your gaming program up and running. Attendance at gaming events will most likely start slow, but as word gets out to your community,

Magic: The Gathering tournament play in Hanover, Germany.

the gamers will come. Program attendance will rise, and with that comes another reward: increased circulation and library usage. Gamers are not one-dimensional beings who only like to play games. They read, watch movies, and, like all of us, have questions that need to be answered. They will become users of your library. Better yet, they will become *huge* supporters of your library. They will tell others how cool the library is and how much neat stuff it has to offer. Word of mouth works. You will see it in action after you initiate a gaming program.

PlayStation 3 console games. Flickr photo by Sergey Galyonkin, used CC BY-SA 3.0.

Types of gaming

The two most popular forms of gaming in public libraries tend to be centered around board games and video games. Both of these experiences offer library patrons a chance to experience gaming in a community setting. There are also many different kinds of games that can be played in the library. Here are some of the terms you may run into when learning about gaming:

Console gaming. Video games that are played through a video-gaming system (such as Xbox 360, PlayStation 3, Nintendo Wii) connected to a television.

Handheld gaming. Video games that are played using a portable gaming device (such as Nintendo DS, Nintendo 3DS, and Sony PlayStation Vita).

Mobile gaming. Games that are played on a mobile device or tablet. Popular examples of mobile games include *Angry Birds* and *Fruit Ninja*.

Role-playing games (RPGs). A quest-based adventure in which the player controls a character or group. Notable video-game RPGs include the *Final Fantasy* series. RPGs can also be applied to card games such as *Magic: The Gathering* or tabletop games such as *Dungeons and Dragons*.

Massive multiplayer online role-playing games (MMORPGs). Character-based games that require an online connection to play and feature an open world that characters are free to roam. Examples of popular MMORPGs include *World of Warcraft* and *Minecraft*.

Teens playing *Settlers of Catan* board game. Photo by Matěj Baťha, used CC BY-SA 3.0.

Board games. This applies to any tabletop-based game that uses a board, items, cards, and other game paraphernalia to play. Board games range from such simple titles as *Candy Land* and *Chutes and Ladders* to more complex board games, such as *Monopoly* and *Settlers of Catan*.

Card games. Games played with a set of cards. Card games could be as simple as playing blackjack with a standard deck of cards or as complicated as special-card-based games, such as *Magic: The Gathering*, or other card games, like *Zombie Fluxx*.

Types of gaming programs

Here are just a few examples of the types of gaming programs you can offer in your library.

Have an open gaming event. Set aside an area for one day, and turn your library into an arcade! Include all forms of gaming, and notice what interests your community the most. Based on this event's attendance, you will be able to gauge where to go with future gaming programs in your library. At this event, you will also be able to identify those in your community whom you can use as a resource to grow your gaming program. It also gives teenagers a great opportunity to hang out and socialize in a safe setting.

Open up your library to card gamers. Most teens who play card games such as *Magic: The Gathering* are always looking for a place to play their game. Traditionally, these games have been played at comic and gaming shops. However, there is always room for these in the library. What's best about these programs is that they often run themselves. The librarian does not need to be an expert in card games to participate; the teens will run the event themselves. Just make sure you feed them!

Bloomingdale (Ill.) Public Library participated in International Gaming Day 2012.

Organize a video-game tournament. There's no better way to create community at your library than having a video-game tournament. Before running a program like this, it is recommended that you try an open gaming event to see what games your community best responds to. Once that is established, set up a tournament, and offer a prize to teens competing. This will be a surefire way to get them interested in the tournament.

Mobile-gaming petting zoo. Technology petting zoos, ones in which the community can visit the library and try out the latest e-readers and tablets, have proven to be popular events for libraries. Why not use this idea and base it around the act of playing mobile games? Invite your community to visit the library to test out a number of handpicked mobile games.

Tie it into the collection

If you're going to have a teen program that offers gaming, you should go the extra mile and tie it into your collections. How so? There are a few simple ways:

Have a circulating gaming collection. A circulating gaming collection allows those attending your gaming events to continue the gaming they're experiencing in the library.

Graphic novels. The visual and story elements in graphic novels are very likely to appeal to gamers, who are playing games that deal with the visual and story elements as well.

Video-game strategy guides. Strategy guides are not only helpful to gamers who want to solve the puzzles in their video games, but they also reinforce literacy in gaming. Teens who play video games and read the strategy guides are engaging in two forms of literacy and are learning to navigate between these two media.

It's a good thing!

Finally, we have to ask ourselves this simple question as we move ahead: What do we really have to lose? We can complicate the situation by getting bogged down in the what-ifs and whys of gaming in the libraries, or we can move ahead and reach out to this section of our community. Give it a shot. You have nothing to lose. You only have wisdom, insight, and hopefully a few new patrons to gain!

SOURCE: Specially prepared for *The Whole Library Handbook: Teen Services* by Justin Hoenke, teen librarian, Chattanooga (Tenn.) Public Library.

Self-directed and free-range programming

by Karen Jensen

IN THIS CHAPTER, we have discussed the basic rationale for and mechanics of programming. Some types of programming are traditionally very popular with teens, like craft and gaming programs. But traditional library programming insists that teens come to the library at a specific time and place, which may not work for a large portion of the target audience. In addition, libraries must address the rapidly changing nature of the teen audience. New technologies are changing the way that teens operate, how they choose to spend their time, how they communicate, and what they expect from those who want something from them in return—which would be teen librarians. Namely, we want them to be users, supporters, and advocates.

Self-directed programming

In a rapidly evolving world, libraries have to think about library programming and how it may be changing. There are ways that libraries can give teens more say in the timing of library programs, like offering opportunities for self-directed programs, such as contests, and other ways for teens to be involved with the library in their own time and on their own terms. This could include online discussions, social-media interaction, and learning about library services and resources hands-on.

Many libraries refer to this as *passive programming*. However, *self-directed programming* is more accurately descriptive. Contests and other nontraditional programming are not passive; teens are actively engaging in an activity on their own time, at their own discretion, and autonomously interacting with the library, which is a worthwhile and desired result for our teen services.

When participating in a traditional library program, teens have to commit to a certain time and place. So you have the best *Hunger Games* program (ever!) planned for Monday night at 7:00 p.m., but that day, the history teacher assigns an entire chapter to read with the promise of a quiz; teens have to do five pages of calculus homework; and then, to top it all off, 300 inches of snow are predicted. Suddenly, the 40 teens who signed up have translated into five teens that evening. Life happens, and there is a lot of competition for teens' time and attention. Self-directed programs, however, allow teens the opportunity to participate in the library on a broader timetable. They help keep the library

Self Directed Programming with Apps

•Upload contest sheets teens can do them on their own time

•Share pictures & do caption contests, trivia and more

•Start a Hashtag – great for marketing while programming
  Example: #3wordbooktalk

•For Poetry Month: Do Instagram bookspine poetry, or do an Exquisite Corpse poem

•Use Facebook Groups to do a teen book discussion group

•Live Tweet while reading a book, a popular tv show premiere, or the Teen Choice Awards

•Do an online scavenger hunt, check-in
See also: Self Directed Programming and Check In @ Your Library

Slide from Karen Jensen's slideshow, www.scribd.com/doc/201441563/Teens-Tech-and-Programming.

out there, actively in the forefront of the teen brain, by having a more continual presence.

The importance of this quiet, ongoing presence shouldn't be overlooked. Contests don't have to be limited to books; they can tap into any part of teen culture and demonstrate what a well-rounded information resource the library is. When planned correctly, they can also help teens learn how to use the library catalog and various library resources within the library. Contests have value because they help promote the library, and they demonstrate the wide variety of ways that the library can be involved in the lives of teens.

Creating a predictable timetable for self-directed programming helps to build participation. A new contest every two weeks can create turnover. Contests can be static, where teens pick up or print off a contest sheet and fill it out to enter, or they can be more dynamic, where teens are engaged in online games. A free-range program may take the form of a lift-the-flap-style poster in the teen lounge that is changed on a weekly basis. Or perhaps submissions of poems, videos, or book reviews are requested continually but collected and published on a library blog on the tenth of every month. This type of contest ensures that you have steady content to share with teens via their social-media pages, and you meet them where they are most often.

To encourage participation, it is good to have prizes. Prizes don't have to be extravagant: A movie-themed contest can have a movie-themed prize of a popular DVD, a box of popcorn, and two liters of soda. The winner of a poetry challenge may win a book of poetry or a rhyming dictionary. Try cultivating some community partnerships and get a local business to sponsor a monthly prize for a nontraditional program. It is marketing for them and a good community partnership for the library. Gift certificates, gas cards, and "buy-one, get-one-free" coupons also work well as prizes, the latter of which is often an easier sell for local businesses as it is sure to bring in more than one customer at a time.

Free-range programming allows you, as a programmer, to be creative. Think outside the box. You can create a wide variety of opportunities, including word scrambles, book-title scrambles, name the quotes, scavenger hunts, matching quizzes, and more. They can be word puzzles or visual puzzles. There is a bit of staff time and research that goes into putting together good contests, but the level of participation will often justify the preparation time.

One of the major challenges to library programming is getting teens into the library for a scheduled event at a scheduled time. There is tremendous value to traditional library programming; we can verify and assert its educational value as we develop programs with specific educational goals in mind. But not all library programming needs to be about something that connects directly to the collection or have an immediate literary tie-in. Teens have tremendous social needs, and if libraries are to be a community resource of value, they must find ways to tap into and meet these needs. If teens value hanging out with their friends so much, and we recognize that this has a valued social component, isn't it in our community's best interest to give them safe places to do this?

The value of hanging out

Every day, sometime after 3:00 p.m., libraries around the world are flooded with spirited teenagers. These teens have been sitting for eight hours in an environment where they are told what to do and when to do it; the imposing quiet of a library can be the precisely wrong environment in this moment for teens. A

teen coffeehouse, open-mic night, or café-type venue is a more informal type of program that invites teens to come into your library, typically after school, in a safe space and simply "hang." Again, this is a more self-directed type of program. Teens are in the library in a library-sponsored program, but they determine how they spend their time within this space. Libraries can offer food, homework help, gaming, and more, and teens are allowed to choose how to spend their time while at the program.

In comparison, much library programming tends to be more organized and structured: craft programs, book discussion groups, Harry Potter parties. Lots of librarians (and their administrators) like these types of programs because they have form, structure, numerical evidence of popularity in the form of attendance, and usually some type of obvious literature or collection tie-in. They also tend to be staff intensive (a lot of staff time is invested in planning, prepping, and marketing); cost more in funds (crafts and speakers in particular tend to cost more); and you can have very mixed results. The truth is, picking a program topic limits your audience from the get-go; the moment you pick a theme, you have limited a portion of your target demographic. Because both types of library programming have value, both structured and free-range, it is important that libraries adopt programming models that balance the two.

The benefits of unstructured programming

It is developmentally appropriate. Teens are peer oriented and on an amazing journey of self-discovery; at the same time, they are moving away from adult authority and trying to navigate life more on their own. A café type of program is a great environment for teens to do all of these things. Here teens can explore relationships, navigate social situations in a safe environment, choose for themselves

---

Assets gained through nontraditional programs

Programs that emphasize "hanging out" promote the following developmental assets:

Asset: **Community Values Youth.** Young person perceives that adults in the community value youth.

Asset: **Safety.** Young person feels safe at home, school, and in the neighborhood.

Asset: **Youth Programs.** Young person spends three or more hours per week in sports, clubs, or organizations at school and/or in community organizations.

Asset: **Homework.** Young person reports doing at least one hour of homework every school day.

Asset: **Reading for Pleasure.** Young person reads for pleasure three or more hours per week.

Asset: **Interpersonal Competence.** Young person has empathy, sensitivity, and friendship skills.

Asset: **Personal Power.** Young person feels he or she has control over "things that happen to me."

Asset: **Other Adult Relationships.** Young person receives support from three or more non-parent adults.

how they want to spend their time, and feel a greater sense of freedom in a safe space.

As you can see, a coffeehouse or café type of program that encourages self-direction in a safe environment helps promote many of the 40 Developmental Assets. By giving teens choices, you are communicating respect and support. These unstructured environments also give teen services staff an opportunity to engage with teens in less formal ways; they encourage and invite teens to provide informal feedback, have one-on-one readers' advisory experiences, and develop healthy relationships with adults who care and can

Unstructured gaming program in the library after school.

serve as mentors and role models. The teens at unstructured programs come to serve as a more informal teen advisory board (TAB); however, because such a large and diverse crowd attends, you get a wider variety of viewpoints and ideas. The truth is, certain types of teens tend to sign up for and participate in advisory groups, and these are often the very teens whose needs we are already meeting fairly well in the library.

It is cost-effective. Programming costs money. And libraries face continuing budget and staff cuts, putting more pressure on staff to decrease costs and yet produce greater results. Staff time is also money. Every minute that you spend on researching and developing a program is a cost to the library; plus, it takes you away from other tasks. Libraries are all trying to find ways to better balance our time, money, and resources. Because there is almost no prep time involved in a café-type program, there is a decrease in expenditures. Also, the inclusiveness of café-type programs allows libraries to reach a greater potential audience.

It is a public-relations gold mine. Communities want and need healthy and safe places for teens to meet, as bored, unattended teens are a common community concern. The library is an answer to the age-old complaint, "I'm bored." Keep track of your statistics and put together good public-relations materials. Make sure patrons, parents, and the community as a whole know how many teens you are serving weekly and yearly. Let them know about the success of teen programming and how it meets developmental needs and benefits the community.

It cultivates a love of the library. A typical library programming goal is to cultivate positive regard for the library, and we do this by creating positive library experiences. Cafés get teens into the library on a regular basis. They meet the widest variety of needs and attract the widest variety of participants. They communicate a trust and respect in teens that results in teens having a trust and respect in libraries. In addition, teens are more likely to start using library resources and collections as they become repeat visitors. More positive experiences will lead to more library supporters.

What's the problem with unstructured programs?

Many library administrators are not as supportive of unstructured programming. They tend to value specific goals and evaluations that demonstrate how those goals were met. They want concrete collection tie-ins. This hesitancy can be overcome by really selling the program. You do have goals: Your goals are to get teens into the library and build relationships with them. Help staff understand teen development and how this type of programming is essential for healthy adolescent development.

To recap, unstructured library programming is valuable for several reasons:

- It meets teens' developmental need for peer-oriented interaction.
- It communicates a level of trust and respect to the teens.
- It gives teens an opportunity to choose how to spend their time in a safe environment with some oversight.
- It gives you and your library a forum to communicate new materials, popular materials, upcoming events, and services.
- It builds a core teen audience for your library.
- It allows you opportunities to develop relationships with teens in your community and better meet their needs (they become an informal TAB).
- It provides the library with valuable public-relations opportunities.

Changing the way libraries do summer reading

Summer reading programs (SRPs) are traditionally an important part of the library programming to many people, and research does seem to indicate that they help teens maintain and often improve important skills in a time when they are outside of the classroom. Some librarians argue it undermines our goals of promoting an intrinsic love of reading by offering incentives to read, but summer reading programs seem likely to be around for the foreseeable future. However, that doesn't mean that summer reading programs cannot continue to adapt and evolve to thrive.

The unconventional summer reading program. No matter how hard we push, not all teens like reading for pleasure. But the library is about more than just books, and it has value in the lives of teens in a myriad of ways. By expanding the way libraries present summer reading clubs, libraries can expand the way they market themselves to teens. Libraries have a variety of programs and services that invite nonreaders into the library, and we can find creative ways to involve nonreaders while respecting them and our libraries' goals.

SRPs are important because research shows that teens who read over the summer maintain or advance their core vocabulary and education level. Plus, story is an important way for all to learn about and engage in both the discovery of our world and self. In most standard SRPs, teens are asked to keep track of their reading, usually by book titles read or number of books read. Let's broaden the scope and goals of the summer reading program to reach out to the nonreaders in our communities. We can put together summer reading programs that still emphasize the value of reading while reaching out to our nontraditional readers and highlighting some of the other, equally important, aspects of our library services.

Time versus books. When libraries ask teens to record their reading in terms of books, our teens are comparing apples to oranges. One teen can read a title from the Harry Potter series clocking in at well over 700 pages, while counterparts are deliberately searching the shelves for the shortest books they can find. Administrators argue that recording participation in terms of books helps to increase circulation, but it also encourages our teens to pursue the lowest common denominator; we may be reaching our

Michigan Summer Reading banner. Flickr photo by Canton (Mich.) Public Library, used CC BY-SA 3.0.

goal of increasing circulation, but we do little to encourage our teens to seek out challenging reading materials to improve their skills over the summer months.

In comparison, recording participation in terms of time spent reading gives a nod to 21st-century reading habits. Many teens today do a large bulk of their reading online by reading various blogs, news feeds, and more. Many libraries allow teens to count audiobooks as part of their participation, so why not expand SRPs to include other types of reading, including online reading, by inviting teens to record time spent reading as opposed to the number of books read? In this way, we are only increasing our audience and encouraging participation.

2003 Caldecott Award medalist Eric Rohmann watches a young artist draw at Tuscaloosa (Ala.) Public Library's Weaver-Bolden branch during a June 2, 2009, program kick-off of the "Catch the Reading Bug" summer library program.

The "bonus" ballot. Is reading the only way that teens can earn prizes in a teen summer reading program? The answer does not have to be yes. Libraries spend a lot of time putting together additional library programs and services and asking teens to participate, so why not reward teens for using them by providing "bonus ballots." Staff are spending the time and money to put these programs together and asking our teens to come, so why not fully integrate them into our SRPs and offer teens the opportunity to gain participation credit for it? By offering a chance to win for nontraditional participation means libraries are encouraging involvement, broadening the scope of SRPs, and reaching out to more reluctant readers. By opening the door in this way, you will get teens into your library who aren't readers, and perhaps on one of their visits, they may finally pick up a book and choose to read it. If nothing else, you are building relationships with nontraditional library teens and helping them form positive opinions of the library.

Online entries. Summer reading programs are a tried-and-true part of the library calendar, and they are grounded in some very traditional beliefs, but some of these views need to change because our audience is changing. Teens spend a lot of time online; it's past time for us to take our SRPs online. Current technology makes it easy for libraries to create SRPs where teens can sign up online and fill out entry forms, reviews, or ballots from home (or school or wherever). Yes, libraries need to continue to have the paper trails in our library; not all teens have the same access to technology. But we want to create a program that includes the greatest number of teens, which means libraries need to engage in multiple ways of reporting.

As teen librarians think about and plan programming for teens, it is important to think outside the box and adapt to meet the changing demands of the target demographic. Teens, more than any other demographic it seems, are early adapters, ever changing, and incredibly diverse. Successful teen librarianship involves keeping involved with the target audience, meeting their needs, and being open to nontraditional ways of doing so.

SOURCE: Specially prepared for *The Whole Library Handbook: Teen Services* by Karen Jensen, teen services librarian, Grand Prairie, Texas.

COLLECTIONS

CHAPTER FIVE

Collections are the backbone of our library service. If we are going to present ourselves as the information centers of our communities, then we must build strong, diverse collections that allow our patrons to support their formal and informal education goals. Teens are a unique age group with distinguishing characteristics; they deserve collections that speak to the truth of their experiences. In this chapter, we will discuss how you can make a case for teen collections in your libraries, how you promote those collections to your teens, and what we mean when we talk about young adult literature.

Collection development: Making the case for teen collections

by Karen Jensen

COLLECTION DEVELOPMENT is one of the most time-consuming parts of being a teen services librarian. We spend a lot of time looking for books, determining if they have value for our collections and if they will circulate, and trying to work within a specific budget, which is often much too small for our needs. To have a good collection, we need sufficient funds, and to have sufficient funds, we need to have a well-circulating collection. Administrators usually use circulation to determine at what levels they are going to fund a collection, despite the reality that a poorly funded collection will by definition be low circulating because a lack of sufficient funds makes it difficult to buy the type and number of materials that you need. It can be an upward spiral or a downward spiral.

But the truth is, we can't have good circulation numbers if we don't have good materials. This means we continually need new materials—and in a timely manner. Libraries don't always have ordering processes in place that allow for the quick acquisition of new materials. And we all know that budgets are shrinking.

In the past few years, the young adult publishing market has exploded. Unfortunately, library budgets have not exploded at the same pace as the market. In fact, those budgets are often shrinking. To develop the types of collections that we would like, the types of collections that best meet the needs of our teens, there are a few things that we can share with those outside the field of young adult librarians: administrators, publishers, and authors.

Sufficient funding

We can't have a high-circulating collection if we don't have the funds and ordering processes in place to build high-circulating collections. Libraries often want to put the cart before the horse and demand it be successful before providing adequate funding. Sometimes, you have to invest in something to see good results.

Collection management essentials

Having an ample budget doesn't mean the path to a healthy collection is an easy one. The following considerations need to be balanced and continually revisited.

- Providing multiple copies of best-sellers to meet demand on a limited budget
- Providing multiple copies of those titles that are classroom assignments
- Having space to store multiple copies of assignment titles that have been rotated out of the curriculum or extra copies of best-sellers
- Replacing materials with a high turnover rate, either through theft or wear
- Retaining or completing lengthy series
- Replacing older, classic titles with updated covers
- Managing the increased demand for multiple formats of titles out of the same-sized budgets
- Getting new and high-demand materials in a timely manner
- Dealing with controversial subject matter and materials in collections that need to realistically reflect the lives of teens
- Creating a diverse collection that represents the rich cultures of the world
- Balancing the reading interests and demands that span the whole age range
- Balancing informational and recreational material

High-circulating collections need time, space, and money to grow. It is the job of the teen services librarian to make sure the elements are in place to develop a good, balanced teen collection. It is also the job of the teen services librarian to make the case to administrators when it comes to putting together the library's budget each year.

Teen publishing is growing by leaps and bounds. Bookstores have entire sections devoted to teen books, and libraries must remain competitive if we want to cultivate users and meet community needs. First, you need to lay the groundwork and create a space that promotes circulation. Weed the shelves to create space for merchandising (see "Merchandising 101: Marketing to Teens in the Library," pp. 141–144). Effectively utilize the teen area to face-out and promote materials. Weeding out the noncirculating items also makes it easier to find the circulating items; less cluttered shelves are more browsable. Remember to keep track of circulation statistics.

When putting together book orders, keep track of the number of books you weren't able to order because of budgets and what additional amount you would have needed. This figure will help lay some of the groundwork to express the budgetary need.

Determine what percentage of the library's yearly circulation statistics is the circulation of teen items. Then, determine what percentage of the library's book budget is spent on teen materials. In an ideal world, these numbers should match. If 10% of your library's overall circulation is represented by teen materials, then your teen book budget should be 10% of the library's overall book budget.

Nontraditional acquisitions

Some libraries still require professional book reviews in order to purchase materials. Not just a professional review, but a positive professional review, or *multiple* positive professional reviews, which will justify spending money to add the material to the collection. But the internet, the blogosphere, and inclusion of books in places like Walmart and Target are all changing the landscape of reading and what teens ask for. In addition, teens want to see tie-in novels to their favorite TV shows and movies, which are often not reviewed. There needs to be ways to successfully include recreational reading in library collections. The professional-review collection-development policies leave teens with two choices: Read only those books that adults have declared "quality" reading materials or read nothing. If reading is a library goal, then libraries must help teens find the types of materials that they want to read, even if they are not the type of materials adults think they should be reading. Libraries should want teens reading something, anything, with the hope that it will be the bridge to reading that finally makes them a satisfied library customer and gets them interested in the idea of reading.

There is tremendous value in the book review, and you will spend a lot of time reading them and using them to make important collection development decisions. However, libraries also need to make sure there are ways to purchase things like the *Charmed* and *Buffy The Vampire* series, or whatever is currently popular. There will always be outliers: those books that we need to have even if they aren't great literature, that aren't purchased through our large discount vendor or with a traditional purchase order, and that aren't published by one of the big six publishing houses. We need to make sure we have collection development policies and procedures in place that allow for the creative and emergency needs of our collections.

New marketing trends

Libraries are traditionally slow adopters. However, libraries can't keep ignoring the success of ebooks. And after ebooks, there will be another new trend or resource that libraries will have to incorporate. Libraries need to look at collection-development policies and budgets to make sure there are successful ways of meeting patron ebook needs. Yes, teens read ebooks. One can make the argument that not everyone has an e-reader and libraries dilute material funding by buying another format of the same titles, but we risk alienating those new adopters as library supporters if we don't prove our relevancy and meet their needs. They will see no need to vote for supporting us because we no longer meet their needs and they have gone elsewhere.

In fact, libraries are already having to reevaluate current thoughts on small and self-published materials, as mentioned in the section above. The bottom line is this: If teens can't find what they are looking for in the library, they aren't coming back because there are so many other ways for teens to find what they want to read. Libraries may be "free," but if teens have continued unsuccessful trips to the library, we still become irrelevant.

Diversity

Publishing tends to run in trends; today it is dystopian, yesterday it was romance, and tomorrow it may be mysteries. It is easy to purchases the latest, hottest title and watch it fly off the shelves, but our collection development goal is not solely about circulation statistics. In order to truly meet the needs of our community, we must build diverse collections. Not just people diversity, which will be discussed later, but book plot diversity. It is true that a lot of teens are looking for the next Hunger Games or Twilight series, but it is equally true that teens have other needs and interests. Our goal is to make sure there are books in our library collections where teens can find themselves represented and validated, not just based upon their race, sexuality, or religion, but based on their interests.

Realistic depiction of teen lives

The teenage years are vast and complex. Most libraries define teen or young adult services as grades 6 through 12, or ages 13 and up. There is a marked difference between a 6th-grader and a 12th-grader. And in the years between the two, a lot happens. Teens will begin to question who they are, what they think about every aspect of life and the world they live in, and yes—they will start to think about sex. Many of them will start to have it. Whatever librarians may personally feel about various issues surrounding the teen years, our job is to remove ourselves from the equation and meet the needs of teens. That means some of the materials in our collections will be controversial. In fact, if they aren't, then we aren't building good collections.

Because of the issue of content, it is important that libraries have intellectual freedom policies in place and that all staff understand and embrace them. In addition, every library should have a procedure and form in place to deal with material challenges, which unfortunately happen. Developing good rapport with staff and helping them understand teens and the need for realistic teen fiction as well as providing for good intellectual freedom training can help prevent patron challenges from escalating.

Periodically, an article appears in the popular press forecasting the end of books in libraries or lauding the paperless library. Although digital books are certainly on the rise, teens are not abandoning their need for and interest in stories—the stories of fictional people, the stories of history, or the information on which they will build their own stories. It is for the importance of the stories that teen librarians must remain dedicated to thoughtful, thorough collection development.

SOURCE: Specially prepared for *The Whole Library Handbook: Teen Services* by Karen Jensen, teen services librarian, Grand Prairie, Texas.

Teen collection development outline
by Karen Jensen

WHEN YOU CREATE A TEEN COLLECTION, you should first look at your available space and budget opportunities. Then, you can use the sample outline provided on pp. 96–97 to develop a yearly collection development plan. Define each part of your library's collection, set the specific guidelines for the collection, list review sources and weeding schedules, and divide up your budget as a percentage of the whole so that you and your administrator can quickly find how monies are being spent in the teen area.

Keep in mind important teen collection goals: popular-demand items with high circulation that encourage a love of recreational reading; school curriculum support and materials of independent investigation; and diversity, a balance of both popular and award-winning titles. Also keep in mind your library's individual collection development policy.

Use an outline

A simple spreadsheet or outline can help organize the overall plan for teen collection development. Although an example is provided on the following pages, the concept is easily personalized, and you may find that over time you will want additional information. The headings include the following:

Collection guidelines: Outlines the specific collection goals for each subclass.

Selection sources: Outlines the review and selection sources for each subclass.

Weeding guidelines: Each library will have specific weeding guidelines; when using the example, it can be helpful to personalize and fill in a weeding rotation schedule. For example, each January weed fiction, each fall weed audiobooks, etc.

Percentage of total: As a guide for collection development, breaking down one's budget into smaller percentages can help you determine how much to spend in each year.

Action items: This section is an ideal location for specific yearly goals, such as expanding the number of multicultural titles held, or meeting needs and interests that come up in an annual survey.

Sample collection development outline

Teen collection overview

Collection guidelines: Collect in most formats for middle school and high school audience. Primary book characters in middle school or high school setting.

Selection sources: School Library Journal, VOYA, Booklist, ALA Youth Media Awards, YALSA "Best of" lists.

Weeding guidelines: Continuously weed. Yearly big weed of items that haven't circulated in the past two years. Replace worn items still in demand.

Percentage of total: Begin at 100%.

Action items: Rotate any displays no less than once a month to promote circulation.

Fiction

Collection guidelines: Limit collection to popular authors and those books that are highly recommended. Purchase optional titles depending on collection gap needs, space, and funding.

Selection sources: See teen collection overview.

Weeding guidelines: Weed heavily items that haven't circulated for two years.

Percentage of total: This will probably be the largest percentage of your collection and require the greatest percentage of your budget.

Inspirational fiction

Collection guidelines: High circulating items.

Selection sources: See teen collection overview.

Weeding guidelines: Due to lower numbers of new releases and the enduring popularity of specific titles, weed items that haven't circulated in three years.

Percentage of total: Determine what percentage of your space and budget you want to spend.

Action items: Define what you mean by inspirational fiction: All inspirational titles or Christian fiction only?

Graphic novels

Collection guidelines: Select well-reviewed novels that appeal to teens.

Selection sources: As in teen collection overview, plus online resources such as the "No Flying No Tights" review website.

Weeding guidelines: Graphic novels typically have a shorter shelf life due to binding issues.

Percentage of total: Determine what percentage of your space and budget you want to spend.

Action items: Maintain high-demand series.

Nonfiction

Collection guidelines: Focus on spirituality, crafting, and other specific teen interests that are non-academic.

Selection sources: See teen collection overview.

Weeding guidelines: Weed items that don't circulate after two years.

Percentage of total: Determine what percentage of your space and budget you want to spend.

Action items: If you don't have a teen nonfiction collection, consider pulling non-academic titles of interest into a small collection for browsing and discovery.

Audiobooks
Collection guidelines: Buy recordings of well-reviewed books and popular titles..
Selection sources: As in teen collection overview. Check YALSA "Best of" lists, Odyssey Awards.
Percentage of total: Determine what percentage of your space and budget you want to spend.
Action items: Remember to promote any downloadable services your library offers to teens as well.

Music CDs
Collection guidelines: Buy mostly music that's in demand with frequent air play, both popular and alternative.
Selection sources: Billboard.
Action items: Determine if you will include these items in your teen collection and develop appropriate guidelines.

CD-ROMs, video games
Action items: Determine if you will include these items in your teen collection and develop appropriate guidelines.

Magazines
Collection guidelines: Subscribe to a wide variety of magazines, both general interest and specialized.
Weeding guidelines: Discard after one year.
Action items: Many magazines are going to online only.

DVDs
Collection guidelines: Buy popular teen DVDs, both feature films and music performances. Limit selection to PG and PG-13 ratings.
Action items: Are teens allowed to check out movies? Consider having a small DVD collection in the teen area of popular teen movies.

SOURCE: Specially prepared for *The Whole Library Handbook: Teen Services* by Karen Jensen, teen services librarian, Grand Prairie, Texas.

Are all lists created equal?

by Casey Rawson

WITH INCREASINGLY DIVERSE service populations, libraries require more titles that feature individuals from varied backgrounds. Many studies have emphasized the importance of giving young adults access to titles in which they can see a reflection of themselves—a character or author who shares their race, nationality, religion, family status, sexual orientation, socioeconomic status, or disability. Yet in libraries with limited budgets and staff, finding titles that accurately represent a particular service population can be time-consuming. As a quick solution, librarians often rely upon ready-made lists, such as YALSA's "Best of" lists or the *Publishers Weekly* bestsellers to make collection development decisions.

Selecting for a diverse population

Michael Cart has said that literature with diverse characters gives adolescents "an opportunity to see their own faces reflected in the pages of good books." Yet it is not only their own reflections that are of value for young adults; encountering characters unlike themselves can be of equal value. As Hazel Rochman states in *Against Borders: Promoting Books for a Multicultural World*, "Books can make a difference in dispelling prejudice and building community; not with role models and literal recipes, not with noble messages about the human family, but with enthralling stories that make us imagine the lives of others."

Providing a diverse collection of young adult literature is not merely about increasing test scores or leisure reading; some researchers maintain that such literature is vital for overall success in life. Rudine S. Bishop argues that adolescents who never see themselves reflected in literature may develop a decreased sense of self-worth and may come to believe that they have little value within either the school or social community.

So why aren't diverse materials more visible in libraries that serve young adults? Studies have identified several barriers to the use and collection of such titles. One barrier is a lack of education and training among educators and librarians regarding diverse texts. Another, perhaps more critical, obstacle is the scarcity of titles written by authors from diverse backgrounds.

Despite these barriers, building a diverse library collection for young adult patrons is possible. This study analyzes three categories of young adult fiction to determine the levels of diversity shown in their protagonists.

Titles

The three categories of literature examined are:

Award-winning young adult fiction. This category includes winners of the Michael L. Printz Award for Excellence in Young Adult Literature, Printz honor winners, and titles on the YALSA Top Ten "Best Books for Young Adults" (now called "Best Fiction for Young Adults") between 2000 and 2009.

Teen-selected top-10 fiction titles. This category consists of fiction titles appearing on YALSA's "Teens' Top Ten" lists between 2003 and 2009.

Bestselling young adult fiction. This category includes the 10 top-selling young adult fiction titles for each year between 2000 and 2009, as determined by *Publishers Weekly* in its "Top Children's Fiction" list. Only items published for ages 12 and up were included.

Books appearing in more than one of the categories were counted only once. Data were compared with the actual demographics of the teen population, from U.S. Census and National Center for Education Statistics data.

Diversity

Protagonists were analyzed according to these categories:

Gender. Male or Female.

Race/ethnicity. White, Black/African American, Hispanic, American Indian, Asian, or Other.

Nationality. Country of birth.

Religion. Christianity, Judaism, Islam, Other, or Not Mentioned

Family structure. Dual Parents, Single Parent, Guardianship by a Relative, Guardianship by a Non-Relative, or Orphan/No Guardian.

Socioeconomic status. Low (lacking some basic needs such as food or shelter), Middle (having sufficient resources to meet all basic needs), or High (having an abundance of resources).

Sexuality. Straight, Gay, Bisexual, or Questioning.

Disability. Disability (physical or mental impairment) or No Disability.

Genre and setting were also recorded for each title. Genre determinations were made with the assistance of the NoveList database and tag clouds from LibraryThing. Four setting categories—Rural, Suburban, Urban, and Other—were used to describe the predominant location of each title.

Results

A total of 248 unique titles were selected for analysis—114 award-winning novels, 74 "Teens' Top Ten" novels, and 92 bestselling novels. Over 90% of the titles were successfully coded for all variables; of those remaining, no book had more than three uncoded variables.

Underrepresented protagonist categories. Several categories of protagonists were underrepresented in the data set across all three study groups. Urban-dwelling protagonists, who comprised roughly one-fourth of the overall sample, are one such underrepresented group. In reality, over half (58.2%) of U.S. residents live in urban areas (cities that have a population greater than 200,000), with the remainder of U.S. residents evenly divided among suburban and rural settings. The award-winning category had the highest percentage of urban settings, at 31.8%; only 20.7% of bestsellers took place in urban settings. For a full breakdown of novel settings, see Figure 1.

Figure 1. Novel setting

	AWARD WINNERS (n=110)	TEENS' 10 (n=73)	BESTSELLERS (n=92)	OVERALL (n=248)	NATIONAL PERCENTAGES
■ Other	9	20	39	60	
■ Urban	35	17	19	64	58.2%
▨ Suburban	32	20	17	65	21.0%
▧ Rural	34	16	17	59	20.8%

Source: Federal Highway Administration

Minority (nonwhite) protagonists are also underrepresented across all three categories of titles. Overall, 81.1% of protagonists in the sample were white; this compares to a national percentage of 56.7% white among children and teens ages 19 and under.

The award-winning titles category exhibited the most racial diversity; in this category, 65.6% of protagonists were white, 10.4% were black, and 4.8% were Hispanic. The bestsellers category exhibited the least racial diversity among pro-

Table 1. Protagonist race and demographic national data

	AWARD WINNERS (n=125)	TEENS' 10 (n=78)	BESTSELLERS (n=136)	OVERALL (n=297)	NATIONAL PERCENTAGES
White	65.6% (82)	89.7% (70)	92.6% (126)	81.1% (241)	56.7%
Black	10.4% (13)	2.6% (2)	1.5% (2)	5.4% (16)	15.3%
Asian	6.4% (8)	1.3% (1)	0.0% (0)	3.0% (9)	4.1%
Hispanic	4.8% (6)	3.8% (3)	3.7% (5)	3.7% (11)	21.3%
Biracial/ Multiracial	3.2% (4)	1.3% (1)	0.0% (0)	1.3% (4)	3.2%
American Indian	2.4% (3)	0.0% (0)	0.0% (0)	1.0% (3)	1.3%
Other	7.2% (9)	1.3% (1)	2.2% (3)	4.4% (13)	0.2%

Source: U.S. Census Bureau. *American FactFinder: 2009 American Community Survey 1-Year Estimates* (2009).

tagonists; in this category, 92.6% of protagonists were white. Hispanic protagonists were particularly underrepresented among these books: Hispanic protagonists comprised 3.7% of this sample, but nationally, 21.3% of children and teens are Hispanic. Table 1 includes complete data for protagonist race.

LGBT protagonists were underrepresented within the bestsellers category, where all 136 coded protagonists were identified as straight or as having no romantic preference within the novel. Gay, lesbian, and bisexual protagonists were found among the award-winning and "Teens' Top Ten" titles, where their prevalence was similar to actual U.S. demographics among teens. See Figure 2 for a complete breakdown of results in this category.

Protagonists raised outside of a dual-parent home (68.2%) were overrepresented in this sample; nationally, 68% of children and teens live in dual-parent households. Similarly, roughly 20% of protagonists in this study were orphans or had no guardian; this is much higher than the actual national percentage of 0.4%.

Figure 2. Protagonist sexual orientation

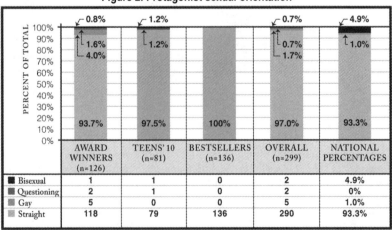

	AWARD WINNERS (n=126)	TEENS' 10 (n=81)	BESTSELLERS (n=136)	OVERALL (n=299)	NATIONAL PERCENTAGES
■ Bisexual	1	1	0	2	4.9%
■ Questioning	2	1	0	2	0%
■ Gay	5	0	0	5	1.0%
■ Straight	118	79	136	290	93.3%

Source: Debby Herbenick et al., "Sexual Behavior in the United States: Results from a National Probability Sample of Men and Women ages 14-94," *Journal of Sexual Medicine* 7, suppl. 5 (2010): 255-265.

Figure 3. Protagonist family structure

	AWARD WINNERS (n=125)	TEENS' 10 (n=81)	BESTSELLERS (n=136)	OVERALL (n=299)	NATIONAL PERCENTAGES
■ Guardianship by Non-Relative	7	3	6	14	1.6%
■ Guardianship by Relative	6	5	36	42	9.5%
▨ Orphan/No Guardian	25	15	27	60	0.4%
Single Parent	43	30	29	88	26.5%
◪ Dual Parents	44	28	38	95	62.0%

Source: U.S. Census Bureau, *American FactFinder: 2009 American Community Survey 1-Year Estimates* (2009).

These percentages did not vary greatly among the three title categories. Results for protagonist family structure are shown in Figure 3.

For award-winning and bestselling titles, higher percentages of protagonists were identified as belonging to the low socioeconomic class (33.6% and 28%, respectively) than the actual percentage of children and teens in poverty in the United States (20%). Full results for protagonist socioeconomic status are shown in Figure 4.

Cross-category comparisons between white and minority protagonists. Looking across all three categories of books, there were 241 white protagonists and 56 minority-race protagonists. When compared to white protagonists, protagonists of color were:

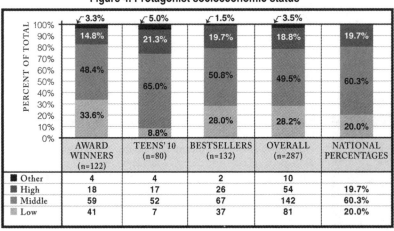

Figure 4. Protagonist socioeconomic status

	AWARD WINNERS (n=122)	TEENS' 10 (n=80)	BESTSELLERS (n=132)	OVERALL (n=287)	NATIONAL PERCENTAGES
■ Other	4	4	2	10	
■ High	18	17	26	54	19.7%
■ Middle	59	52	67	142	60.3%
Low	41	7	37	81	20.0%

Source: U.S. Census Bureau, *American FactFinder: 2009 American Community Survey 1-Year Estimates* (2009).

- more likely to be featured in realistic fiction (42% of minority protagonists versus 25.7% of white protagonists) and historical fiction (26% versus 8.9%) titles;
- less likely to be featured in fantasy (10% of minority protagonists versus 31.9% of white protagonists), humor (0% versus 8.9%), and action and adventure (2% versus 5.8%) titles;
- more likely to be male (58.2% of minority protagonists versus 46.1% of white protagonists);
- more likely to be identified as religious (25% of minority protagonists versus 8% of white protagonists);
- less likely to be part of a dual-parent home (25.9% of minority protagonists versus 33.2% of white protagonists) and less likely to be raised by a related guardian (5.6% versus 16.4%);
- more likely to be an orphan or to have no guardian (27.8% versus 18%) and slightly more likely to be part of a single-parent family (31.5% versus 28.6%);
- more likely to be in the low socioeconomic class (44.2% versus 24.3%) and less likely to be in the high socioeconomic class (7.7% versus 21.7%);
- more likely to be identified as gay, questioning, or bisexual (5.4% versus 2.5%);
- more likely to have been written by a male author (59.2% of books featuring a minority protagonist were written by males versus 48.9% of books featuring a white protagonist);
- much more likely to have been written by an author of color (38.3% versus 1%); and,
- more likely to have been written by an author from the United States (83.3% versus 68.4%).

Discussion

Where should librarians turn to find ready-made lists that reflect the diversity of their service populations? The results of this study show that if YA librarians rely only or mostly on bestseller lists for collection development, many young adults from diverse backgrounds will be underserved. The bestsellers list was fairly balanced in terms of protagonist gender, contained a large percentage of foreign-born characters, and included a diverse range of titles as far as protagonist family structure and socioeconomic status. However, nonwhite, LGBT, and religious protagonists are underrepresented on this list, as are protagonists identified as having a disability and those living in urban areas.

The "Teens' Top Ten" list fared a bit better than the bestsellers list in some categories and a bit worse in others. It featured slightly more urban, LGBT, disabled, and nonwhite protagonists. However, this list also has deficits in comparison to the bestsellers list and to national demographics: Male protagonists are underrepresented, as are protagonists in the low socioeconomic class, and religious protagonists are still rare.

Overall, the award-winning books most closely matched the actual demographics of the U.S. teen population, although even this list had some shortfalls. This list was fairly balanced in terms of its protagonist gender breakdown and included a higher percentage of urban protagonists than the other two groups. The award-winning titles had the highest percentage of nonwhite protagonists and included at least one protagonist from each racial group identified by the U.S. Census (the only list that did so). This list also included the highest percentage of religious protagonists and the highest percentage of protagonists from the low socioeconomic class (who are actually overrepresented on this list compared to national data). Award-winning titles featured LGBT protagonists at a rate consistent with national estimates. They also featured disabled characters more commonly than titles in other groups.

So does this mean that librarians can fully rely on award-winning title lists? No. Aside from considerations of readability and popularity of these texts versus bestselling titles, the award-winning list still falls short in some aspects of diversity. Along with the other lists, the award-winning list:

- lacks adequate representation of Hispanic protagonists,
- underrepresents protagonists in urban settings,
- underrepresents religious protagonists, and
- is heavily skewed toward a small number of genres.

Hispanic protagonists are severely underrepresented on all lists in comparison with the actual demographic data for U.S. adolescents and children. This could be because there has not yet been a major movement among scholars, parents, teachers, and librarians to push for titles for and about Hispanics and Latinos as there was for titles for and about African Americans in the United States in the 1970s. As the Hispanic and Latino population in the United States continues to grow, a movement for these titles may be on the horizon.

All lists underrepresent urban-dwelling protagonists. However, this may be at least partially explained by the large numbers of historical fiction and fantasy titles included in this study. Although books were coded as having urban settings if they took place in cities of the past or in fantasy cities, large numbers of these books took place in rural settings or had other or mixed settings.

Across all categories, religious protagonists comprise a small minority; protagonists from non-Christian religions are particularly rare. Most protagonists in the "other" religion category practiced a fictional religion rather than an existing one (for example, two of the protagonists in G. P. Taylor's *Shadowmancer* practice a religion that resembles Christianity but is not). Religion is a major part of life for many, if not most, children and teens in the United States; one recent study found that 65.3% of children and teens ages 6 to 17 participate in religious activities once a month or more. The lack of young adult titles that address this aspect of teen life is puzzling; the idea that authors view religion as somehow taboo seems to be an inadequate explanation, since authors and publishers seem perfectly willing to feature other, even more sensitive issues, such as teen sex, pregnancy, drug use, and physical abuse. More research into this question is necessary.

Each of the three lists is heavily skewed toward one or two genres. Thus, relying on any one of these lists would result in a collection that is lacking in several key areas. The award-winning titles are biased toward realistic fiction and historical fiction; fantasy, science fiction, action and adventure, and sports novels (all popular genres) are comparatively neglected. Among the "Teens' Top Ten" books, fantasy and realistic titles are included at a high rate at the expense of other genres. Among bestsellers, fantasy and humor novels together comprise the majority of titles.

In fantasy titles, 31.9% of the protagonists were white and only 10% were minority protagonists. Of the five minority protagonists, one was black (again in *Shadowmancer*), and the remainder were classified in the "other" category because they were described as being of a fictional race. Science fiction was a bit better; of the four minority protagonists, one was Asian, one was Hispanic, and two were others (alien). The tendency of authors to feature minority protagonists in realistic or historical fiction is an interesting trend. It may be an outgrowth of a repeated call among researchers for "culturally conscious" or "enabling" texts that challenge racial stereotypes, provide literary role models for minority teens, and connect with teens' cultural heritages.

In this sample set, nonwhite protagonists were more than twice as likely to be identified as gay, bisexual, or questioning as white protagonists. The reasons for this are unclear; perhaps it is the case that authors who feature protagonists who are marginalized in terms of race are also more willing to feature protagonists who are marginalized in terms of sexuality.

One question that this research does not address is why so little protagonist diversity (at least in several of the dimensions studied here) exists in bestselling young adult novels. To some extent, the market controls what sells and what doesn't, and it could be the case that books with minority protagonists are truly not as appealing to wide audiences. Are white, straight, middle-class teens uninterested in reading about characters who are different from them? If so, could this be because the large majority of the books that they have read and enjoyed do not feature minority characters? Are minority teens not purchasing books? If so, is this because they simply don't want to read, they can't afford the books, there are not enough characters like them in the books to which they have easy access, or some other reason? How does the marketing of young adult titles differ between books featuring minorities and other books? How much might those differences account for the dearth of minority protagonists on bestsellers lists?

Conclusion

Whether or not libraries are ready for them, millions of children from diverse backgrounds will soon be finding their way into young adult collections for the first time. Whether they come back may well depend on whether the books they find there include characters whose backgrounds reflect the diversity they see in themselves and in their communities. And whether they find those books depends on whether librarians are willing to embrace a broad view of diversity—looking beyond simply protagonists' race or ethnicity—and take the time to locate and purchase books featuring protagonists from marginalized groups who are portrayed accurately and compassionately.

If, as a profession, librarians can commit to doing this, then the overall diversity of our collections will increase along with the rising diversity of the populations we are serving. And perhaps, if every library in the country begins ordering titles that feature diverse characters, we might even rewrite the bestsellers list and change the face of publishing in the United States. That is a lofty goal, and one that only people—not lists—can achieve.

SOURCE: Casey H. Rawson, "Are All Lists Created Equal? Diversity in Award-Winning and Bestselling Young Adult Fiction," *Journal of Research on Libraries and Young Adults* 1 no. 3 (June 2011), online at yalsa.ala.org/jrlya/2011/06/.

Weeding
by Heather Booth

1. "Books are for use.
2. "Every reader his or her book.
3. "Every book its reader.
4. "Save the time of the reader.
5. "The library is a growing organism."—*S. R. Ranganathan*

LOVE IT OR HATE IT, weeding—the process by which items are systematically removed from a collection—is essential to a well-maintained teen collection. Whether it is done naturally without much intervention, continually and gently, or periodically with a strong hand, every collection needs to be weeded. Some items will wear out and fall apart and need to be withdrawn, others will become outdated and need to be retired, and others need to be removed because they did not find an audience.

Why weed

Weeding is Ranganathan at its most basic. If an item is not being used, it does not belong in the collection. The length of time an item should remain on the shelf, waiting to be checked out, will vary depending on the type of material, the space limitations, and its relative popularity compared to similar items. Additionally, use need not be indicated only by circulation statistics. A book's usefulness may be that it represents a unique viewpoint on a historical event; or it is a superb example of the experience of teens in a minority culture; or it is frequently used in-house, despite rarely being checked out, which is the case for many more controversial books. In these cases, weeding a book for lack of circulation would be a mistake.

Weeding saves the patron's time as well. The sleeker the collection, the easier it will be for teens to find the perfect item that meets their needs or interests, both when browsing and when looking for a specific item. And finally, the library is ever growing and changing. And just like the garden plants that must be pruned or thinned or weeded to allow the newer, more useful, more beautiful plants to thrive, so must our collections let go of items as they grow.

When to weed

There are many different timetables for this, but in the teen collection, it is important to consider the cyclical patterns of use. Weeding at the height of summer or in the midst of winter break is not advisable. These times are when most teen collections will see their highest circulation. Not only will the teen librarian be busy at these times of year, but books that need examination will be checked out, and this may bring new life to titles that have been sitting for a while on the shelves. A school library will see a different pattern, and summer will likely be the best time for weeding in this setting. Some collections are massive enough, and some of our time limited enough, that weeding needs to be done continually throughout the year, addressing a shelf a week, a section a month, a letter of the alphabet every two weeks. For others, weeding will be most efficient in one fell swoop during a lower traffic time of year.

Reasons to weed

The main reasons to weed your collection are condition, currency, circulation, and space, and here's how to do it.

Condition. Begin with the easiest: condition. Teens do not want books that look like they've been dragged through the dirt, gnawed on, or used for scratch paper or batting practice. Even if these tattered tomes are long-standing favorites—especially if they are—replace them with fresh new copies.

Currency. When weeding for currency, consider the nonfiction as well as the fiction. There is certainly no place for outdated medical advice or unauthorized biographies of flash-in-the-pan stars from 15 years ago. Likewise, shelf space will be better spent on fiction that keeps its pop-culture references current or ambiguous, displays contemporary social mores, and has cover art that today's teens find relatable. This is not to say that the collection doesn't have space for classics or historically significant works, but the goal for most public and school library teen collections should be meeting the needs of the teens in your community today and tomorrow, not existing as a time capsule for our own reminiscences.

Circulation. Weeding for circulation seems simple, but most librarians will shudder when they come face-to-face with the reality that an old favorite, or a great book that just never took off, has circulation numbers low enough to land it on the chopping block. The circulation range limit for weeding will vary, depending on the size of the collection and the rate of turnover. When considering how long a book should be allowed to sit on the shelf without being checked out, remember how fast a teen generation turns over. A book that hasn't been checked out in five years is a book that was last checked out a year before this year's seniors entered high school.

Space. For many librarians, the true test of our weeding mettle will come when we are faced with space limitations and are forced to consider removing books that are in good condition, current, and have moderate circulation numbers but are being outperformed by other books. Weeding for space works the same way the other three do, but it pushes the librarian to make tough decisions about the relative usefulness, value, and popularity of similar books.

For many, it is helpful to work from preset guidelines. Weeding with rules, instead of "by feel," will result in consistency and a less emotional experience. For a good overview of various weeding procedures and guidelines, read ALA's "Library Fact Sheet 15," *Weeding Library Collections: A Selected Annotated Bibliography for Library Collection Evaluation* (ala.org/tools/libfactsheets/alalibraryfactsheet15). In it, you will find ample resources for school libraries and small collections and referrals to advice that can easily be applied to your teen book and media collection.

Ultimately, we must remember that the teen library collection is not ours; it is for the teens in our community. We are the caretakers of a collection that belongs to others. We do not serve them well and we are not good caretakers of their collection if we do not keep their need for an up-to-date, well-maintained, frequently weeded collection at the forefront of our priorities.

SOURCE: Specially prepared for *The Whole Library Handbook: Teen Services* by Heather Booth, teen services librarian, Thomas Ford Memorial Library, Western Springs, Illinois.

YA book blogs and how they can help you develop your collection

by Abby Johnson and Melissa Wheelock-Diedrichs

BLOGS ARE POPPING UP all over the internet, and they can cover a multitude of subjects that teen librarians may find useful for collection development. There is definitely still a place for traditional review journals, but in this section you will find information to help you navigate the world of blogs and use them as a resource for developing your collections.

What is the blogosphere?

The term *blogosphere* collectively refers to all blogs (frequently updated websites with journal-style posts) on the internet. Regular features called memes encourage wide participation across the blogosphere, gathering bloggers together to review nonfiction books, post about poetry, or explore the review copies bloggers have received in the mail. Bloggers have also developed annual conferences for networking and professional development. The annual KidLitosphere Conference is held in the fall in a different city each year, and the Bloggers Conference has been developed out of the annual BookExpo America, held in the spring.

Why pay attention to blogs and blog reviews?

The two most important reasons to follow blog reviews are content and communication. The format of blogs allows flexibility in length, publishing dates, and content. Blogs also allow open communication between the publisher of the blog and the librarian.

Reviewers in traditional journals have to keep their reviews short and to the point. Blogs, without those length limitations, can include information that isn't available in traditional sources. Bloggers often provide reviews of items such as series books and audiovisual media that are not comprehensively covered in traditional review journals. Bloggers are also often able to provide reviews of new and upcoming titles more quickly than print journals, thus enabling collectors to stay on top of new titles that people are talking about.

The other reason to pay attention to blogs and blog reviews is the communication aspect. Blogs allow readers to comment on blog posts and to ask questions. Good bloggers are diligent about answering those questions and responding to comments. This allows librarians to build relationships with those bloggers, which opens a dialogue. As you get to know the bloggers, you can evaluate how their opinion of a book compares to your own. This interaction will help you make better-informed decisions.

Finally, and, perhaps most important, is the connection to teen readers. There are teens out there blogging about books, and this is a wonderful resource to the collection development librarian. Anyone who has worked with teens knows what we think is good isn't necessarily what teens think is good. These teen bloggers will help you stay in touch with the interests and needs of your teens.

How do you find reliable blog reviews?

There are hundreds of book blogs on the internet, and they are easy to find, once you start exploring. Remember that anyone can write a blog, and for that reason, selectors must read blog reviews critically and pay attention to authorship. Look  for an "About me" section with information about the blog's author. Reviews should contain enough information to let selectors make an informed decision about a book's place in the collection. Check the backlog of a blogger's content to make sure she is consistently posting thoughtful reviews. If the blogger has reviewed something you've read, check to see if she covered relevant information. This can give you a good indication of the quality of reviews being written on the site.

Be wary of bloggers who only post positive reviews or whose reviews do not contain a great deal of actual content. There is certainly a place for bloggers who may only post "buzz," including book trailers, lists of highly anticipated upcoming books, etc. These blogs can inform selectors about upcoming books,  but there is a difference between buzz (read: free advertising) and thoughtful reviews. The best way to make sure you're utilizing reliable blogs is to read content critically and make decisions about which blogs are most useful for your collection and the needs of your patrons.

Where do you start?

Audiobook Jukebox (www.audiobookjukebox. com), a directory of blogger audiobook reviews.

Book Blogger Directory (bookbloggerdirectory. wordpress.com), a directory of book bloggers of all genres.

The Book Smugglers (thebooksmugglers.com), thoughtful reviews of sci-fi and YA books.

The Cybils Awards (www.cybils.com), annual book awards given out by bloggers.

Forever Young Adult (www.foreveryoungadult.com), reviews of teen books and popular TV shows.

Guys Lit Wire (guyslitwire.blogspot.com/), reviews of books for teenage boys.

The Hub (www.yalsa.ala.org/thehub/), YALSA's own YA lit blog.

I'm Here, I'm Queer, What the Hell Do I Read? (www.leewind.org), Lee Wind's blog on YA books with GLBTQ characters and themes.

KidLitosphere Central (www.kidlitosphere.org), a directory of children's and YA book blogs.

Stacked (www.stackedbooks.org), frequent in-depth reviews from YA librarians.

SOURCE: Specially prepared for *The Whole Library Handbook: Teen Services* by Abby Johnson, children's manager, New Albany–Floyd County (Ind.) Public Library, and Melissa Wheelock-Diedrichs, teen librarian, Kokomo–Howard County (Ind.) Public Library.

The next big thing in ebooks

by Erin Bush

EBOOKS ARE NOT THE NEXT BIG THING. They spent several years as the Next Big Thing, but now that e-reading is possible on cellphones and tablets as well as computers and e-readers, they are officially a Very Big Thing and have been for awhile. What's still just beginning to be explored, though, are the possibilities that e-publishing holds for enhancing the reading experience. Some writers and publishers are exploring interactive creations, such as hidden clues and puzzles for readers to find online, game tie-ins, interactive maps, and more; there's even a term, *transmedia*, for this kind of experience, which connects reading with other activities. However, there's another Next Big Thing spawned by e-reading—it's less technologically intensive than transmedia, but still has the potential to change how we read.

Before e-publishing, if authors created works in their fictional worlds that weren't novel-shaped, their options for sharing them with readers were limited. They could write short stories and try to publish them in anthologies, but there was always a risk that the anthology's editor wouldn't take the story or that the author's regular readers wouldn't find it. Highly successful authors might have a chance to publish a collection of their own stories or a limited-edition printing of a novella. Most of the time, though, those sorts of side stories probably never saw the light of day. Certainly, books like J. R. R. Tolkien's *The Silmarillion* and the *Unfinished Tales*, which provide great insight into the author's creations, were far more the exception than the rule until e-publishing made it possible to produce and share them without the expense of printing.

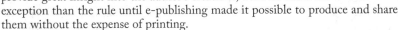

The trend toward publishing this kind of material directly in electronic format has been gradual; authors have been sharing excerpts from upcoming books on their blogs for about as long as authors blogging has been a trend. And some have stretched the possibilities of electronic publishing pretty far already—for example, Catherynne M. Valente, author of the lovely fantasy *The Girl Who Circumnavigated Fairyland in a Ship of Her Own Making*, first published the novel herself in installments on her blog, then offered it for download before it was conventionally published in print.

But it seems to have been within the last couple of years that publishers have gotten involved, working with established authors to give electronically published short stories lovely covers that fit with the rest of a series and making it easy to download them on the most popular e-reading platforms, Kindle and Nook. I first observed this trend in romance fiction for adults, and in 2012 in particular it spread to YA in a big way.

Young adult authors who've e-published short stories in the world of their established series that year include Veronica Roth, Taherah Mafi, Lauren Oliver, Sarah J. Maas, Rae Carson, and many more. The content can range from short retellings of key scenes from the perspective of a character whose point of view we don't get in the main series, as in Veronica Roth's "Free Four: Tobias Tells the *Divergent* Story," to longer tales, such as Rae Carson's "The Shadow Cats." This novella is both a prequel to Carson's epic fantasy *The*

Girl of Fire and Thorns and an alternate-point-of-view story focusing on main character Elodie's older sister, the crown princess. In Dan Wells's "Fragments," a short story set in the dystopian universe of *Partials*, Wells expands his world building by telling a story set two decades earlier with new characters in another part of the world—China—rather than the Long Island setting of the first book. Seeing these multiple perspectives and getting access to aspects of the world building that might otherwise have remained in the author's mind changes the reading experience. The feeling is a bit like immersing oneself in the sort of inventiveness and perspective shifting that's often found in good fan fiction—except these inventions are created by the authors themselves.

Publishing these stories in e-format seems to be a win for authors, publishers, and readers. Authors get to share stories that might otherwise have sat in a drawer or on a hard drive somewhere and know that those stories are being read and discussed by their most devoted fans. Publishers get to keep the attention of readers between books in a series and ratchet up the excitement and anticipation for a new title. Readers get more stories—and often at a price that's very reasonable for teens. Most of these e-published short stories sell for $2.99 or less on the major bookstore websites—some are even free. For all of these reasons, e-publishing short stories and other "extra" material in popular series appears to be a Next Big Thing that will only get bigger.

Are there any disadvantages to this trend? Possibly. If publishing extra ebook-only material becomes standard, something all the big names in young adult fiction are doing, those readers who don't read ebooks, or who can't find the stories because their computer, smartphone, or e-reader access is limited or nonexistent, may start to feel that they are getting a lesser reading experience. Many libraries also seem unsure about whether to purchase these exclusively e-published short stories. In my own region, where there are several large city and country library systems, some have purchased them and some have not.

What do you think? If you're a fan of these popular YA authors, do you gobble up e-published short stories, or are you indifferent to them? If you're a librarian, does your library system carry them in its ebook collection or not? What is the system's rationale for the choice?

As someone who read *The Silmarillion* multiple times growing up, I tend to think in terms of "the more story, the better," so despite the potential disadvantages, this is one Next Big Thing that I can get excited about.

SOURCE: Erin Bush, "The Next Big Thing in E-books," The Hub, October 29, 2012, online at yalsa. ala.org/thehub/2012/10/29/the-next-big-thing-in-e-books/.

Booktalking: Tips from a pro
by Joni Richards Bodart

A BOOKTALKING PROGRAM offers numerous benefits.

- Booktalking overcomes our most frequent phobia—public speaking. And it's the best way to start doing it, with kids who don't have English or history or whatever class that period after all.
- Booktalking gives more contact with the kids. You can get information on collection development, programming wants and needs, and class as-

signments. They can get ideas on reading, teen advisory boards, and the cool activities and programs you've planned. And they can get to know you and discover you are really a real person!

- Booktalking increases circulation—always a result of booktalks, and always a plus—and can put more money in your book budget.
- Booktalking spreads influence. Like a stone dropped into a quiet pool, after your booktalking presentation, the ripples begin to spread. You don't have to convince all of the teachers in a school that you should visit their classes—teachers will convince each other. You don't have to booktalk to every teen—they spread the word themselves, and peer recommendations are always the most powerful.
- Booktalking promotes recreational reading. Reading more frequently means reading better, and reading better enhances self-esteem.
- Booktalking develops skills. It also helps develop higher-level thinking processes, and reading helps students' visualization skills and creativity as well.

Defining the booktalk

Book Talk *noun* (buk) (tawk)
1. A conversation about a book that one's read, infused with joy and emotion. Best if done daily.

What *is* a booktalk?

- It's not a book review; it doesn't evaluate.
- It's not a book report; it doesn't tell the whole story.
- It's based on the assumption that the book is good.
- It's a commercial or sales pitch for a book that convinces someone else to read it.
- It isn't static but dynamic, interactive, always changing to fit the booktalker and the audience—but always including whatever's necessary to draw in the listeners.

Four unbreakable rules about booktalking

1. **Don't talk about a book you haven't read.** If you're using someone else's talk, you may not know that there's an error in it or not realize when you have made a mistake yourself that makes the talk inaccurate. More important, it isn't *your book*, about people you know and want to share with your audience—the characters in the book are just that, characters, and not your friends. And that's what a booktalk is—introducing your audience to your friends in the book.
2. **Don't talk about a book you don't like.** You won't be able to sell it to anyone, since it is your enthusiasm that sells the book.
3. **Don't tell the ending.** Why would anyone want to read it if you do?
4. **Do your own thing.** Develop your own style of booktalking that works for you. Don't try to copy anyone else—be yourself. And remember—rules can be broken, but be careful how you break them, and break them only for a good reason.

Using someone else's talk

There are many sources of published talks—books, websites, and blogs. If you are going to use someone else's talk instead of writing one of your own, you need to make sure it will work for you. Read it aloud, and see if its rhythm, language, and style fit with yours; if not, change it so it does work. This may mean changing the words, the length of the sentences, the point of view, the length—whatever you need to change to make it work for you. Continue reading it aloud and changing it until you are satisfied. At that point, it's no longer someone else's talk—it's yours! Of course, if the talk sounds right for you when you read it aloud the first time, then changes aren't necessary. If the style of the talk fits yours, you can use it as is.

Writing your own talk

If you are going to write your own talk, you need to take notes while you read or as soon as you finish the book. The format of the notes doesn't really matter. Do your own thing—figure out what works for you. Include author, title, bibliographic info, page numbers for the scenes or lines that you want to use,

characters' names, plotline, genre, whatever you think you might need when you go back later and try to write a talk without rereading the book. If you can keep the book near at hand until you write the talk, use paper clips or tiny sticky notes to mark those pages you need to remember. This saves time relocating that elusive title or scene.

And as you read, keep your purpose in mind, and read for booktalking. This is different than reading for pleasure or to review. Look for scenes or hooks you might want to use, and be aware of what props might work with the book. Read as if you were the age the book is intended for—use your inner teen! Consider reading the book twice: once for enjoyment and once to build your talk. When I read for booktalking, I focus on the first quarter of the book and absolutely no more than the first half.

When you start thinking about how to write your talk, start with the hook—what made you pick up the book, and what made you keep going? You might have found a phrase, a line or two of dialogue, or a scene that caught your attention as you read the first part of the book. Will that hook work in a booktalk? Was there a character you really identified with? A scene that grabbed you? A sentence that sang in your head? An intriguing plotline? An unusual mood or writing style? Focus your talk on what was most exciting for you. Not everyone will focus their talk on that title the way you did. That doesn't matter—this is *your* talk, and it is based on what *you* found exciting.

Your first sentence is the key—it makes sure the audience's attention is on you. Start in the middle of the action. Use short sentences and lots of action. And remember, your words will be spoken, not read—read your talk aloud after your first draft so you can hear how it sounds. If you have information on the author, you can use it to make him/her more real. If you use the language of your audience, make sure any slang is current.

Keep the purpose of your talk in mind. Know where you're going and why. Plan a beginning, middle, and end, and have a reason for each. Omit details, and let your audience discover some things on their own. Don't oversell a book—it will come across as false. And don't feel obligated to talk about books with subjects you aren't comfortable with.

Know when to stop—and do it. Your talk should be as long as necessary, but as short as possible. Tell only enough to make someone want to read the book. Make the last sentence a grabber just like the first one. It's a hook also—it lets the audience know that there is something more happening that you haven't told them about.

Content perspectives or approaches

When I began to do booktalking workshops, back in the 1970s, I had to define and explain how to do it, and one of the first things I did was to define the different content perspectives used to focus the booktalk. They are based on the *focus of excitement* in the book, which can vary from one person to another. Write about what is important to you in the book, what gripped you and made you want to keep reading.

Plot summary. Sketch the plot in broad strokes, omit minor plotlines and details, and let the audience discover them themselves. Lead up to the climax, and stop. "To find out what happened . . ."

Anectote/excerpt/short story. This is for episodic books or short story collections—you can tell one scene or story completely, including the ending, and finish with "And that's only *one* of the stories/adventures/things that happened." The scene needs to be typical of the book, and not too far into the story, so you don't give too much away. You can also talk about short story collections by doing mini plot outlines or character descriptions for several of the stories.

Character description. Describe the main character in detail, from first- or third-person point of view. You can tell about or become a character, or briefly describe several characters. Using first person can be very moving, getting into emotions of the character. It's okay to become either male or female, just as long as you make sure your audience knows you are speaking as the character, not as yourself. Be sure to mention your character's name early on, as in "My name is Dillon Hemingway, and I'm 17 years old" (*Chinese Handcuffs*, by Chris Crutcher). You can also become a minor character and describe the main characters or setting. I have had some people tell me that it's good to become a character using first person if you are nervous about being in front of a group, because you can let the character stand up there and talk instead of you.

Mood based. A mood-based talk is the hardest to describe, and it works for an unusual writing style or mood. Use phrases or sentences to convey the writing style, but be careful about reading from the book. It separates you from your audience, and can be a physical barrier, and you may not be able to read aloud as well as you think you can. Do listen to a recording of your reading before you base a booktalk on it. Use your voice, pitch, pace, rhythm, and tone to convey the mood of the book and to create the mood for the audience.

Taking notes

Most people want to have notes with them, especially when they are beginners. I still take notes with me! There are several ways to so this, so you will need to experiment and find out what works for you. You can use:

- the whole talk (this is what I do)
- an outline
- the first sentence
- key sentences
- characters' names

Practicing your talk. Practice everything all at once: talk, body position and movements, gestures, what you do with the book, what you do with your notes. It's easier to remember everything when you practice everything at the same time. Gestures can help you remember words, and vice versa.

Don't memorize. Make your talk into a cartoon strip. Break it up into different pieces or scenes, and memorize their order. Then fit the text to each scene. Deliberately use different words and phrases when you practice. Work from your outline, or just don't look at your talk while you practice, even if you get stuck. Give yourself time to unstick yourself before you look at the talk. Remember—this is just practice. Practice till it sounds like you're just talking.

Speak slowly. Give the audience time to hear and *understand* what you're saying.

Stay flexible. Change your talk if it doesn't work—it's not set in stone. Get feedback from peers on your performance, and pay attention to the way teens respond to your talk. If your hooks don't work, change them.

Time your talk. It shouldn't be more than three minutes long, and many people do great talks in half that time. You want your talks to be as long as necessary but as short as possible.

Planning a booktalk for a specific group

Learn about the group before you start selecting books:

- The reading level (vary around this some, on both sides)
- The ratio of males to females
- The age range
- The size of the group
- Are they readers or nonreaders?
- What titles were read recently for assignments?
- What titles have most of the group read, are reading, or plan to read?
- What are the special needs or interests of the group or establishment? (This is especially relevant to visiting religious schools, detention centers, or other establishments that may have additional requirements or restrictions.)
- What is the purpose of your visit? What does the teacher expect of you?
- Are both fiction and nonfiction okay?
- Does the group want a thematic approach or mixed bag?

Delivering your booktalks

Get there early so you can set up books and talks; make sure you have water; and catch your breath.

Make sure the teacher stays in the room (you're the entertainment, not the disciplinarian) and models the behavior s/he wants from the class, i.e., *listening*. And it's okay to leave if the teacher can't control the class, especially if it's a substitute. You have the right to be listened to and treated with respect. Explain to the teacher, the librarian, and if necessary the administrator, and reschedule.

Wear comfortable clothes and shoes. I always have pockets for my hands.

Relax. Take a deep breath or two. Speak slowly. Project. Make eye contact; it makes it personal and helps keep the rowdies in line.

Stay in control of your stage fright. You are an actor, and your audience won't know if you made any mistakes or are scared to death unless you *let* them know it!

Keep talks and books in presentation order. This is especially important if you're a beginner, since that way it's easier to use the written talks for support.

Don't read the title from the cover. Show it to audience as you say it.

Stay flexible with interruptions. Keep your sense of humor!

Don't beat up on yourself about your mistakes. And remember that *everyone* is entitled to a bad day once in a while!

Talk slowly enough to give your audience time to really hear what you're saying, and use pauses to create emphasis and tension or suspense. People talk faster than they hear, and you need to let them have time to absorb what you're saying.

Enjoy yourself and have fun. Enthusiasm can cover many flaws, make mistakes less obvious, and help your audience have a good time, too.

Interact with the kids afterward.

Take annotated booklists you can hand out with the titles you talked about and also some read-alikes.

SOURCE: Specially prepared for *The Whole Library Handbook: Teen Services* by Joni Richards Bodart, associate professor, San Jose State University School of Library and Information Science.

Readers' advisory: Listening is an act of love

by Heather Booth

THE STORYCORPS PROJECT, in which loved ones tell stories of their lives to one another, is a good lesson to the readers' advisor. Especially to the teen readers' advisor. One of the basic ideas of this oral-history project is that listening is an act of love. The recordings in this project are not just conversations or interviews but invitations to communicate, to ask for and to receive a bit of something sacredly held, to listen completely, and in doing so, to reach a greater understanding of someone. Quite often, we think of readers' advisory (RA) as getting the right book to the right person. But we have failed ourselves and our patrons if, before that can happen, before we press crisp pages into eager hands, share the excitement of a perfect match, or hopefully extend an olive branch to a reluctant reader, we do not listen.

Listening is an act of love, and listening to teenagers completely, asking open questions that invite them to tell us more, and gently moving from one topic to the next when it appears they have given us all the information they are comfortable or able to give is at the heart of RA to teens. If we can listen to them talk about the books they have liked, the stories that moved them, the information they seek to find, the connections they hope to make, we are telling them that what they have to say is important. It counts. We hear them. Their interests are worth our time and energy. And we are going to do something about it.

RA presents the ideal opportunity to do this. Asking for recreational reading is more personal than asking for help with a homework assignment but not so intimate as asking for informational resources on sensitive topics. If we can demonstrate our listening skills in an RA interaction, we position ourselves to be the person teens can trust when they need more information or are seeking to share their time with us in a teen advisory board (TAB) or program, and this then extends to the library as a whole—we become a trusted space in the community. When beginning a job as a teen services librarian, we don't automatically have the relationships with the teens or with the community (in most cases) that tell people that we're willing and able and ready to listen—about everything from what kind of snacks we should request for the vending machine in the lobby to what the big research paper is, to what help a college-hopeful teen needs to make it there. That kind of give-and-take is something that takes time to build. This is where RA is an indispensable service that must be part of all teen services librarians' repertoires.

Prove to teens that you can help them find something they like reading, and they will believe you when you tell them that you want to know what programs will appeal to their peers, what databases they find most useful, and how the library can serve their demographic better. For reluctant readers, or the very picky, your willingness to listen and try to meet their needs will pay off even if you never successfully find a book that they enjoy. The care you take with their requests and the seriousness with which you approach your suggestions demonstrates that you are there for them and will try.

RA belongs in every library that serves teens for the same reason StoryCorps encourages family and friends to share memories and experiences. "Each session represents an act of love and respect: minutes set aside to ask important questions and listen closely to the answers." Teen librarianship is not a job that will bring most of us traditionally recognized fame, fortune, or glory. But for each connection we make through listening and extending a hand (with a book or without) to the teens we assist, we are showing our love for the work, for the teen, and for the material, and in doing so, we will earn the kind of success that those people who share the small details of their lives do when they share their stories. We lay the foundation upon which a future is built.

SOURCE: Specially prepared for *The Whole Library Handbook: Teen Services* by Heather Booth, teen services librarian, Thomas Ford Memorial Library, Western Springs, Illinois.

Readers' advisory for teens
by Heather Booth

READERS' ADVISORY is more than just passing on suggestions of good books. It is a skill that is part science and part art, with a healthy dash of mind

reading. The science comes in the classification of various types of books into genres and categories, grouping them together in a useful and meaningful way, and knowing where and why any given book fits into that scheme. The art of readers' advisory involves masterfully articulating various elements of a book to pique interest and entice the prospective reader. And mind reading definitely can help in detecting just what a patron means when he says he wants "just anything good."

Fortunately, strategies and resources are available to assist those of us who are not part of the Psychic Friends Network to build our skills in the art and science of readers' advisory. This section will provide an overview of the concepts of readers' advisory, although it can only skim the surface of very deep water. Those who seek a more comprehensive introduction or a more in-depth look at effective readers' advisory techniques for adults are encouraged to see Joyce Saricks's *Readers' Advisory Service in the Public Library* (ALA Editions, 2005). For those who are serious about establishing or expanding a readers' advisory service or are seeking to improve their own readers' advisory skills, Saricks's book is an indispensable resource.

Reference for recreational reading

The simplest way I have found to explain readers' advisory to those unfamiliar with the concept is to liken it to reference work for recreational reading. When working with teens, you may often have the opportunity to do readers' advisory for homework assignments. This is not exactly recreational reading, but the same concepts and practices apply (see Chapter 8). As with reference work, patrons approach the desk seeking information or can be spotted with a perplexed look wandering the floor. Also as with reference work, you will need to conduct an interview to ascertain exactly what type of information the patron is looking for. And most important, as with reference work, you will suggest a variety  of materials based on what the patron has asked for, not what you think the patron should have. Thus, a readers' advisory exchange can be broken down into three distinct parts: the approach, the interview, and the presentation of options and resolution. This is true whether you work with teens or adults, though when working with teens, you may need to make some minor stylistic adjustments to traditional readers' advisory services.

The approach

Quite obviously, the key to a successful approach phase is to be approachable. Because some patrons may assume that librarians do not want to be bothered or that only serious informational reference questions merit attention, they never take advantage of readers' advisory services, even though they would benefit from or enjoy them. Some patrons may approach us and describe exactly what they want, but far more patrons will look for a book on their own and not think to ask at the service desk. Many library patrons do not realize that asking for help in finding a good book for leisure reading is completely legitimate and even encouraged. We can work to change this misconception by focusing on our approachability. Welcoming facial expressions, acknowledging patrons when they enter our area, and offering assistance are great starts.

Because teens see us as authority figures (or at the very least, as adults), approachability and an open, positive attitude are of utmost importance. Remember that teens often face challenges in obtaining good customer service based solely on their age and appearance. Their resulting wariness of age bias will often carry over into their interactions with library staff. This is not to say that inappropriate behavior should be tolerated in hopes that teens will see us as cool and come to us for reading suggestions. But acknowledging societal preconceptions that teens face can help inform the manner in which we approach them.

When offering assistance to teens, being specific about what you can offer is often more helpful than a general offer. You could simply ask, "Can I help you?" or

---

Reading your teens

No one wants to be like the pushy salesperson who lunges at customers the minute they walk into the store, yet our teens need to know that we are serious about our offers of help. The clues below will help you determine which teens to approach and which are content browsing on their own.

Approach if a teen
- Is alone
- Is browsing books and talking about books with a friend or parent
- Is "lingering," meandering through the stacks, soaking it all in
- Picks books up and skims through them, reads flyleaves, and so forth
- Is browsing pathfinders, reading articles posted in the area, or otherwise absorbing materials
- Makes eye contact with or smiles at you when you are in the area

Wait until next time if a teen
- Is just hanging out and socializing with friends
- Is engrossed in reading
- Avoids eye contact
- Is wearing earphones
- Is browsing an area with sensitive materials and does not exhibit any of the above signs of approachability

---

"Did you find what you were looking for?" But by observing a teen's behavior and tailoring your response to that specific situation, you can often initiate a fruitful readers' advisory conversation. For example, if a patron has picked up a teen chick lit title, you can start off by saying, "You know, a lot of people who liked that book are also reading books by this other author." If someone is browsing the new fiction, you can clarify the type of help you can offer by remarking, "If you don't spot one that looks good, I would be happy to help with some suggestions." Because teen patrons may not be familiar with the services we can provide, offering assistance with specific tasks can let teens know that we have skills from which they can benefit and that we are willing to help.

At our readers' advisory desk, we have many read-alike booklists and other thematic lists available, and we are close to a web public access catalog (PAC). Readers' advisory interviews may begin when teens are browsing the lists and we ask if they are looking for a particular list that we could help them locate. Teens who do not know how to find what they are looking for are often drawn to these printed aids, so they may say something like, "No, nothing in particular, I just can't remember the name of the book my friend suggested." Or when a teen is lingering over the web PAC, we may approach and offer specific help, either with navigating the catalog or by suggesting a book if general keyword searches are not fruitful. These are wonderful openings for a readers' advisory interview.

In our library, the new fiction section is very close to the readers' advisory desk. Because of this configuration, we are able to initiate many readers' advisory interactions while sitting at the desk. However, the new fiction is

All you need to know about the approach phase in an RA interaction

1. Be present. Move out from behind the desk. Patrons rarely linger around the service desk—they want to be where the books are. That is where you also should be to offer the help that they need.
2. Be approachable. Smile and let your patrons know that you are happy that they are in your area.
3. Be specific in offering help. "Can I help you?" works only if a patron knows what kind of help is available.

---

only a small fraction of the collection as a whole, and that section is not the place to find most browsing teens.

Good practice involves seeking out patrons who may be in need of help or might be open to but unaware of readers' advisory services. To find them, move out from behind the desk now and then and take a stroll through the fiction area. You may encounter a patron staring at her favorite author's shelf, lamenting the fact that there are no titles she has not already read and not knowing which other authors she might enjoy. Or you may run into someone who has not been in the library since he did his third-grade state report but has some free time, wants to read some fiction, and does not know where to start.

At the same time, you might come across patrons who value their silent wanderings in the stacks and want nothing to do with suggestions or readers' advisors. Whatever the case, we have found that the positive results gained from approaching patrons far outweigh the occasional negative reaction. This concept is particularly important in teen readers' advisory, especially if your library's teen area does not have a service desk.

The interview

Any librarian familiar with reference interview techniques will be able to adapt those techniques to a teen readers' advisory interview. Like a reference interview, a readers' advisory interview can include such behaviors as active listening, repeating information as you understand it ("So, you're looking for an author who writes like John Green but isn't American?"), asking open-ended questions, and maintaining objectivity and withholding judgment. However, because of the highly individual nature of reading interests, readers' advisory interviews are more effective when conducted in a conversational style rather than in the methodically structured manner that works so well in reference interviewing.

Saricks describes a readers' advisory interview as "a conversation, with readers telling the readers' advisor about books and their leisure-reading tastes and the readers' advisor listening and suggesting possible titles." She goes on to explain that this conversation can be more important than finding the perfect book because it establishes in the patron's mind that discussing leisure reading is a welcome and rewarding activity to engage in with librarians.

During the interview, the librarian should try to use appeal factors to ascertain just what type of book the patron is looking for. Appeal factors do not speak specifically to the content of a book but rather to the elements that a reader may be drawn to or repelled from. In addition to its story line, a book's language, pacing, setting, characterization of people and situations, and "discussability" all contribute to a reader's enjoyment. In fact, a

---

The vocabulary of appeal

Using the terms below during a readers' advisory interview can help you identify the factors that contribute to a teen's preferences in leisure reading.

Pacing: breakneck, compelling, deliberate, densely written, easy, engrossing, fast-paced, leisurely paced, measured, relaxed, stately, unhurried.

Characterization: detailed, distant, dramatic, eccentric, evocative, faithful, familiar, intriguing secondary (characters), introspective, lifelike, multiple points of view, quirky, realistic, recognizable, series (characters), vivid, well-developed, well-drawn.

Story line: action-oriented, character-centered, complex, domestic, episodic, explicit violence, family-centered, folksy, gentle, inspirational, issue-oriented, layered, literary references, multiple plotlines, mystical, mythic, open-ended, plot-centered, plot twists, racy, resolved ending, rich and famous, romp, sexually explicit, steamy, strong language, thought-provoking, tragic.

Frame and tone: bittersweet, bleak, contemporary, darker (tone), detailed setting, details of [insert an area of specialized knowledge or skill], edgy, evocative, exotic, foreboding, gritty, hard-edged, heart-warming, historical details, humorous, lush, magical, melodramatic, menacing, mystical, nightmare (tone), nostalgic, philosophical, political, psychological, romantic, rural, sensual, small town, stark, suspenseful, timeless, upbeat, urban.

Style: austere, candid, classic, colorful, complex, concise, conversational, direct, dramatic, elaborate, elegant, extravagant, flamboyant, frank, graceful, homespun, jargon, metaphorical, natural, ornate, poetic, polished, prosaic, restrained, seemly, showy, simple, sophisticated, stark, thoughtful, unaffected, unembellished, unpretentious, unusual.

SOURCE: Joyce G. Saricks, *Readers' Advisory Service in the Public Library*, 3rd ed. (Chicago: American Library Association, 2005), 66.

---

novel with a plot that differs greatly from a reader's typical interests could still be enjoyable if other appeal factors draw the reader in.

Everyone knows the saying, "You can't judge a book by its cover," but equally wise is the idea that you cannot judge a book by its plot. The way an author tells a story can be just as compelling as the story itself—or more so. Literature's great plotlines are recycled again and again, but what keeps them alive, in part, is the artistry the author lends to the tale. Consider the following descriptions of a book whose plot sounded as if it could not be further from my interests but that I absolutely loved because it contained appeal factors that I look for.

Plot-based description: Orson Scott Card's *Ender's Game* is a science fiction story about a young boy recruited into a futuristic military training school as the last great hope for saving the world from an evil alien race.

Appeal-based description: Orson Scott Card's *Ender's Game* is full of strong, relatable, and complex characters. It is told from multiple perspectives with moderate pacing, though it does have several fast-paced action sequences as well. Part family drama, part adventure, part coming-of-age story, it is a unique and provocative novel providing much fodder for discussion.

Given the plot-based description alone, readers may expect a breakneck-paced, action-packed, plot-driven story told in short chapters and may be surprised by the sometimes contemplative tone or the philosophical and political issues dealt with in parts of *Ender's Game*. In contrast, without mentioning the plot at all, the appeal-based description provides enough information for prospective readers to judge if the book sounds like what they are looking for. They may still be turned off by the plot, but knowing what the

> **All you need to know about the interview phase in an RA interaction**
>
> 1. Exhibit good interview behaviors, such as active listening and asking both open-ended and specific questions, to get to the root of the patron's request.
> 2. Speak in a conversational style to help patrons understand that you are happy to discuss leisure reading and that you welcome their return for future readers' advisory services.
> 3. Use appeal factors when asking patrons about their preferences as well as when describing potential reads.

appeal factors are will give them a sense of what the experience of reading the book will be like.

The presentation of options

When presenting the fruits of our readers' advisory labor to a patron, it is useful to keep in mind two of S. R. Ranganathan's laws of library science:

2. Every reader his or her book.
4. Save the time of the reader.

Law number 2 could be a readers' advisory motto. We must believe that there is a book out there for each reader. It is not always easy to find that book, but we have better luck if, rather than trying to find exactly the right book ourselves, we use information from the readers' advisory interview to offer the patron several options and allow the patron to determine the most suitable book. Finding that book may take several tries, especially when you are working with teens or patrons who have particular likes or dislikes. Using the tools and guides discussed later in this book will help greatly in narrowing down the choices, but doing so can still take time. When working on a particularly difficult request or helping a patron who seems to have a reading interest that you just cannot meet, remember law number 4. As tricky and time-consuming as the request may be, you can achieve a much faster result than the patron could by wandering up and down the aisles.

You can also save a patron time by pulling several books off the shelf and allowing her to peruse them. Using the basic plot points and clearest appeal factors, give the patron a 30-second booktalk before leaving her to choose from the titles you have selected. Often, when a patron mentions a particular title she enjoyed, we can use that as a point of reference. For example, if a patron is looking for something to read after having enjoyed Carolyn Mackler's *The Earth, My Butt, and Other Big Round Things*, the books pulled can be related to that title. Megan McCafferty's *Sloppy Firsts* is similar, but lighter and more focused on friends and dating than on the family. Or Kathleen Jeffrie Johnson's *The Parallel Universe of Liars* could be described as similar in that the main character is also on her own in figuring out who she can rely on and how she feels about those around her. The great joy in readers' advisory comes when, weeks or even months after a conversation with a patron, she returns to your desk to tell you that you found the book that speaks to her.

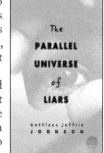

Librarians should attempt, to the best of their ability, to find the type of book the patron has requested, even if they may not personally enjoy or appreciate that type of fiction. Connecting the process of readers' advisory to good reference practices, if a patron approached the reference desk asking for information on how to

---

All you need to know about presenting opinions after an RA interview

1. Remember, there is a book out there for every patron, even if it takes a while to find it.
2. Save the reader's time by giving brief descriptions of the books after pulling them off the shelves to hand to your patron.
3. Listen to what the patron is asking for and try to give her just that, reserving judgment of the literary value of the request. The goal in readers' advisory for leisure reading is to give the patron what she wants to read, not what you think that she should read.

---

obtain a divorce, the librarian would not give him something called *Every Marriage Can Be Saved*. The librarian would of course be seen as imposing a personal view on a patron, which would be inappropriate. Recreational reference—readers' advisory—is no different. This is an especially important concept for readers' advisory work with teens.

Teens are constantly being told what they should do—from what to wear, to how to do their schoolwork, to how to improve their general behavior. The bulk of this, one hopes, comes from well-intentioned adults who care about teens and want to see them succeed. One great way to help teens succeed in life is to help instill in them a love of and an interest in reading. But that cannot be achieved by attempting to foist good-for-you books on blossoming readers. Instead, readers' advisory for teens functions on the concept that reading of any kind in any genre is valid and should be encouraged. So when a young teen comes looking for a romantic book, steering her to Jane Austen's *Emma* because it fits the description, or to Margaret Mitchell's *Gone with the Wind* because you loved it at her age, should probably not be your first, or at least your only, response.

Concluding the readers' advisory interaction

Once you have presented various options to the patron, end the readers' advisory interaction in a way that invites future contact. Even if the patron did not want to engage in a lengthy conversation about finding a book, saying that if he needs help next time, you would be happy to make a suggestion can go a long way in establishing the library as a friendly place in which to discuss fiction and recreational reading.

Sometimes a patron's request really strikes a chord or is so open-ended that the options could be limitless, and you may find yourself giving the patron more books than he is ready for at the moment. In situations like this, it is important to give the patron—especially a teen patron—an out. This lets him know that the choice of what to check out is up to him and that you will give him as many or as few suggestions as he feels he needs. Pay attention to the patron's attentiveness and body language. If you see an overwhelmed, eyes-glazed-over look, take a moment and give him a graceful way to end the conversation. You may be pleasantly

---

Open-ended ways to end an RA conversation

- If you take a look at these and they aren't what you want, just let me know, and I'll be happy to try again.
- We'll be here if you need help finding something next time.
- Next time you're in, let us know what you thought of the book.
- Do you feel that you have enough suggestions, or would you like me to pull a few more possibilities?
- Have I overloaded you yet, or could you use a few more titles?
- Do any of these books sound interesting, or should I pull some different options?

---

surprised to hear that the patron really could use just one more book or that he thinks that the first one you mentioned is exactly what he is looking for. On the other hand, you may discover that what you thought the request was and what the patron actually wants are very different things. This pause in the conversation will allow you to change directions and also lets the patron know that his interests really do matter, that you are hearing what he is asking for and doing your best to give it to him.

What makes teens so different?

Readers' advisory for teenagers differs from readers' advisory for adults not just in the selection of materials that we offer but also in the manner in which we conduct ourselves. Whereas an easy rapport may form between two adults discussing a book, we must remain aware that because teens most often encounter adults as teachers, parents, or supervisors, they may be caught off guard or surprised by our usual manner, be it poised professionalism or more laid-back joviality. Though we need not handle our teen patrons with kid gloves, being aware that emotional volatility is part and parcel of adolescent development may help our interactions, especially when we have trouble understanding or communicating ideas. Just as we might kneel down to speak to a toddler or raise our voice to speak to someone who is hard of hearing, adjusting our manner to meet the developmental stage of teenagers can lead to a more effective readers' advisory interview all around. Consider the following:

- The words that we speak make up only 7% of what a listener believes about our message; the remaining 93% is influenced by tone of voice (38%) and nonverbal cues (55%).
- Sarcasm or good-natured teasing can work against congruent communication—communication that avoids conflict and allows feelings to be expressed—which has been shown to be most effective with teens. It can easily be viewed as criticism when the intent may be completely benign.
- Teens and adults read and interpret facial expressions with different parts of their brains. The prefrontal cortex, the part of the brain that most accurately deciphers facial expressions, is the part that adults use for this task. However, in teens the prefrontal cortex is still developing. In its stead, the amygdala—sharply attuned to emotional responses such as fear—interprets facial expressions. The difference can lead to misunderstandings because the adolescent brain does not yet interpret subtle facial expressions in the most accurate way, nor does it interpret them through the same mechanisms as an adult brain.
- Teens view respect, sharing of time, and openness as the three most important ways in which adults can show that they are interested in providing help.

The research on the way that adolescents absorb messages indicates that we can best communicate with teens by being clearer and more direct than we might be with adult patrons. We need to make extra efforts in our readers' advisory conversations to display our attention to and interest in what teens are asking for and saying. Our body language and facial expressions should reinforce the sentiments we express as

5

clearly as possible. Due to the unique developmental qualities of adolescence, active and empathetic listening becomes more important when working with teens. We need to allow teens to express their ideas or interests before offering interpretations or asking clarifying questions. While teens are talking, we need to focus fully on what they are asking or telling us and resist the temptation to do catalog searches or write down names of authors and books that we are itching to tell them about. We need to devote at least the same amount and quality of time to our teen patrons as we would to our adult patrons. And most important, we need to show genuine respect for our teen patrons—their likes and dislikes, their reading interests and aversions, and their personal qualities—to demonstrate that we are helping adults who want to assist them in finding recreational reading.

Conclusion

Readers' advisory can both bring great pleasure to our patrons and be a challenging and enjoyable activity for staff. Though it may appear to require a daunting amount of knowledge, be consoled that every book or review we read and every conversation about books that we have increases our skill. It is easy to be intimidated when observing skilled readers' advisors working with patrons—it really does appear that they are mind readers at times. However, the people who make readers' advisory look easy usually have years of experience in its art and science. Remember that at the core of the service is a conversation about books. Whether you are working with adults or teenagers, the skills are the same. However, given teens' perceptions and sensitivities, you may need to adapt your conversation style a bit. Through active listening and careful practice, anyone who has the desire to give high-quality readers' advisory service will be able to do so.

SOURCE: Heather Booth, *Serving Teens through Readers' Advisory* (Chicago: American Library Association, 2007).

Awards, lists, reviews, and readers' advisory possibilities
by Francisca Goldsmith

AT EACH ALA MIDWINTER MEETING, I listen to and watch the immediate responses as YALSA's media awards are announced, fascinated by how many interpretations audience members make of what doesn't win and what the winning titles say about those who selected them. Over the years, I've served on three YALSA awards committees. For way longer, I've been reviewing books and media for an array of professional journals *(Library Journal, School Library Journal, Booklist, VOYA, Public Libraries, Busted)* and a couple of general reader publications; my typical annual review production numbers somewhere between 100 to 150 titles, mostly assigned to me by editors.

As a fairly long-term readers' advisory practitioner and instructor, I read widely

beyond what I review and what I judge for lists and awards. What I hope to provide here is some focus on how all these different book and media considerations differ in both purpose and approach.

First, a review is one reader's considered view of a title's merits and shortcomings, with the sometimes added inclusion of prescribing for a specific audience. Committee work, on the other hand, whether for an award or for list-recognition purposes, involves, by definition, the important difference of multiple viewpoints being expressed as decisions are considered, let alone made. A reviewer eats a piece of chocolate and then writes his or her judgment of it, making use of previous chocolate-eating knowledge but also of potential consumers of this chocolate, while a committee is composed of members with different taste preferences, chocolate-consumption experiences, and familiarity with the diverse climate and diet realities of prospective chocolate eaters.

Second, an award is a singling out, an identification of the exemplar, while list creation highlights particular elements of individual items without prioritizing the highlighted elements. Everything in the box of chocolates shares such attributes as sweetness, cacao, and designed shape, but some of the pieces may have nuts, some may be chewy, and it's not the committee's work to tell us that nuts are better than soft centers but to make sure the best of both are well represented.

Third, each award has stated criteria that are essential to the identification of the exemplar. Putting forth the highest cacao-content chocolate as the exemplar isn't appropriate when the stated criteria for the exemplar are that the chocolate be mixed with an equal portion of sugar and be available for mailing to all climates at all times of year. Putting forward the highest cacao-content chocolate as the exemplar when the criteria are that the chocolate be available in ounce-sizes and shaped like a daisy may be appropriate—if the highest cacao-content contender happens to be portioned in ounce-sized pieces shaped like daisies.

So where does that get us upon learning what won and what got listed when we've already read reviews and also read presumed contenders? Sometimes, when hearing the award and list news, I've gone back to refresh my familiarity with the criteria by which specific selections were made, and I see that I was so focused on how delicious the dark-dipped, cream-centered pieces in the chocolate box tasted that I'd forgotten that the particular award is for the salted nut to chocolate ratio.

Other times—most times—I delight in having my attention pulled to a title or several titles that flew under my personal radar, because while I'd read all year, I am not a superhuman who can consume the full outpouring of publishing that fits the minimum criteria (such as year of publication and distribution availability), and I know that committee work changes the very literal conversation about other qualifying aspects and elements, such as recognizing a voice as authentic or if a series title can stand alone.

In 2012, my reading experiences included serving as one-ninth of the 2013 Printz Committee, a vantage point from which I want to bring perspective to your own reading opinions and plans. We'll start by looking at the 2012 universe as it can be described quantitatively (or, what's that box of chocolates hold anyway?).

- 9 committee members spent
- 12 months reading and discussing, both online and during
- 36 hours of face-to-face meetings about
- 698 titles produced for young adults by
- 85 publishers distributing in the United States

The way to work with all those variables is to stick true to the criteria for the award. In the case of the Printz, for example, these include the fact that Printz Honor Books are not "runners-up" but are determined by a process that has a beginning only after the award winner is decided. That isn't true of *all* awards, but it is true of this award. And it's not true just for the 2013 committee but for each standing Printz Committee. Rules like this one keep the award consistent from year to year, even while the committee members and the books themselves necessarily are different.

The luxury of committee discussions, in contrast with review writing for professional journals, is sheer words. Instead of making a case for or against or simply describing in 150 words or so, discussions include back and forth between both impressionistic talkers and pithy talkers. In contrast with young adult literature reviews in general periodicals, on the other hand, award committee discussions occur among a group with deep and broad expertise in young adult literature and young adults and so is focused on the specific criteria of this award, as opposed to what sells, what cultural tropes seem of the moment, or what the works under consideration might "teach."

Although access to reader opinion burgeons with book blogs, and publishers crave starred reviews in some vetted resources, the award committee's work, while it is underway, doesn't correspond directly with that public sphere. After the committee work is said and done, the exemplar determined and announced, having the award is part of the wonderfully ample universe of resources we have from which we can do readers' advisory work.

But the award isn't about finding the perfect book that will magically fit any reader; it's the book that shows off to highest possible degree, in the refined judgment of a committee, that the award criteria are embodied in it during this annual award cycle. It's the blue-ribbon bonbon among the year's confections, not the one piece of chocolate that all tasters would agree as making the perfect breakfast food.

SOURCE: Francisca Goldsmith, "Awards, Lists, Reviews and Readers' Advisory Possibilities: It's Not Just One Big Chocolate Shop," YALSA The Hub, February 11, 2013, online at yalsa.ala. org/thehub/2013/02/11/awards-lists-reviews-and-readers-advisory-possibilities-its-not-just-one-big-chocolate-shop/.

Are you reading YA lit? You should be

by Gretchen Kolderup

I'M A YOUNG ADULT LIBRARIAN, but I didn't read young adult lit when I was a teen myself. I was a precocious reader and desperate to be treated like a grown-up, so I read books for grown-ups because anything else was just too puerile for someone as obviously mature and sophisticated as I. It wasn't until I was in my mid-twenties, working on my MLS and realizing that I wanted to work with teens, that I discovered there was a huge, glorious world of excellent YA lit that I had completely missed. Now it's almost all I read.

Outside of YA circles, I sometimes find myself having to justify my tastes to others. Yes, a lot of why I read YA lit is because I work with teens. But even if I were to switch careers, I would continue reading YA lit because it's *good*. That's not to say adult lit isn't, of course, but YA lit has a freshness that I really enjoy, and it rarely gets bogged down in its own self-importance. YA lit is also mostly free of the melancholy, nostalgia, and yearning for the innocent days of childhood that I find so tedious in adult literary fiction.

I think the reason some grown-ups look down their noses at YA lit is because they haven't read any of it recently, so they don't know how good it's gotten—or how different it is from what they might imagine it to be. While there are still books that deal with Big Issues, the "problem novel" of the 1970s and 1980s has been eclipsed by more slice-of-life contemporary fiction, romances, fantasies, mysteries, sci-fi stories, and genre-blending tales that defy categorization. For as much attention as the Twilight series has gotten, it's certainly not all that's out there.

Much more than a genre

I think it's a lack of exposure to contemporary YA lit that makes adults refer to it as a "genre." Much of the time when people say "the YA lit genre," what they really mean is *category* rather than *genre*, and that's fine. However, I recently attended a talk by an author who had been writing adult genre fiction and was working on her first YA novel, and she kept referring to the characteristics of the YA genre, as if all YA books were somehow fundamentally the same. When we can hardly even agree on how to define YA lit, how can we so easily reduce it to something as strictly delineated as a genre?

This author characterized YA lit as first-person, coming-of-age stories told in 300 pages or fewer. Though it's true that a lot of YA lit is written in the first person, about 54% isn't, according to a 2009 study by Melanie Koss and William Teale. Furthermore, although there certainly are shorter titles being published for teens, every single book in four well-known YA and upper-middle-grade series— Harry Potter, Percy Jackson, Twilight, and the Hunger Games—are all longer than 300 pages.

But what about that coming-of-age bit? Koss and Teale found that "overall trends in subject matter included a shift away from coming-of-age stories to a focus on books with themes of fitting in, finding oneself, and dealing with major life changes." YA lit isn't so much about that moment when the protagonist becomes an adult (or sees how to do so, or realizes why he or she must do so some day), it's about discovering who we are within the context of our society. That's much more universal.

So it seems silly to me to call YA lit a genre, to pretend that it's all somehow the same. But if it isn't a genre, just some part of the greater world of fiction, what can we say about it? How does it compare to fiction for grown-ups? And what makes it worth reading even if you're not a teen?

What we talk about when we talk about YA lit

Before I begin to answer these questions, I should clarify what I mean when I say "YA lit." As hard as it is to define, I should at least try to specify what I *don't* mean. Just as there is no age at which a child instantly becomes an adolescent or an adolescent becomes an adult, the flow from children's lit to YA lit to adult lit doesn't divide itself neatly into specific age ranges. Although this article will discuss some middle-grade titles that have crossover appeal to both children and teens, I won't be addressing the lower end of middle-grade fiction.

I also won't be writing much about stories written for those in their late teens or early adulthood; there seems to be a disappointing gap in fiction aimed at college-aged people. When I say "YA lit," I'll be mostly talking about fiction, and fiction aimed at those in late middle school and high school.

There's a difference, smaller now than in the past, between what is written for teens and what teens actually read. Historically, what might have been called literature for youth was fiction that was essentially an instruction manual intended to create well-mannered young people, didactic tales of what happens to disobedient children, and the problem novel of decades past—essentially what adult writers thought teens *should* be reading. Fortunately, these days libraries and booksellers are classifying what teens *want* to read as YA fiction. My library has titles in our YA collection that are also in the children's collection, and our YA lit section also includes books ostensibly for grown-ups that have appealed to teens, such as *Catcher in the Rye* and *Treasure Island*, as well as more contemporary adult titles with teen appeal.

YA lit is similar to adult lit

YA lit is a quickly growing field: The market has expanded by 25% in just over a decade, and publishers and authors are clearly aware there's money to be made here. There's even a recently published book about writing YA lit in the "Dummies" series, attesting to the commercial growth of the YA sector of publishing.

One notable trend is the success of book packagers, such as Alloy Entertainment, that develop ideas for new series and then contract out the writing to authors who work closely with editors to flesh out the stories, which are then sold to publishers. The books are designed to be commercial successes, and in 2008, 18 of the 29 titles that Alloy produced made the *New York Times* bestseller list for children's lit. Their series, which include the Gossip Girl, Luxe, and Sisterhood of the Traveling Pants books, are often created with movie and TV tie-ins in mind.

Book packagers are not new, nor are they unique to YA lit: They have been around since the Stratemeyer Syndicate churned out Nancy Drew and Hardy Boys books, and they create coffee-table books and self-help series for grown-ups as well. Although the YA titles created by packagers are certainly different beasts creatively than books that are conceived and crafted by individual authors, they sit side-by-side on shelves of libraries and bookstores, expanding the range of what's available to readers of YA lit.

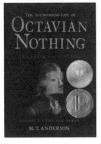

Like books for grown-ups, YA lit has stories that are written to be bestsellers, such as the Gossip Girl series or the Maximum Ride books, as well as more literary fiction with sophisticated tones, themes, motifs, and character sketches, such as M. T. Anderson's *The Astonishing Life of Octavian Nothing, Traitor to the Nation* and Tim Tharp's *The Spectacular Now*. In some ways, YA lit has become a lot like literature for grown-ups: It is both commercial and creative, it covers a spectrum of critical literary quality, and it has titles across many genres.

YA lit is different from adult lit

YA lit is also different from fiction for grown-ups. There don't seem to be as many westerns. The romances are a little different. It's not hard to find more gentle mysteries, though unlike mysteries for grown-ups, YA mysteries are a lot less likely to include recipes for desserts. Less superficially, the tone of YA lit is often different: There's less retrospection, less melancholy and nostalgia. Often, though not always, YA lit is more story-focused. All of this, I think, reflects the differences in the minds and lives of teens compared to adults.

One of the biggest differences in the landscape of YA lit is that there's more genre-blending than in adult literature. It may be because teens' literary tastes are still developing, while adults are more likely to have very particular reading habits, but I think it's also because the newness of YA lit allows for innovation.

For all the flack they get, the Twilight books are a great example of genre-blending. They have vampires, but they're not horror stories. And the paranormal element is only one aspect of the story: Much of its appeal is in the romance of forbidden love. There's also an action element, featuring vampires versus werewolves (or good vampires versus evil vampires, or good vampires plus werewolves versus the vampire establishment).

Anna Godbersen's Luxe series is set in 1899, but its focus isn't the events of the time so much as the intrigues and romances of the young elite. The first book begins with the funeral of the lovely, beloved Elizabeth Holland and then jumps back a few days so readers can follow how it all happened and discover the secrets she and her peers kept and exposed. Yes, it's historical fiction, but it's really a delicious, scandalous romance.

Libba Bray's Gemma Doyle trilogy (which begins with *A Great and Terrible Beauty*) is another genre-blender. Sixteen-year-old Gemma, who has been raised in India, has a vision of her mother's mysterious death before it occurs. Gemma is forced to return to her father in Victorian England, who then ships her off to a boarding school. The girls there initially snub her, but as Gemma begins to discover and develop her powers, she gathers her own clique. Throughout all of this, Gemma is being observed by the beautiful, mysterious Kartik, who has followed her from India. Historical fiction, supernatural powers, a boarding-school setting, and a romance all come together in a book that was selected by teens for YALSA's "Teens' Top Ten" list as well as by librarians for YALSA's "Best Books for Young Adults."

Even the Pretty Little Liars series isn't just about rich girls being catty. There is a lot of that, along with plenty of designer-brand name-dropping, but foremost on the protagonists' minds are the messages they have been receiving from a friend of theirs who went missing years ago, and presumably died. Figuring out who it is that knows all of their secrets before those secrets get spilled is the mysterious core around which the boyfriend-stealing and backstabbing swirls.

What's currently happening in YA lit

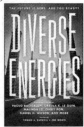

One characteristic of YA lit that differs from adult lit, and is so fundamental to the field that it drives what gets published, is the quick turnover in trends. Inspired by the success of the Twilight saga, lots of other paranormal-romance stories have been published in the last few years. More recently, as the Hunger Games series has risen to popularity, we've been seeing more dystopian tales, though I think even that wave is starting to crest, and we'll soon see a new theme or archetype or proto-genre rise to take its place.

The point is that currency is key. While there will always be fans of paranormal romance, a lot of teen readers tell me they're "so over" vampires, werewolves, and fallen angels. In the same way that youth culture is focused on what's new and trendy, so is YA lit, which means librarians need to remain alert to new publications and weed aggressively. It also helps YA lit create an environment that encourages innovation.

Perhaps driven by the same desire to be where the money is being made, we're also seeing a lot of new series and trilogies. Series and trilogies certainly aren't new in YA lit, but they're a huge proportion of what my library has on its shelves and what my patrons are reading. As I write this, seven of the top-10 titles on the *New York Times* bestseller list of children's chapter books are part of a series—and the *New York Times* also has a separate children's series list. Even debut authors often start out with the first book in a trilogy, as evidenced by Veronica Roth's *Divergent*, number eight on the *New York Times* list of bestselling chapter books for children.

This prevalence of series is a double-edged sword: If you like the first book, you know what to read next, but some of my teen patrons are starting to express a desire for a book that "just ends" rather than leaving unanswered questions for the next installment. Although it's not as much a problem as it is with manga series, which may have several-dozen volumes, if you're trying to start a YA collection at your library, it's hard to decide if you should get all 13 books in the Gossip Girl series plus the four additional novels in the spin-off series, or buy 17 other titles.

Other recent trends in YA fiction include books told from multiple viewpoints (*Will Grayson, Will Grayson; Nick and Norah's Infinite Playlist; Please Ignore Vera Dietz; Confession of the Sullivan Sisters*); novels written in verse (books by Ellen Hopkins, Sonya Sones, Sharon Creech, Virginia Euwer Wolff, and Lisa Schroeder); and retold, twisted, and fractured fairytales (*Beastly, Princess of the Midnight Ball, The Iron King*, and *Into the Wild* as well as stories by Shannon Hale, Donna Jo Napoli, and Robin McKinley).

Historical fiction seems to be getting a makeover, too: I've been seeing a lot of historical fiction that isn't focused so much on the events of that time period (you know, the kind of historical fiction you read in school because your teachers knew it was a stealth history lesson) but is instead a romance or a fantasy that just

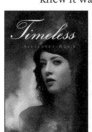

happens to be set in another time period (*The Luxe, A Great and Terrible Beauty, The Season, The Vespertine*, and *Wrapped*). I've also recently noticed a number of historical fiction titles that involve time-travel to blend in characters with more modern sensibilities (*Revolution, The Time-Traveling Fashionista, Steel*, and *Timeless*).

One trend that's received a lot of media attention recently is the perceived "darkness" in today's young adult literature. It started with "Darkness Too Visible," a June 4, 2011, article in the *Wall Street Journal* by Meghan Cox Gurdon about her concern over the mature content that can be found in today's YA lit. Her article sparked a flurry of counterarguments, but I think this "darkness" really attests to the reality of teens' lives today and our growing trust in them to be able to handle reflections of that reality. That's not meant to imply that all YA books are dark: There are certainly gentler titles. YA lit is big enough that there are stories for every reader, just as there are with titles intended for grown-ups.

Adults reading YA lit

In short, you should read YA lit because it's good. It's fresh and exciting, and there are interesting new things to find. It's so good, in fact,
you may not realize you're reading YA lit. A nonlibrarian friend had
enjoyed Paolo Bacigalupi's Nebula– and Hugo Award–winning *The
Windup Girl*, so he read *Ship Breaker* (which won the Printz Award
and was a National Book Award nominee) when it came out. He was
astonished to learn that this book, with its dark themes and tone, was
a YA title.

Another recent trend in YA lit is adult authors making their
youth-lit debuts. Candice Bushnell, Carl Hiaasen, Kelley Armstrong, Kathy
Reichs, Clive Barker, Terry Pratchett, John Grisham, and James Patterson have
written YA or middle-grade books. Adults who are curious about YA lit might
follow a favorite author and see where it takes them.

You certainly won't be the only adult reading YA lit. In addition to those of
us who work with young people, "regular" grown-ups are joining in.
A *Los Angeles Times* article from March 2010 featured some of these
adult readers of YA lit. On August 6, 2010, the *New York Times* explored some of the reasons for that interest. Surveys showed then that
"the percentage of female YA fans between the ages of 25 and 44
has nearly doubled in the past four years," and "today, nearly one in
five 35- to 44-year-olds say they most frequently buy YA books. For
themselves."

Adults who want to read stories of high literary quality won't be
disappointed with YA lit, especially if they begin their sampling with
award-winning titles.

In 1996, after more than a decade of dormancy, a National Book Award category for young people's literature was resurrected. This award isn't just for YA lit
(it can go to titles for a younger audience or to nonfiction), but the YA lit titles to
which it is awarded are of the highest literary merit.

The *Boston Globe–Horn Book* Awards are a prestigious award in youth literature. It has a fiction and poetry category that recognizes winners as well as up to
two honor books.

The Michael L. Printz Award has been administered by the ALA's Young
Adult Library Services Association since 2000 and recognizes winners and honor
books that "exemplify literary excellence in young adult literature."

While it's true that not every YA title will appeal to grown-ups—some really
are best appreciated by teens—there are many with crossover appeal. Here are a
baker's dozen of mine:

Alexie, Sherman. *The Absolutely True Diary of a Part-Time Indian* (Little,
Brown, 2007).

Anderson, Laurie Halse. *Chains* (Simon & Schuster, 2008).

Anderson, M. T. *The Astonishing Life of Octavian Nothing, Traitor
to the Nation, Volume 1: The Pox Party* (Candlewick, 2006).

Bacigalupi, Paolo. *Ship Breaker* (Little, Brown, 2010).

Blundell, Judy. *What I Saw and How I Lied* (Scholastic, 2008).

Cornish, D. M. *Monster Blood Tattoo, Book 1: Foundling* (G. P.
Putnam, 2006).

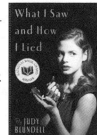

Green, John. *Looking for Alaska* (Dutton, 2005).

McCormick, Patricia. *Sold* (Hyperion, 2006).

Marchetta, Melina. *Jellicoe Road* (HarperTeen, 2008).

Ness, Patrick. *The Knife of Never Letting Go* (Walker, 2008).
Sepetys, Ruta. *Between Shades of Gray* (Penguin, 2011).
Yancey, Rick. *The Monstrumologist* (Simon & Schuster, 2009).
Zusak, Markus. *The Book Thief* (Knopf, 2007).

A few closing thoughts

YA lit is big and getting bigger. YA lit is good and getting better. YA lit is a diverse mix of genres and styles and themes and tones, and it spans the quality spectrum just like books for grown-ups do. While YA lit is written with teens in mind, it has evolved beyond the coming-of-age concerns that first popularized the category and now fully merits adult readers' attention.

Another thing I love about YA lit is the way authors connect with fans and speak with passion about their field. Many YA authors have Twitter accounts that aren't managed by a publicist (Maureen Johnson's interactions with her fans are especially hilarious), and the YouTube channel John Green (left) runs with his brother has created an entire community of Nerdfighters who spent the summer of 2011 reading and discussing *The Great Gatsby*—for fun. Ellen Hopkins spoke passionately at YALSA's 2010 YA Lit Symposium about the response she has received from readers of her books that say that she, through her books, saved their lives. That kind of connection and mutual support is awe-inspiring.

What I think is most exciting about YA lit is that the kids who are reading it now are our next authors, both of books for grown-ups and books for young people. The exciting, innovative stories they're reading now are what will shape their imaginations and sensibilities when they go on to become writers themselves. That fills me with hope for our literary future.

SOURCE: Gretchen Kolderup, "Are You Reading YA Lit? You Should Be," July 27, 2011, In the Library with the Lead Pipe, July 27, 2011, online at www.inthelibrarywiththeleadpipe.org/2011/are-you-reading-ya-lit-you-should-be/.

MARKETING

CHAPTER SIX

Although most librarians have little or no experience in marketing, they will be called upon to do it daily. Marketing includes not only promoting the library as a whole, but promoting the various services and materials that the library offers. This means that we have to promote the fact that we have teen services behind the doors of our library, often to both staff and teens alike. In addition, librarians are called upon to market individual events, such as programs and yearly teen summer reading clubs as well as the individual titles on our shelves.

Librarians employ a wide variety of skill sets and techniques to engage in marketing, including giving booktalks, making displays, and creating signage. The goal of marketing is to generate use, to promote goodwill, and to keep the library actively in the forefront of your community's mind. If libraries want to be vital parts of communities, then they need to engage community members in dialogue. That is marketing.

See Appendix D for an annotated guide to marketing resources.

Marketing: An introduction

by Karen Jensen

MARKETING IS EVERYTHING YOU DO to position the library as *the* place to be in your community. Advertising is not marketing. Promotion is not marketing. Merchandising is not marketing. But they are all a part of marketing, a piece of the whole. Marketing is everything you do to brand your library, and your teen services program, with your audience.

Everything you do is another building block in creating the overall image for your library and teen services program—every piece of paper you put out, every poster you put up, the overall look of your teen area, the number and types of programs that you do. Think of your overall teen services program as a piece of pointillism art: Each action is one small pointy stroke of your paintbrush, and as your teens pull away from the canvas, they begin to see the whole picture. What do you want that picture to look like?

Everything you do—and everything you don't do—sends a message. Think of your customer experiences. When you walk into a store, what do you notice and how does it make you feel? Your teens are doing the very same unconscious assessment when they walk into your library. Every action, every piece of paper, and every program either reinforces that message or detracts from it. We have to be conscious as librarians that we understand what we are doing and why we are doing it. Then we have to convey that message to our audience: our teens.

This is one reason to have a detailed service plan (see Appendix A, "A Sample Teen Services Plan," pp. 187–190), and periodically evaluate it to make sure your goals are on track. Your marketing plan helps you meet your goals and provide quality service to your teens.

Some of the basic plan components include advertising (promotion) of specific events, merchandising in-house, and putting together a comprehensive marketing plan. Because people spend their entire college years learning how to do marketing, this is going to be a quick and dirty overview. But there are some good resources throughout to help you. An annotated guide to some useful marketing resources can be found in Appendix D, "Marketing Resources: A Guide with Annotations," pp. 193–194.

The quick marketing overview

There are three basic steps to marketing: defining your audience, defining your message, and delivering your message.

Defining your audience. Understanding your audience is key to effectively reaching them with your marketing messages. We know that teens today are incredibly visual, and as of this writing, 95% of them are online. This information helps us define our message and find ways to transmit it to our audience. For additional information to help you understand your audience, check out resources like Ypulse (ypulse.com), the 2002 *Frontline* series on the teenage brain, and the 40 Developmental Assets developed by the Search Institute (www.search-institute.org/content/40-developmental-assets-adolescents-ages-12-18). In addition, the Pew Research Center puts out yearly reports that give essential snapshots into the lives of teens today that we should consult, because understanding who your audience is will help you understand how best to reach them.

There are five basic things that we know about teens that influence our marketing strategies:

- Teens are highly visual.
- Teens are fluent in multimedia.
- Teens spend a great deal of their time online and engaged socially.
- Teens value independence and respect.
- Teens are peer oriented.

Defining your message. Your message will be unique to your library. Identify key components that you want to address in your marketing strategies that emphasize the value of the library in the life of teens. You may want to come up with a quick, simple slogan that highlights this message to put on your pieces, a tagline that becomes synonymous with your library. The message is not announcing the time or availability of a specific program. The message is what teens will gain from the program, event, or service. The message could be as simple as, "You belong

---

Ten quick marketing tips and a good reminder

1. Know your audience.
2. Use consistent messaging—make sure everything you do reinforces the message.
3. Impressions matter—you want to make a good impression each time. In addition, think of each time you are in the public eye—whether through a flyer or a program—as an impression. The more times the public sees you, the more you become ingrained in their consciousness. You want to make multiple impressions to improve their recall.
4. Grow. Change. Be responsive—one of the biggest threats to libraries is the rate at which we respond to changes in the cultural zeitgeist. Pay attention and stay on the cutting edge.
5. Toot your own horn—marketing is not a time to be subtle or modest. You want to be honest, but don't be afraid to toot your own horn.
6. Use the best tools—not all tools are created equal. Determine the best way to get your message across effectively and pursue it.
7. Marketing is emotional—you want to make positive emotional connections with your audience; you are trying to build a relationship. Appeal to the emotion.
8. Word of mouth can make or break you—this is a fact. Word-of-mouth advertising is one of your best tools. So do everything you can to generate positive word of mouth by creating a positive library environment. Make it easy for teens to share their positive experiences via your social-media outlets.
9. Pay attention to marketing trends—marketing is not static. Find a few resources that you value and keep yourself updated on current and coming trends.
10. We are more than books—market it all.

Reminder: As you market your library, please remember to get outside the building. Libraries traditionally have a tendency to put signs up in their buildings and post things on their websites. The problem with this strategy is that libraries are preaching to the choir; regular users are already coming to the library. Get outside of the building, and put signs, flyers, banners, and more in new traffic areas to draw new users into the library.

Don't just put things on the library's website, but ask to share information on popular local sites of interest. If part of the goal of marketing is to attract new users, libraries must get outside of their comfort zone and normal routine to get that information to new users in new places.

6

here" or "We help you get where you're going." Once your library understands the message it wishes to convey, framing that message will be easier, and the way you deliver the message will make much more sense.

Delivering the message. With elements one and two in place, you know how to find the best and most effective ways to get the message to the audience. In education, there is an emphasis on the fact that there are different types of learners; this is also true when considering the ways in which you deliver your message. Although you are reaching one general audience, teens themselves vary, and you'll want to deliver your message in more than one way in order to reach the greatest possible number of teens within your community. It's not enough to make a sign and put it up; you need to investigate a wide variety of ways to get your message to the audience that reach out to those who are visual and auditory. You need to go where the teens are, both in your community and online.

Some of the ways that you can get your message to your audience include signage both in-house and at popular teen hangouts in your community, social-media outlets like YouTube channels and Twitter, and local resources like the newspaper and the schools.

SOURCE: Specially prepared for *The Whole Library Handbook: Teen Services* by Karen Jensen, teen services librarian, Grand Prairie, Texas.

Crafting your marketing plan
by Karen Jensen

BEFORE PUTTING TOGETHER A MARKETING PLAN, consider the various components involved. A good marketing plan is composed of two pieces: positional pieces (which identify the library and its services, competition, and useful strategies) and background pieces (which include marketing research, objectives, and targets).

Positional pieces

Mission statement. Every library should have a mission statement. And your teen services plan should start with a mission statement that supports the library's mission statement but is specific to your teen services goals.

Identifying library services and value. If you want to sell your teens (and your administrators and your community) on library services, you need to make sure that you understand what they are and what the value to them is. Identifying the services and value to teens will include such items as

- Lifelong learning at no cost to the patron on a wide variety of topics of interest
- Resources to support educational success
- Information on a wide variety of topics of interest and need
- Recreation through programming and information that supports recreational interests
- Value—saves users money on materials and provides free entertainment and family activities through programming

- Expert help in finding appropriate resources and information
- Free internet access and technology

Identifying library competition. You need to identify both your direct and indirect library competition. All libraries face some general competition, but there is also competition unique to various communities. And because we are working with teens, we need to be able to identify unique competitors that speak to teens but not the general population.

Direct competition: Local and online bookstores and large retail chains, local and online video service providers, historical societies.

Indirect competition: Internet, time absorbers (other area programming, school activities, leisure activities).

Positioning. Before you can market your teen services program (or your library), you have to know what you are trying to market. How do you want to position yourself? For example, your library may describe itself in the following ways:

Valuable, both financially and as a service organization to the community.

Professional, bringing the best and widest variety of resources to the community through information specialists.

Service oriented, focused on providing a high level of customer satisfaction.

Entertaining, in supporting the community's entertainment needs through both resources and programming.

Strategies. Things to consider: What marketing strategies will you use to promote your teen services program and its various parts? What are you currently doing? What would you like to be doing? This is the place to lay out your vision for the future and how the library fits into teen lives.

Background pieces

Marketing research. Here is where you need to spend some time tracking how your library users find out about library materials, programs, and services. Do a basic survey to get their input. If you have programs that you ask patrons to register for, ask them when they register how they found out about the program. If you do program evaluations at the end of a program, ask them how they found out about the program.

Marketing objectives. So you're putting together a marketing plan—but why? What do you hope to accomplish? Before you can proceed, you need to make sure you have clear marketing objectives.

- To increase the library's presence in the community through marketing and outreach.
- To introduce new patrons to the library through targeted marketing and outreach activities.
- To increase circulation and use of services by having a more visible presence in the community and by bringing in new patrons.
- To try new marketing avenues and evaluate their effectiveness in promoting the library in the community and bringing in new library users.

Target markets. Next, identify your target market: Who are they? Where can you reach them? What do you need to know about them? Collect local census information to get specific numbers and distribution for local communities. Use adolescent development facts and research current marketing trends to identify key facts about the audience. This information increases the likelihood of success.

Marketing summary

The marketing summary focuses on two main components: *traditional (standard) methods*, which are those methods already being used by the library that it will continue to employ, and *new strategies*, which are untested methods that the library would like to investigate to determine if they will help reach a different audience and increase the library's visibility in the community.

Standard promotional strategies. Standard promotional strategies include those strategies that the library is already doing. When calculating the cost, include printing costs, subscription costs, and advertising costs, and put a dollar value on the amount of staff time it takes to engage in the strategies being discussed.

New marketing strategies. When considering new marketing strategies, do your research. What new avenues are available to you locally, and what will the projected cost be to incorporate these strategies into your plan? Again, these cost projections should include real costs involved and an estimation of staff time, which also has a price attached to it. Here are some marketing strategies you may want to investigate:

- Paid newspaper advertising
- Paid online advertising
- Promotional banners and billboards
- Direct mailings
- Creating email lists for mass distribution
- Utilizing a text-messaging service

Expense forecast. After outlining strategies, put a realistic expense forecast on each individual strategy. When discussing budgets with administrators, it is important to have a realistic financial plan for promoting teen services. There is little point in putting the time and energy into teen services if the library is not going to invest adequate staff, time, and resources into promoting those services.

Evaluation

As with any plan, make sure there are ways of evaluating whether the library is seeing any benefit from the various marketing strategies being utilized or trialed. The information needed includes knowing where patrons are learning about library programs and services and determining whether the library is seeing an increase in attendance or usage after initiating new marketing methods. There are some simple ways that the library can gather this information:

1. If program registration is required, ask patrons how they heard about the program as part of the registration process.

2. Utilize the poll features on social-media sites and website, and ask patrons to rank how they find out about library programs and services.
3. On a quarterly basis, compile statistics and examine which vehicles are generating the most amount of traffic for the library.
4. Using circulation reports, monitor the impact of various programs on circulation statistics by comparing daily totals over a period of time. If circulation rates begin to increase, it is reasonable to surmise that new marketing methods are generating new traffic resulting in a circulation increase.

Proper evaluation also helps justify the expenses and aids in good decision making for future planning or in times of budget planning.

SOURCE: Specially prepared for *The Whole Library Handbook: Teen Services* by Karen Jensen, teen services librarian, Grand Prairie, Texas.

Graphic design basics for non–graphic designers

by Karen Jensen

ALTHOUGH SOME LIBRARIES have marketing departments, small libraries are usually forced to create their own promotional signs and flyers. Like marketing professionals, graphic designers spend years studying the concepts of layout and design to make graphics with the greatest impact. There are, however, a few quick tips that can help nondesigners create quality, professional-looking signs and flyers. If you do your own promotional materials, creating quality materials is important to successful marketing. Some of the design elements you want to consider include the following:

Fonts and colors. Designers recommend limiting the main scheme of a piece to two or three colors and font choices. They should be complementary colors and readable fonts. It is important to choose legible fonts; some fonts only work well and become readable in bigger sizes. Everything needs to work together and be in harmony; don't let one element pull the eye too much or distract from the overall message.

Typography. Speaking of fonts, text is also a graphical element. Headlines and text all need to be considered in the overall design process. Typography is in fact considered quite the art form, and there are entire texts written on the subject. The most important part in considering typography is to make sure it is readable, that it matches the overall design scheme, and that it helps emphasize the message.

The graphics is the thing. When considering design, make sure to include pictures or clip art of some sort. Keep in mind that copyright applies to images. To avoid copyright issues, consider creating your own images, easily done today with a smart phone and a few good apps. If you don't have the time or inclination, there are a variety of free stock images found online. If using multiple images, it is important that they match stylistically to make the piece look uniform in thought. For example, if one image has a bold black outline, then they probably all should. If one image is a line drawing, then the other images should also be line drawings. Us-

Logo created with free Cool Text Graphics Generator.

ing the same type of graphics creates a sense of visual uniformity and purpose; it conveys a sense of intentionality and professionalism, which validates your message.

Basic layout. Americans read from left to right in a Z pattern, so you want to place the important content elements in the top left, middle right, then bottom left and back to the far right corner. When someone approaches a work to visually scan it, their eyes will customarily focus on these locations just as if they were reading a text.

Justify the text. When designing a flyer, initial instincts seem to promote center justification. However, choosing to either left- or right-justify text creates a crisper line and makes a better use of the space.

Symmetry is not cool. Part of the reason why center justification is not ideal is because, artistically, symmetry is a bad design goal. Although we humans tend to instinctively prefer symmetry when we look at faces, symmetry is not typically found in nature: Look at the tree lines that you admire so much; they are not symmetrical. When you choose symmetry as a design layout, the eye doesn't know what elements are important, your viewer doesn't know where to focus, and the important parts get lost.

Size really does matter. Thinking again of typography, differentiating text size helps the viewer understand the hierarchical importance of the text. This is why a headline is bigger than the message. The headline grabs your reader's attention. Then the next element is slightly smaller to let the reader know what the next step is. You can also help make these distinctions by consistently using different colored text throughout your document. By choosing the right design elements, you guide your reader through the document and help him or her focus on the important elements, which include the who, what, when, and where.

White space is your friend. White spaces are those graphically and textually blank places on your page, although they are not necessarily truly white. For example, if your background is blue, then your white space—the space that allows the eyes to rest—would also be blue. The use of white space allows your readers to have a place to rest their eyes and avoid overdesign. When dealing with teen viewers, you can get away with less white space than you can with an adult audience. Teens spend a lot of time engaging with visual media and are used to video games, graphic novels, and highly stylized magazines.

Borders are also your friend. Borders help wrap it all up in a clean bow. They present a clean edge that again helps define your space and helps direct your viewer's attention. That said, sometimes it looks cool to break through the border.

If it works for the piece, break the rules. As with all rules, sometimes it works to break them. If it works for the piece, then go with it. Take time during the day to thumb through popular teen magazines and online sites for design and layout ideas. If you find a design you like, adapt it for your purposes.

Verb up your image. When writing marketing text, there should be a strong emphasis on verbs. When putting copy together, think about the audience: teens! Teens are *active*. Even if they are just sitting around, they are still "hanging" and "chilling," which presents a sense of activity. By leading with verbs, your copy invites teens to be a part of something. Verbs are an important brushstroke in a marketing plan. You want to let teens know that there is something unique, amazing, and powerful happening at the library—something they want to be a part of. Don't warn them that they won't want to miss out; show them your marketing materials and let them come to that conclusion on their own.

Think of the awesome verbs that invite engagement: *capture, feed, explore, discover, crave, win, delight, share, fascinate, captivate.* In the right context, you can even use *hang* and *chill*, depending on the overall goals. The bottom line is this: Viewers wants to know what is in it for them, and that message is made clear by starting with a verb. As they read it, there is an unspoken "You" or "You will" that begins the message: "Create exciting pieces of jewelry," "Travel through the library after hours and see if you can survive." It's attention-grabbing and exciting, and it makes readers put themselves into the action. They won't want to be left out.

The temptation is to use *being* or *helping* verbs, or to use the verb *read*. Of course, we are promoting reading, but libraries should present a more multifaceted image. Libraries are not, after all, only about books. Try to start everything you put in the hands of your teens with a verb. Invite them to *do* something, to be a part of something. That something can be a guided activity, a program, or it can be a moment that is self-guided, using your materials and resources. It can be an event. It can be a process. The overall message is this: When you step into this library, you will *do.*

Validate your message. When marketing is thoughtful and intentional, it sends an important message to the audience: We are professionals, we have value, and we are successful. Everything done by the library reinforces or negates this message. Planning and evaluating will help librarians ensure that they are sending the right message.

SOURCE: Specially prepared for *The Whole Library Handbook: Teen Services* by Karen Jensen, teen services librarian, Grand Prairie, Texas.

Merchandising 101: Marketing to teens in the library

6

by Karen Jensen and Heather Booth

WHAT IS MERCHANDISING? Merchandising involves promotional activities, including advertising, point-of-purchase displays, and in-store promotions, designed to show a product or service in a favorable light so that it will be purchased by the business community and/or the consuming public (from Answers. com). Basically, from the library point of view, you are positioning your merchandise (books, program information, services) in-house in a way that encourages library patrons to check out your materials. There is a reason why stores do displays—merchandising: It works!

Merchandising is one part of your overall marketing plan. It is an internal component. And it, like all marketing and promotion, should be purposeful and planned. Take a walk around your teen area and find creative ways to display your materials and programming information, and highlight your services in high-traffic areas. High-traffic areas are key; you want your information to be seen, so make a space for it that makes sense.

For example, do you have tables for sitting in your teen area? You can do little mini displays on each table using either a wire book display holder or collect four or five titles and display them using two bookends.

What do you merchandise?

Promote new acquisitions and materials of interest to your patrons in a consistently purposeful and attractive-looking manner. Chances are, you are already doing this by having various book displays.

You can also promote services, such as online content and programs. If you make a dedicated space for your patrons to find upcoming program information, they will know where to come each time they visit and find it. In your teen area, you can create a basic space as simple as a blank wall with clear labeling, or get creative and put up billboards, a variety of clipboards, etc. Your goal is simply to create a routine (a dedicated space) that allows your teens to find the information quickly.

What are your merchandising goals?
- Increase overall "attractiveness" of the library.
- Increase the library's display capabilities and prompt impulse selections.
- Increase the use of various collections.
- Keep the merchandising areas and techniques fresh and appealing. When you go out shopping, look at the displays in the stores you visit to get ideas.
- Keep your various display areas neat at all times.
- Provide a wide variety of materials on display; collection diversity is our goal, and it should be a display goal as well.

What are your merchandising areas? Merchandising areas should see a lot of traffic. You may have a cozy reading nook tucked away in the teen area with a little space perfect for a display from which a teen could grab a book and dive right in, but unless teens are actually using the space, the display will go unnoticed. Consider higher traffic areas such as the following:

Tabletop and counter displays. It's easy enough to put a book face-out on the desk in front of you each time you sit down. Use it as a conversation starter. Put a sticky note on it with three words to describe the book. Change it frequently so that patrons never know what to expect and seek it out just to see what is there.

End-cap displays. There are many attractive slat-wall options for libraries, but

if the type of shelving or cost of installing these pieces is a barrier, consider requesting some of the removable variety. These are just as effective, less expensive, and are easily removed to be used elsewhere if the shelving configuration changes.

Face-out book displays. Keep your collection weeded to a size where you can face-out book titles on the three rows that are most visible and easily accessible to patrons. Patrons do judge a book by its cover, and covers create "sales." The more books you have faced-out in your teen area, the more your circulation will increase.

Shelf-top displays on lower shelving. Any shelf that ends at eye level or lower is an excellent candidate for a display. Save teens some browsing time (and their necks) by pulling some great books out of each section and placing them face-out on top of the shelves. Or give each section of shelving a display theme. Horror for the left, romance for the center, mystery for the right, or something similar.

Stand-alone displays. If all other display options go unnoticed, consider a stand-alone display for the simple fact that you can put it in the way. Does a daily parade shuttle teens from the front door, around a corner, and straight into the teen area? Consider putting a display on the parade route in a place that they have to adjust their path. Nothing will shock someone out of their habits and get them to look around faster than something breaking their routine.

Spring display, Vernon Barford Junior High School Library, Edmonton, Alberta. Flickr photo by Enokson, used CC BY-SA 3.0.

Make merchandising a part of your daily routine. Walk through your teen area several times a day to make sure that the shelves look neat and tidy, that display holes are filled, and that your area is sending the message that you want it to send. The time and money we put into our teen areas send a message; they let teens know how much, or sometimes how little, we value them. When we create teen-friendly spaces and keep them neat, clean, and energetic, we send the message that we want to send—we value you here at our library. As a bonus, spending time in the teen area gives you time to interact with and talk to your teens.

Basic merchandising guidelines

Merchandising goals: fullness, neatness, variety. Vary the color of book covers so they don't blend in and cancel each other out. Contrast pulls the eye in quicker than conformity.

Emphasize diversity of the collection.

Make sure books represent a variety of genres, religions, ethnic groups, time periods, etc. (unless there is a specific theme to a display).

As you merchandise, pull any damaged or excessively worn materials and evaluate for either repair, replacement, or removal.

Check the displays daily, and replace books that have been on display for more than two weeks without circulating. These can be interfiled back into the collection and replaced with other titles.

Make sure all titles are *facing out* so that the patron can make direct eye-line contact with them and clearly read titles.

Do not fan out or place books at an angle. *Why?*

* The spine can be read only from one angle.
* The covers are obscured.
* It's hard to put a book back, so it makes customers more reluctant to pull things off the shelf. One effective strategy some librarians use is creating an aesthetically appealing arrangement of books and then intentionally removing one or two so that teens can see that the books can be taken.

A word about merchandising signage. When you put up large displays, you'll want to include signage to let your patrons know what your theme is and what

6

materials they can expect while browsing the display area. As with anything you put out for the public to see, you want this to be clear, neat, and professional. That doesn't mean it can't be fun, artistic, creative, or whimsical. It just means that you want it to look like you know what you're doing, that you put a little bit of effort into it, and that your audience is worth spending the time on.

 Many libraries have access to and use die-cut machines, which are certainly an easy and appropriate way to create signage. You can also make signs and posters in a wide variety of publishing programs, including Microsoft Publisher. If you are adventurous, you can download GIMP (a free online photo-manipulation program) and spend time learning how to use it. It is a great program but has a much steeper learning curve than Microsoft Publisher. Read the section on graphic design basics, pp. 139–141, for some information on design and layout for your signs.

Whatever type of in-house signage you use, be sure to keep an eye on it for wear and tear. In fact, if you can, laminate or place signage in acrylic sign holders. This helps keeps corners from curling up, etc.

Remember, we want our promotional activities to be:

Purposeful—demonstrate to the public that we know and care about what we are doing.

Cared for—keep them neat, clean, and attractive.

Successful—the more we have to work at keeping them neat and attractive, the more it means books are being checked out. That's a good thing.

SOURCE: Adapted from the South Jersey Regional Library Cooperative, Trading Spaces: Do-It-Yourself Toolkit (www.sjrlc.org/tradingspaces/toolkit/index.shtml#tipsheets).

Booktalking in your local schools as a marketing opportunity
by Karen Jensen

WHAT DOES EVERY LIBRARIAN LOVE? A captive audience! You want to get into your schools, into the classrooms, and develop relationships with your teachers. One of the best ways to do this is to develop a booktalking program. In its most basic description, a booktalk is a short introduction—think commercial or movie trailer—for a book. What you want to do is give *just enough* information about a book to tantalize teens and then leave them salivating for more! If you have done a booktalk properly, your audience will be on the edge of their seats asking, "What happens next?" And your answer is always, "You have to read the book to find out!"

Going to the schools for booktalks accomplishes several things. The most obvious is promotion of specific titles in the collection, but there are many more benefits to the library and to teen services:

• It demonstrates that the library cares about leisure reading and helping teens find books that they might enjoy by discussing appeal elements.
• It gives the librarian an opportunity to share other events and new services at the library with teens. You don't need to dive straight into the books once the teacher has introduced you. Take a moment to introduce

yourself and mention an upcoming program or two.

- It positions the librarian and the teacher as allies and helpers. The librarian becomes an endorsed resource this way.
- It establishes the tone for teen services at your library. If you go into a booktalk with a dry, by-the-book talk, that is the impression teens will take away of your services as a whole. Being dynamic and engaging will likewise convey a lot about your approach and the way teens will experience the library.
- Booktalks move books. Your circulation will increase, which is good for you, but it also means that more teens are reading, which is good for the teens and the teachers.

A booktalking program can be an effective tool in your school-library relations' toolbox. What you want to do is develop relationships with teachers who will keep you coming back again and again into their classrooms to introduce new books to their students. It can be once a month, once a grading period, or at the very least before winter and summer breaks. So you have to sell yourself to the teachers to get your foot in the door, and then you have to deliver the goods. In addition to this overview, be sure to read the excellent advice from Joni Richards Bodart on pp. 110–115.

Making contact

Do some research and put together a really good introduction for your area teachers about booktalks. Let them know what booktalks are, why they want to let you do them, how they support the curriculum, and how they encourage students to read. Make it short, simple, and visual: you are marketing a service to them. Your basic selling points:

- Teens find that reading is more enjoyable and that they are more likely to finish a book *if* it is a book they select for themselves.
- Booktalks introduce teens to a wide variety of books and allow them to make those successful choices.
- By giving teens these tools and opportunities, booktalks increase reading pleasure. Booktalks = more reading success, more reading variety, and more reading enjoyment!

In your introduction, mention several different types of booktalks that you would be prepared to do. For example, you could highlight new books, award winners, books that dovetail with a thematic unit, or books that are just great reads for an upcoming break. Explain how much class time your visit might take, and include any stipulations or requests. For example, if your circulation system allows mobile checkout, would you check books out to teens on-site? How much advance notice will you need to prepare special booktalks? Are there specific days of the week you prefer? Which grade levels will you visit? Will the teacher need to be in the classroom while you are present? (The answer to the latter should be *yes*. You are a guest and should not be expected to handle classroom management, nor should the teacher use you as a lesson plan and call a sub in for the day of your visit. Unfortunately, these issues do arise on occasion.) Will you provide a list for all of the students with additional titles? And finally, don't forget to leave as many methods of contact as you have. Teachers have a very busy daily schedule, and whatever mode of contact makes it easiest to communicate is what you should strive to offer.

Wait until the second or third week of school and send a letter of introduction and brochure to each language arts or English teacher and each school librarian. If your local schools use literature circles or reading across the curriculum, involve other related departments as well. Ask the school principals if you can have a few moments to speak at a teacher in-service day and give some sample booktalks. Do everything you can to get your foot in the door; *then wow them.*

Creating a package

Start out by creating for yourself a basic building block of about 20 booktalks for the best teen books that will reach the greatest audience. Be sure to write your booktalks, practice them, and keep them readily available. As you read a book, create an electronic file (or an old-fashioned index card if you prefer) that gives a basic description of the book, the appropriate audience, and a hook for that book. What is it that will help you sell this book to teens? You want to include a wide variety of books and talking styles, including some Booktalk 2.0 styles discussed below. Here are some basic booktalk rules:

- Read the book.
- Like the book, or understand its appeal.
- Write the right booktalk for that book.
- Practice makes perfect.
- You're a librarian, you can always borrow prepared booktalks from publishers or other librarians!

Play to your strengths

Honestly, I am not a funny person (well, not intentionally anyway). I can never even remember the punch line to a joke. So I don't try to do funny booktalks. Teens would see right away that I am out of my element. To sell a book, you have to be *authentic.* Don't try and sell a book you hate. Don't try and sell a book you know nothing about (really, you should read it). And don't try to be something that you're not. You want the teens to trust you because you are trying to get them to do something . . . so be authentic. Trust is vital.

However, even if you've found your comfort zone, you still need to be able to employ a wide variety of styles. Booktalking expert Joni Richards Bodart discusses the different types of booktalks as being character-based, mood-based, plot summary, or anecdotal in Chapter 5. This will help you develop the tools you need to be a successful booktalker.

Get your audience involved

Remember, in an ideal scenario, you will go to a teacher's class and booktalk to each and every period. This means that you can be entertaining each class for anywhere from 15 minutes up until the entire period, depending on what you and the teacher agree upon. So you want to make it fun for the teens—get them involved.

Ask a question and get them talking. For example, when booktalking *No More Dead Dogs* by Gordon Korman, ask them if they have read *Where the Red Fern Grows* and how they felt when the dogs died.

Take a portion of the book and make it into a short readers' theater.

Create a short news show or interview that ties into a book. Believe it or not, a lot of the same techniques your children's librarian employs for story hour can also be successfully used in a fun, interactive booktalk. So make cards with words on them, and ask teens to yell them out every time you show them the card. Ask teens to sing, dance, act, and get involved. It doesn't have to be you standing up in front of them.

Tech it up (Booktalks 2.0)

Today most classrooms have a computer and an overhead projector in them, so take advantage of this. Download book trailers onto a flash drive, and share them. You can download a wide variety on YouTube or at various publishers' sites, or visit Naomi Bates (naomibates.blogspot.com) and use hers, or follow her directions for making your own.

You can also create PowerPoints or basic images to share and give that "wow" factor. I find these to be particularly useful when I want to booktalk a book that is never on the shelf—this allows me to show them the cover. In fact, I now almost always create a visual presentation of some sort to go with my booktalks. The visual reinforces the verbal. Plus, I can leave it behind in the classroom for the teacher and students.

No, really—get teens involved

Teachers are always looking for creative ways to help students explore literature and share what they have read, so get students to write their own booktalks and create their own book trailers. You can share what they do in the classroom in a wide variety of ways in your library with the proper permissions and platforms, such as on a web page or social-media page or display screens in your teen area.

Make their trip to the library successful

I have always been amazed when visiting the classroom how students will write down titles and come up and ask you about them. If you can, find a way to check titles out to the students at the end of the day. I have written down book barcodes and library card numbers and gone back to the library and checked them out. But what if the teens don't have library cards yet? Chances are, they are going to come in to the library and ask about the book—but they won't remember much. So you need to make sure all public service staff know not only that you visited a school and booktalked, but what you booktalked. Make sure all staff have a list of the books, a copy of the cover so they can know what it looked like, and a general book description (or a copy of the actual booktalk). You can do this electronically or in print, or both. Then, when a teen comes in and says, "This lady came to our library today and talked about this book set in the future where everyone has a job given to them," the staff member can pull out the list and determine that it is *The Giver*, by Lois Lowry. Teens are satisfied, coworkers feel informed, and everyone walks away having a successful library interaction.

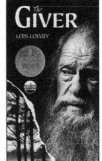

6

Screenshot from Scholastic video booktalk with *Hunger Games* author Suzanne Collins.

Also, if you make slides, print them out and display them in your teen area. And if the books are not checked out, put them on display. Whatever you do, make sure teens can check out the books (buy multiple copies!) or put them on hold. There is nothing worse than coming into the library to ask for a book and no one there knows what you are talking about.

Also, don't forget your school librarians. Take the information to them and introduce yourself. Chances are some of the students will go looking for the books at their school library, so help the school librarian find them there if the school owns them. We want teens to have successful library experiences, whether at their public library or their school library.

It only takes one

If you play your cards correctly, you can establish a good repeat customer relationship with at least one teacher—and if you visit one teacher's classroom every month for six or seven periods, well, that is a lot of booktalks. At one library where I worked, I visited one particular teacher's classroom every month for five years. The great thing about this was that after a year, I had a really good backlog of booktalks to draw from the next year. All you have to do is add the new books that you read. And that teacher could be counted on to spread the word to other teachers, who would occasionally take me up on my offer. Best of all, it was amazing getting to know those students throughout the high school years.

There is nothing to lose in a booktalking situation, and so much to gain. It's an excellent opportunity to connect with teens and an important piece of the teen services' overall marketing strategy.

SOURCE: Specially prepared for *The Whole Library Handbook: Teen Services* by Karen Jensen, teen services librarian, Grand Prairie, Texas.

Make the most of your teen services social media

by Karen Jensen

SOCIAL MEDIA MAY BE a more recent development, but it shows no signs of going away anytime soon. It is an effective and easy tool that libraries should be utilizing to connect with their communities and promote themselves. The tool of choice may change, but the concept is here to stay. Social media is a great way to remind teens of upcoming programs, new books, popular-culture tidbits, great homework sites, and more. Social media is also a good way to stay connected and get valuable feedback from our target audience.

Social media does pose some unique challenges, however, and libraries should have policies in place to help staff navigate the murky waters of having an online presence. Of note, when creating an online presence, make sure it is not tied to your personal accounts but to your library accounts. You always keep your personal stuff personal and separate from your work. In addition, should you leave the library, this allows them to maintain the accounts and keep the contact that you have already established with your community. Your library may want to explore creating a social-media policy to help outline what staff can and can't do using the library's Facebook page. In addition to having a main library page, you should have a teencentric one that allows you to meet your teens in their world. The goal of your library's online presence is to promote, share, and engage.

Promote your services

An online social-media presence is a quick and easy way to maintain frequent contact with your audience. It allows for the development of some regular, ongoing features while giving room for moments of spontaneous interaction. Thus, when the news breaks that the latest big seller is being made into a movie, libraries have quick and easy ways of sharing that news.

Patrons also like the familiarity and predictability that comes with having regular, ongoing features. Not only do they know what to expect, but they come looking for it as you develop a rapport with your audience. For example, start off each week with "First Day, First Lines"—post a first line from a new book or an old favorite. Or post a popular line, and see if teens can guess which book it is from. Here you are doing readers' advisory but in a fun and engaging way.

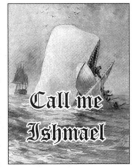

Libraries can promote upcoming events by saving event flyers as JPEG files and posting them. This gives you something visual to share when inviting teens to programs. Any file can be saved as a JPEG and shared on most social-media sites.

- Share book trailers—make your own or repost others.
- Have an online scavenger hunt: Ask a question that requires teens to use your online catalog or databases to answer. Teens will learn library resources and research skills while having fun.
- Don't forget your magazine collection. Most of your magazines have online counterparts—send a link to a pertinent headline, and invite your teens to come in and browse through your magazines.
- Create quick, simple online contests to share. Or download in-house contest flyers as JPEG files, and upload them to share.
- Share your book reviews—keep them positive but honest.
- Online RA—have a weekly day and time for a chat session, or post readers' advisory lists, like "If you like *Twilight* . . . you will also like."

Get your teens involved

When looking for ways to engage teens and tap into their talents, don't forget about social media. Teens can create artwork to share, vote in various polls, participate in online discussions, and more:

- Take pictures of your teens in your teen area or at programs and post them (make sure you abide by your library's photo policy if you have one). This is a great way to do a "Look Who Go Caught Reading" type of thing. You can show teens in action, or get creative and make awesome pictures using a variety of tools.

- Make up your own awards and get teens voting. Teens can also vote in popular awards-show categories, such as the Printz Awards or things like the Grammys and Oscars.
- Push out links of interest to teens. Links of interest can include news about books being made into movies, campaigns like "It Gets Better," PSAs, movie reviews, and more. Spend time browsing sites like *Seventeen* magazine, popwatch.ew.com, TV Squad, or Teen.com. Don't forget to add the occasional humor, like Cake Wrecks. See what your teens have to say.

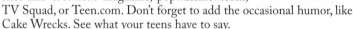
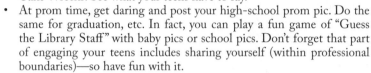

- At prom time, get daring and post your high-school prom pic. Do the same for graduation, etc. In fact, you can play a fun game of "Guess the Library Staff" with baby pics or school pics. Don't forget that part of engaging your teens includes sharing yourself (within professional boundaries)—so have fun with it.
- Contests—Post a cleverly cropped picture of a Transformer or some other pop-culture reference and see who can guess what it is. There are no limits to the creative ways that libraries can engage teens by having teens guess what pictures are, provide captions, and more.
- Have an online book-discussion group or topic chat. Everyone meets online at a certain day and time and chats away.
- True or false. This simple game is great for Facebook. Put a whimsical true-or-false challenge out there, and see what kind of response you get.
- Have a tech lab where teens create pictures or posters, then share them. This is a great way to teach teens tech skills and have teen-generated content to share. Use tools like Publisher, PowerPoint, or GIMP. Get ambitious and let teens make their own videos (outside the library or part of a program) to share. Teens can even make commercials for your library or summer reading club, book trailers, and more.
- Post movie and TV clips and trailers.
- Have teens advise on collection development. Polls and open-ended questions can be used to gain interest into reading habits, get feedback on potential titles for purchase, and so forth.
- Post popular new music videos. Share music videos and post booklists of books that share the same theme. Or create playlists from teen fiction. *The Perks of Being a Wallflower* and *Just Listen* are just a couple of titles that have built-in playlists. Many authors share their book playlists online.

The keys to using social media as a marketing tool all have to do with staying current. Use the right tool for the audience. Pay attention to current trends and adapt accordingly. Keep the sites you maintain updated regularly and frequently. Most social-media sites have blogs dedicated to using that site effectively; visit them often to learn the latest tips and tricks. Also, be sure to check their terms of service because they do change—sometimes frequently—and individual sites have specific rules about use, especially about legal issues like offering contests and giveaways. And finally, keep a sense of humor and have fun with it, too, because if teens aren't having fun interacting with the library online, they won't do so in the future.

SOURCE: Specially prepared for *The Whole Library Handbook: Teen Services* by Karen Jensen, teen services librarian, Grand Prairie, Texas.

INVOLVEMENT

CHAPTER SEVEN

Effective librarians don't just serve teens, they get them involved. Involving teens in library services helps them build important life skills while giving librarians the input and feedback they need to ensure high-quality, successful teen services. As librarians, we could guess at what teens want, but if we take the time to ask them, we are much more likely to actually engage them. Large corporations do this successfully using focus groups, online resources, and various social-media tools, and libraries should take a page out of their playbook. The following is a discussion of why teen involvement is important, how to get teens involved, and how to put that involvement to the best possible use in your library.

Teen involvement:
Putting the teen in your teen services

by Karen Jensen

WHEN PEOPLE ARE INVOLVED in a product or service that your library offers in a hands-on way, you are generating buy-in and loyalty. We need to get teens to stop thinking of it as "the library" and to start thinking of it as "my library." One of the best ways to do that is to involve teens in all aspects of our library program, from designing the teen area to putting together programs, so that teens have that sense of ownership and buy-in. There are a wide variety of ways that this can be accomplished successfully.

Getting teens involved in your teen area. If you have a dedicated teen area, shouldn't the space somehow say this is "your space"? There are a variety of ways that teens can be involved in your teen space to help create that sense of ownership. Even if you already have a space set up, there are some small things you can do to bring your local teens into the space in creative ways.

At the most basic level, if money is tight and you want to get something up quickly, you can simply take pictures of your teens in your teen area and at your programs and use them to decorate the walls. If you have a camera (or a camera phone) and a color printer, you have everything you need. You can do straightforward pictures or use smartphone apps like WordFoto, Photo Booth, and Diptic to create fun and interesting images. With more time to tackle the steeper learning curve, the free online photo-manipulation program GIMP is useful for manipulating your photos and giving them that little something extra. You can upload photos to make collages or include teen pictures in your homemade readers' advisory posters. Make a visual statement to an audience that is very visually oriented. Don't just tell them the library is fun—show them!

You can also get teens involved by allowing them to create and share original artwork in the space. There are creative ways that you can go beyond a simple bulletin board to give the teen area some dramatic flair. For example, a variety of clipboards mounted to the wall allows for the easy changing of teen-created artwork. You can also use picture frames that will allow for the easy rotation of artwork. If you have the technology, teen artwork can be scanned in and displayed in a streaming display on a digital monitor. If you are really bold, you can even get teens to paint a mural or make signs for your area.

When it comes time to revamp your teen area, put together a focus group or consult your teen advisory board (TAB) to get its input on purchasing furniture, naming your space, or organizing the space. Put together a survey and ask teens what they like, what they hate, and what they would like to see in the teen area. When they see themselves involved and reflected in the teen area, that sense of ownership translates into goodwill and the promotional word of mouth that all organizations desire.

Getting teens involved in your teen programming. Sometimes trying to find creative library programs that will interest teens is difficult, but there is a great resource for us that we don't often consider: the teens themselves. Teens are singing, acting, making short films, designing websites, making miniature models, and so much more. They have talents and hobbies that they want to share, so give them a place to do it. Go beyond an *American Idol*–type program or a talent show and allow teens to share their talent—whatever it is—and create a dynamic, ongoing library program for teens, by teens.

Tired of trying to come up with program ideas, I declared 2005 the "year of the teen" and let my teens do the programming. I went beyond a TAB and canvassed my community to determine what talents my teens had that they wanted to share. I created an application with a deadline, selected the programs, met with the presenters, developed publicity—and then let the teens do all the work. One teen shared how to make recycled Capri Sun purses (before you could buy them in the store), another teen shared about her travel experiences, and more. The best part is when teens are doing the programs, they recruit their friends to come.

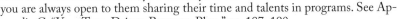

Another great thing about this type of programming is that it really taps in to the 40 Developmental Assets. It expands on what we try to do with TABs and takes it to the next level: It's not just a group of 12 or 20 teens giving program ideas but is open to any teen in the community. And it doesn't have to be on a limited basis; you can let your teens know that you are always open to them sharing their time and talents in programs. See Appendix C, "Your Teen-Driven Program Plan," pp. 187–190.

Promote, promote, promote. Not only is there benefit to the teens when doing teen-originated and teen-led programming, but there is benefit to the library as the teens become your promoters: they are going to want their friends to come. They will hand out flyers for the library, promote it on their social-networking sites, and talk it up to their friends. Including teens in this way creates stronger buy-in, and teen buy-in increases word-of-mouth promotion, which is your most successful type of promotion.

Teen advisory boards. Teen advisory boards or teen advisory groups (TABs or TAGs) are a very popular way to get teens invested in library services. See the following section by Amy Alessio for more information on TABs.

Getting teens involved as volunteers. Libraries are huge fans of teen advisory groups, but they require a certain amount of inflexible time dedication that not all teens can make. TAG meetings take place at a specific time and place. In comparison, you can put together a teen volunteer program that allows teens to be active in the library with more flexibility. Volunteer programs can be structured so that teens can choose their own dates and times to come in.

The advantages of a teen volunteer program. Many teens need volunteer and community-service hours for various classroom credit, extracurricular activities, or as a graduation requirement, so why not invite them to fulfill these obligations at the library? While working with teen volunteers, the library is helping teens serve their community and learn the value of giving back. For those teens who have a lifelong investment in the library, from storytime on through to their teen years, volunteering is an excellent way for them to remain invested in the organization, and who knows—you just might be nurturing a future librarian in the process. Working one on one with teen volunteers allows for the opportunity to build mentoring relationships and get valuable feedback from your teens.

The challenges of a teen volunteer program. Just like managing a paid staff, a staff of teen volunteers requires a lot of time in training, scheduling, and maintaining good communication. For some teens, the majority of this time will be at the beginning of the volunteering period, and they will smoothly sail through their tasks. But for many, especially for those who are in their first work-like setting, much more handholding and repetition of instruction will be required. There are sometimes difficult issues that come up that you must address. As a library begins to rely on its volunteers to accomplish specific tasks, unexpected absences for illness, vacation, or other activities will weigh heavily. Additionally, this mentoring relationship will inevitably include instruction on basic work etiquette, how to handle visits from friends, and how to handle oneself with patrons.

Remember, your goal is teen involvement. There are a variety of ways that this goal can be accomplished, whether getting teens involved in your teen area, program planning, teen advisory groups, or creating a teen volunteer program. Mix and match teen involvement in the way that works best for your library and your community, given the resources that you have. More detailed information on assessing your teen community and structuring the types of involvement programs best suited to your audience are addressed in the following section.

SOURCE: Specially prepared for *The Whole Library Handbook: Teen Services* by Karen Jensen, teen services librarian, Grand Prairie, Texas.

Keeping the teen advisory board relevant and real
by Amy Alessio

CONGRATULATIONS! You have had a teen advisory board (TAB) for a while, and the board members have planned many fun programs. Or maybe you have had some great teen summer events and want to develop a regular teen advisory board. This section is for both of these groups, but it is more than suggestions of activities or group control ideas. It will also address what to do when the TAB stops working, or won't start. Sometimes a group of teens gets really involved in a particular topic and this section will also provide ideas for subgroups of teen advisory boards. Persistence in matching teen input and interests can help all library teen services grow and continue to be relevant in any situation.

Signs of a successful teen advisory board

What makes a teen advisory board successful? Signs of this may vary by situation, but basically a TAB that is working will have teens who want to return each session and who want to be involved with the library. Criteria staff may want to see from a teen advisory board may be that the teens are giving input that positively impacts library services and are willing to volunteer to help with services. Either of these sets of criteria can mean that the TAB can be a few members, or 25 to 30 members, depending on the library situation. Groups larger than that make for challenging meetings and may need to be broken into smaller groups by grade or project.

Meetings need to be welcoming and at a time that works for teens. They should be consistent, such as the third Wednesday of each month, or the first and third Friday afternoons. Staff can coordinate meetings, but letting teens lead the discussion may be most successful for participation.

If meetings are held at dinnertime, pizza or sandwiches should be served. This is as important as offering coffee at an adult early morning meeting! Often teens have activities after school after a very long day and will be hungry. Having meetings at 5:00 or 6:00 p.m. can mean more attendance if teens are in a lot of after-school or evening activities or if they want to come before doing homework at the library.

When teens show investment in the outcome of suggestions, the TAB is working very well. If they suggest having a crafts night where they help younger kids come learn crafts, they should come to help run it. If they suggest new things for the teen website, they should provide copy or design it.

Groups can take a while to gel. Meetings can have some similarities and routine but should be flexible and have fun events as well. For example, perhaps the first 30 minutes of meetings is devoted to eating and library business; then a fun activity fills the rest of the time. This can be up to the teens and can involve anything from book trivia to food crafts, dessert, or themed projects. Having teens make a haunted gingerbread house at the October meeting each year is a favorite tradition at the Schaumburg Township (Ill.) District Library. The event is filmed and posted on the teen website for further publicity for the teen advisory board. Other ideas for meetings include having guest speakers for Black History Month or Veterans Day, having teens work on a big art project to auction for charity or to hang in the library, having a contest for best new ideas, and other interactive events.

Applications can be a way to find out which teens really want to be a member of the teen advisory board, but they should not be exclusive. Teens have enough instances where they are cut from activities or have to apply for something they want. If too many teens want to be on a teen advisory board, perhaps the library can offer juniors and seniors separate volunteer groups. Or teens could be split by interests.

Sample application questions follow:

- Why do you want to volunteer at the library? (This is especially good for avoiding situations where parents are making teens come.)
- What do you like best about the library?
- What do you feel should be changed about the library?
- Do you find pleasure reading, listening, or viewing materials at the library?
- Do you use the library teen site? The library's general site?
- Which library teen programs interest you?
- What kinds of projects would you like to work on? (Consider offering a list of volunteering options and allowing them to circle some.)

Invite teens also to list special skills. If many are good at designing websites, that could be a great project for the TAB. If half of the teen advisory board applicants love anime, maybe a separate advisory board devoted to that subject needs to be created. Those teens could plan an anime club and festival and help with collection development. A section on separate groups or interest-driven teen advisory boards is provided at the end of this chapter.

It is hard to encourage leadership among teens while also being inclusive to all. Electing officers may feel like a rejection to teens who did not win, and they may not return. To make this experience as welcoming to self-conscious teens as possible, consider instead putting a rotation of teens in charge of projects or duties

7

rather than having officer positions. For example, some teens could coordinate the collection of website content. Another could sort patron suggestions for the teen collection or help with weeding projects.

Another way to welcome teens is with incentives. All ages appreciate these! If only a few attend at first, and the teens want to plan big programs requiring more volunteers, offer an incentive to bring a friend in the future. This can be inexpensive, from clearing fines to offering extra checkouts above video game or DVD limits or allowing extra time on the library laptops.

Ready for a change?

Teens are only teens for six years. Junior and senior high schools can encompass up to seven years. During that time they undergo tremendous changes. Interests and abilities will change in particular as physical and emotional maturity take place. Time commitments increase as teens get older, especially after they have their drivers' licenses.

Having a teen advisory board stop working in the fall when it was going well in the spring or having one with dwindling attendance and enthusiasm is not a sign of staff failure by any means. New activities and meeting times compete with library events. Trends and interests of current teens change across communities. Capturing a teen's interest in the library teen advisory board may be an accomplishment that will last only two to four years. So the parameters of a TAB will also change over time.

Flexibility is essential, and the projects of the group may reflect the interests of the age of the group. For example, an older group may take on larger community-service projects, while younger teens may want to focus mainly on volunteering in the library. In the time after a group loses stronger older members, recruiting and regrouping becomes a focus.

Having a group made up largely of older teens is a clear sign that change is coming. Another easy sign to see is when a group is so large that meetings are out of control. This will vary by number of staff available, library situation, and even the nature of the teens attending. Staff will know when meetings are no longer in control. Can any type of order be called to discuss ideas? Are there more teens than projects? Then it is time to split the group in some way.

Some signs that a group is no longer working can be harder to detect. When staff gets to know teens and siblings, and the meetings are small and peaceful, it may seem like the group is working well when a change is needed. For example, a teen advisory board that has been running for a long time now has a group of dedicated boys who rush through the business portion to play games each month. They are not interested in volunteering at other events and like to hang together as a group only. This group may simply need their own space and theme, such as a gamers advisory board. Maybe they would be interested in getting together more times to play games or on different equipment or on a network. They have become a special-interest teen advisory board, and new direction is needed along with the new group.

If the group is planning the same activities each season, and the events they run are experiencing declining enrollment, change is needed. For example, the TAB wants to run a summer prize auction each year, based on books read. The auction has become less popular, but the group puts a lot of time and energy into planning it, dropping other needed volunteer activities, such as making cards for a local senior center. Consider offering a second meeting focusing on the card making after the scheduled TAB time, or on a different day, with a broad charity crafting focus. Bring in a paper artist to inspire new ideas and excitement about the card project. Work with the TAB to recruit more members or to survey the community to learn what needs to change about the summer event. Discover which elements of the auction make it so appealing to the TAB and see if other events can add those elements. Maybe a Teen Read Week online auction with book reviews would get the TAB excited.

There are cases where a group is working but struggling. Sometimes marketing or a couple new members can give a group a shot in the arm to continue. For example, the charity knitting café for teens met weekly at the Schaumburg Township District Library for eight months. In September, enrollment dropped. This is not unusual for fall, when teens enter new grades and activities. The leader warned the group that unless numbers increased to at least three students per week, the group would be ending at the end of October. Staff encouraged new volunteers who were completing their service hours required for graduation to join the group and knit for charity as part of their time in the library. These efforts yielded another member. Upon learning the group would be switching to monthly rather than weekly due to declining enrollment, the remaining teens asked if they could film a commercial about the group. Staff hired a teen filmmaker who had helped with other programs to work on the script with them, film it, and edit it. The resulting ad featured "Super Knitter," who encouraged people to learn to knit so they wouldn't be cold. It was humorous and was put together quickly. Within two weeks, more teens were coming. The group grew to 17 weekly knitters on average  by the following February. So although there are going to be times when a program needs restructuring, attempts to save a group are well worth it.

Making the change happen

In each of the above scenarios, staff had to consider what was working and how to utilize those elements into a new or different type of teen advisory board. Before listing what is not working or what is bad about a particular program, list what is good and what is working right now. What worked in the past is no longer relevant to the teens.

There is always something working. If no teens show up, have online suggestions been turned in? Is another program popular? Is there a particular event for which teens still like to volunteer? Is circulation of a type of item going up? Are hits on a teen library social-media site increasing? With a staff willing to serve teens, there is always something working well, even if it does not seem that way.

Tell the teens. Take a break from the program that is not working. With brochure deadlines six months in the future, this can be hard to predict, but even taking a break from the teen advisory board for a planned three to four months in

7

the summer or in the coldest part of the winter can allow needed time to regroup. Cancelling an advertised program is not optimal and may discourage teens who come by accident from returning. Plan a break when a program has not been working for a while.

Next, staff needs to figure out what is wanted or needed from the teen advisory board. Listing this, then discovering what teens want or need, can be illuminating. For example, staff may want teens to volunteer at a desk during summer reading registration. Teens may list that they wanted to help with that, but it was always held during their basketball camp each year. If staff offered evening volunteering shifts, or moved the summer dates up or back one week, this would work better. Staff may want teens to plan Teen Read Week activities, but teens may all have homecoming events during that time. Staff could change the events to encompass a Teen Read Month. Where possible, some adjustment may find a better fit between teen and staff needs.

Discovering what teens want and need involves surveys. Paper surveys are harder to collect and tally, but a bookmark with a survey in it may get the attention of regular teens even more often than posting it on the website. Trying both methods is best. Be sure to ask what dates and times are best to attend a teen advisory board, and list choices of activities for teens to circle interests. Staff may discover interest in the formation of other groups as well.

Staff may also want to visit community centers with teen groups and survey those teens. Offer incentives for filling out surveys, and offer a generous timeline to fill them out. Having a survey during the first week of the school year will help no one. Keep the survey short and simple, for the sake of staff and the teens.

Involve more staff from different departments. Part of making a fresh new group will be new ideas. Are there teen or college staff members who could give ideas? Survey them before the new group begins. Some may want to be more involved, and finding a place for them could help retain new teens. Technology staff may also have ideas on how to engage teens, both in person and virtually. Staff from adult and youth departments may have ideas on recruiting older or younger teens. Staff who have teens at home are yet another good resource for ideas on what would make an advisory board successful.

Consider offering surveys periodically, such as during Teen Read Week or National Library Week each year, on a particular topic, to help keep teens used to filling them out and to keep services relevant. Or offer surveys at the end of each program with monthly drawings for prizes. One survey may cover elements of the collection, such as magazines. Another may list program ideas from the teen advisory board and solicit more opinions on those options. If a lot of online interest and discussion happens, the teen advisory board may become a cohesive virtual group. This group may be interested in coming in for quarterly meetings or events or just to help with particular projects or services. Being flexible and ready to run with teen interests and input will make different types of groups work at different facilities.

Involve the teens who were involved before. They may have a perception that the program is being changed to get away from them personally. There may be cases where strong personalities dominate a group and splitting of a group is needed, but staff will still want to harness strong leadership qualities. Some will not return after a break, but many will be excited by changes they helped develop and by the new energy and direction. Plan a month when the program will restart and mention it frequently to the teens involved even if a specific date and time is not set up. If patrons ask about a program that is being restructured, a definite date for the restart is seen as a positive sign and something to work toward.

Consider partnering with another agency to offer a teen advisory board. Perhaps a local YMCA or other youth group needs more members as well. If the goals of the group dovetail with library ideas, perhaps the group could meet one month at one facility and one month at another, providing ideas for both. This is more of a logistical challenge and a marketing one, but the reach of the group is doubled through both facilities. Or perhaps the area youth group would be open to having meetings at the library.

If there are only a few teens left who are interested in serving on a library teen advisory board, perhaps that group could give ideas virtually for a time period. Set up an email group or a Facebook site where teens can chime in about  topics, meeting times, and more. If teens are participating enthusiastically through virtual channels yet are not eager to come in, the teen advisory board can work that way for a while at least. Ask the group for input on reading-club themes, other program suggestions, collection ideas, and more, just as would happen with a live teen advisory board. Take pictures of library displays and ask for opinions. It may happen that a group will grow naturally and want to meet in the library, or the group may continue feeling comfortable with the online channels. Encourage those teens who give constructive opinions and actively participate to bring a friend to the meeting of the new club; then offer a small prize when they do.

If a date has been set to restart the in-person teen advisory board, put the best marketing steps forward possible. Consider tying in the new group to a library celebration, such as summer reading, Teen Read Week, or National Library Week to join the momentum of other marketing efforts. Make the meeting itself an event. Think about what made programs in the past year popular. Was food a draw? Video gaming? The first meeting of the new teen group should have elements of popular things without taking away from the purpose of the event. For example, a new teen advisory board with a volunteering focus could have pizza, a raffle, and a mini contest for ideas of service projects. The meeting itself could have time set aside to create blankets (see below) for a local shelter.

Some fun activities planned will help attract teens. But finding ways to let the teens know about the event is also a challenge. In addition to getting as much information out in library and community brochures as possible, attractive posters, signs, and bookmarks can help. Bookmarks could have a list of new books and media on one side, and program information on the other. The bookmarks can be put in the books and video games teens like to check out. They can also be stuck in reserve items waiting to be picked up. Some could be placed at park-district events or at other community locations where teens like to gather. Perhaps school media centers would be willing to put out bookmarks or put up posters. Schools may be willing to have an announcement read.

Online marketing is faster and cheaper, and it potentially scores a larger reach. Posting consistently is the best way to grow marketing on teen library Facebook or other social-media sites.

With a new focus and advertising, the group has a great chance to catch on and revitalize teen library services.

7

Theme teen advisory boards

Is a group that features video games and gaming programs a teen advisory board? It can be. It could be a group of teens who weigh in on collection development in a particular area and develop programs or marketing for that area as well. Several times throughout this section, the idea of breaking off groups around interests has been mentioned. Here are some ideas for what themed clubs could do.

Gamers group

To continue the video-gaming group discussion, a gaming group could be very advantageous for libraries.

Helping to run events. The teens may be knowledgeable about the latest technologies and platforms and know which would work well for library programs. They would also be familiar with the assembly and gaming equipment and be able to run gaming events and help with the labor-intensive setup and cleanup. They could help run gaming events for senior citizens, family events, young children, or their own age group.

Reviewing games. With so many different media types to purchase for libraries, gamers-group teens could be given gaming magazines ahead of other patrons and be asked for a list of titles to purchase. They could also mark their favorites and make suggestions for themed lists to be posted on the library website, such as role-playing games, movie-based games, Wii Fit board games, and more. Teens in this group may also want to provide tips or YouTube commentaries of favorite games for the library website.

Demonstrating equipment. Gaming equipment is expensive, and the library will want to get appropriate use out of the pieces. Gamers-group teens could demonstrate products and equipment in the library lobby before special events or after school. They could also demonstrate tips on a popular game on a big screen. They could do this for different age groups, as with the programs. Teens could make live demos of games such as Angry Birds, with balls, books, and stuffed birds, to attract younger members to programs or as a special event.

Holding meetings. Gamers-group meetings could involve their own mini tournaments on new games each time, followed by some discussion about the collection or upcoming events. Meetings could have themes such as online gaming, networked games, or games themed by platform. If there is a lot of interest in online games such as Minecraft, teens may choose to run or host workshops or events based on those topics. Additional topics might be game design and online animation. Special classes such as those could be held after regular gamers-group events.

Exchanging games. Gamers-group members could participate in game swaps during meetings or at another designated time.

Crafting for charity

Crafting for charity does not require Martha Stewart–level talent from teachers. Teens need only enthusiasm for a particular craft or project. Staff can provide guidance and resources for further teaching, along with basic instruction, to foster enjoyment and rewarding results. Supplies could be solicited from the community, or leftover items utilized from other library projects. Meetings could start with a demonstration of a new technique. One technique may catch on, such as knitting, and eventually the group will work exclusively on that. Guest teachers from staff or the community may be willing to share expertise with the teens for low or no cost. Teen crafters may also wish to share their crafts with younger children in the library or out in the community. Demonstration days of the craft with information about charities being helped could even be held in the lobby or meeting rooms for all ages to involve more people in helping the charities. Here are some more ideas for a group that wants to do crafting for charity:

Cards. There are always places in the community where someone needs cheering up. Staff could contact senior centers in the area to ask for a list of birthdays. Teens could create cards for those seniors involving a variety of techniques, including quilling, three-dimensional aspects, calligraphy, layering, and more. Online searches may provide addresses for local or faraway servicemen and servicewomen who would enjoy receiving supportive cards.

Blankets. National organizations such as Project Linus (www.projectlinus. org) or Warm Up America (www.craftyarncouncil.com/teacher-resources.php) have places for crafters at all levels to send blankets or squares for those in need. Local hospitals may have a need for lap or baby blankets. Homeless shelters or veterans organizations may also be able to use blankets. Among the several ways of making blankets for charity are polar-fleece knotting, quilting, knitting, and crocheting. Teens could even sign squares of fabric for a larger quilt.

Clothing. Knitting and crocheting can also be extended to making hats and scarves for charitable organizations. These projects could be done in conjunction with clothing drives for local or larger-area needs. Hospitals may have a need for booties or hats for particular sizes of babies, such as preemies.

Animal blankets. Animal shelters may be able to use created blankets. They may not be as particular about the quality of the finished project, so this may be a perfect project for beginning crafters.

Auctions. As the teen crafters become more skilled, they could host auctions to raise money for designated community charities, such as food pantries. This could either be done with the creation of a large item, such as a quilt for auction or raffle, or through auction or sale of several created items. The Schaumburg Township District Library celebrates National Library Week each year with raffles of products from each department. For example, one year each department decorated rain barrels for a recycling or green theme. The teen advisory board created a galaxy theme. The barrels had numbers, and patrons or community members purchased tickets for a small amount. Winners were drawn for the rain barrels, and the money went toward a township charity. Other decorated items from other years included piggy banks, boxes, watering cans, and plates.

7

Bookin' teens

A group of teens may want to be more involved with the book collection at the library, from helping with purchases to promoting it. This type of group could easily be adapted to magazines or other media as well, especially graphic novels. Here are some ideas for activities a book advisory group could do:

Purchasing. Many libraries take teens on field trips to local bookstores or give them a dollar amount and have them look at review journals. At the very least,

this group could compile a list of titles for purchase.

Curating. The teen book group could maintain a list of series they like and review those periodically. They could also keep a list of favorite authors and post that list online for teen patrons. The teen book group could help pull books for weeding from printouts and see if there are any the library should keep.

Reviewing. Teen book fans could post online book reviews at regular intervals and encourage discussion of those titles or other ones.

Programming. The teen book group could design and run summer, winter, year-round, or special-occasion book events by setting parameters, choosing themes and prizes, posting reviews from participating teens, or working at a registration table. Book-review auctions are popular at libraries, though they are labor intensive. Teens could choose prizes, help promote this, and run bidding online or in person.

Offering readers' advisory. The book group would create themed lists regularly and read-alike titles to go with current movies and bestselling teen books. These could be posted online or put in books. The group could also help create attractive displays in the library.

Anime group

Similar to the book group, an anime group would specialize in that genre, including movies and books. Here are some ideas to expand the interests of these teens and to attract others also interested in anime or manga:

Purchasing. This group could be given an allowance and review sites or go on a field trip to a comics store or bookstore. Staff could help teens decide how much should be allotted to series already owned and how much for new material. Staff would also help with age and content guidelines.

Series curating. Series are the hardest aspect of anime and manga collections to maintain. Teens could review which book and DVD collections need to be kept up, and which could be weeded. They could maintain summaries of the major series story lines and read-alikes for staff and for the teen website. The anime club could view DVD series or other movies for reviews as well.

Holding technique classes. Meetings for the anime club should involve Pocky (chocolate-cream-covered biscuit sticks) or other Japanese snacks and elements of techniques that interest teens, for example, drawing and painting or comics-writing classes. Digital-animation technique would be another area of interest. Perhaps a teen or a student from an area college could help teach these things to keep costs down. Teens could also teach these things for younger children at the library if they are interested.

Offering culture classes or resources. Basic Japanese classes or Japanese culture may be areas where teens outside of the club could be attracted as well. The anime club could help promote resources featuring these topics on the library site or with displays.

Hosting festivals. Many libraries offer anime movie festivals, with classes in between viewings. This could be a major task for the anime club to design and run each year.

Web designers

Teens and technology go well together, and harnessing those skills can help library staff with saved time and training. Keeping up with social-media sites is hard but necessary to attract teen attention, and help with those areas would be welcome at any library. Here are some ideas for web-savvy teens:

Monthly contests. Teens could design and implement simple monthly contests on the library teen Facebook page or websites with media prizes or book-fines-clearing prizes. These contests include trivia, simple questions with prizes for the first five who answer, or photos where teens guess what the area of the library featured is.

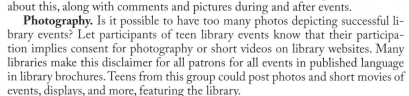

Upcoming events. The most important function of the website or social-media sites is to let other teens know about fun upcoming events at the library or in the community. Teens could post information about this, along with comments and pictures during and after events.

Photography. Is it possible to have too many photos depicting successful library events? Let participants of teen library events know that their participation implies consent for photography or short videos on library websites. Many libraries make this disclaimer for all patrons for all events in published language in library brochures. Teens from this group could post photos and short movies of events, displays, and more, featuring the library.

Meetings. This group may want to have meetings virtually or in the library to learn about and test new gadgets. A perk for this group would be access to experts brought in to teach fun new things. They could divide up who wants to post what on which site for the library, and evaluate which marketing efforts are working well. This group could test new social-media platforms for the library and advise staff.

Programs and classes. This web-savvy group could also demonstrate technologies for patrons or have sessions where patrons could bring in phones or simple gadgets for teens to help work. For example, teens could help seniors program contacts into a phone. (The library would let patrons know that the teens are doing their best and are not experts and are not responsible for erased information or damage.) This group could also teach audiences about simple technologies or basic web design.

Volunteens

This group would be different from the teen advisory board (TAB) in that these teens would train and help with designated library or community efforts on a consistent basis. It could be part of the TAB or a group that meets just after TAB meetings. Rather than librarians assigning tasks that staff need completed and sending the teens on their way, make this experience more rewarding for all involved.

Have teens fill out skill lists and keep those updated. There is no point in assigning teens to help with youth programs if they are not good with young children. Some teens may prefer to help with teen events, behind the scenes at the library, or with senior citizens. Try to match teens to skill sets. Keep lists for all departments of what tasks need to be done so teens and staff always have something to assign when teens arrive, no matter which staff member they encounter.

Know which staff members work best with teens. Administration could encourage staff to participate with teen volunteers and offer rewards or incentives

for doing so. If a teen has to help with a task alongside a staff member who is not good with teens, try to make it easy, so the teen will not have to ask many questions. Encourage staff to be flexible and understand that teens are teens, and this is not their life's work in most cases.

Offer variety for teen volunteers. Offer real responsibility where possible to allow teens to become invested in the work, just as adults prefer in their own work. Volunteers should be encouraged to interact with patrons if they are interested in that type of work, but not be given so much responsibility that it is stressful for them. Volunteering for its own sake comes more with maturity and may not come as easily to teens. If staff do not have time to train or work with volunteers, it may not be a good time to offer volunteering opportunities.

Offer rewards and growth. Regular encouragement and occasional thank-you events go a long way toward retaining volunteers. Excellent volunteers could be trained to work in the library or offered unpaid internships that would enhance college applications.

Handling disappointments with extreme care makes life easy for everyone. Letting a teen know about rules ahead of time and then enforcing them is difficult but necessary. But letting a teen go from a volunteer task should not mean the end (encourage that teen to get involved in other ways). Rules should not be so rigid that teens have difficulty in following them. For example, a teen who is a no-call no-show without reason should be let go, but the case is different for a teen who joins a sports team or lands a role in a play and is suddenly unable to make shifts. The latter teen could be moved to another task, offered a virtual task, or invited to come back when the season is over, whereas the former is likely someone who is not invested in the library and should probably move on to other activities.

Student trustees

Offering teens a voice on the adult library board is a win-win situation. Teens can learn about how the library works, and adults get the perspective of younger patrons. The teens can also help bring library news out into the community and provide positive public relations at events. Here are some guidelines for making the experience positive for all involved:

Allow adult board members to be involved in interviewing candidates. One board member and one staff member could be coordinators of the program. Teens could do simple reports to allow them a chance to give ideas or opinions outside of meetings. Teens should be encouraged to speak at meetings but perhaps not to vote, depending on how board members are elected or appointed in a particular state.

Have two trustees. If one cannot make meetings, be reasonable about expectations with teen commitments. Having two helps cover bases and provides different perspectives as well.

Offer some perks for being a student trustee, such as no fines for a year or dinners with authors or other presenters they may enjoy. At the same time, invite them to pose for reading posters and to appear at National Library Week events and for interviews.

Limit terms and encourage trustees to come to TAB meetings. This helps keep communication going about teen library service needs and concerns.

Encourage teens to write articles about the library for websites or their school newspapers. They could also facilitate focus groups in the community for teens.

How does the TAB fit in?

Elements of all these subgroups could be done by teen advisory board members. There may not be enough involved teens to have subgroups, so staff could help TAB members do work in each of those areas. Meetings could be themed on a particular topic. Maybe teens make the cards for soldiers at Veterans Day or work on the website before Teen Read Week. Teens may enjoy a particular task or area a great deal, and then a mini group would section off to focus on that. For example, some TAB members may love volunteering with the younger children or enjoy running video-gaming programs. All group members find their own comfort area, and staff may have interest in a particular area and fuel enthusiasm in that direction.

Duck Tape Mania sign made by teens at Asheboro (N.C.) Public Library. Flickr photo used CC BY-SA 3.0.

If a couple of subgroups have split off, they too could work together. Both the web-design group and the anime group may be interested in online animation classes. Crafters and volunteers could have crafting days where patrons of all ages could help with projects.

New interests and groups will form and change as teens grow older, and the process will begin again. The teen advisory board is a starting point, and smart staff let them lead the direction to ensure participation and positive experiences for everyone.

SOURCE: Specially prepared for *The Whole Library Handbook: Teen Services* by Amy Alessio, librarian, Schaumburg (Ill.) Township Library.

7

ISSUES

CHAPTER EIGHT

Free speech, teen issues, guy readers, sexuality, and more. Just as our society wrestles with a wide variety of issues and our teens wrestle with their issues, libraries also wrestle with issues of their own. What happens when books contain content that might be controversial? How does a library address diversity? What do we do about nonreaders? How do we connect with teen guys, so often described as reluctant library users? In this chapter, we look at a slice of the variety of issues that come up in teen services, including intellectual freedom, diversity, GLBTQ lit, guy readers, teens of color, reluctant readers, readers in detention centers, and the Relational Reading Revolution. Although we have attempted to include a representative sample of the most common issues we encounter, the variety of life situations and needs that our teens experience is vast, and we encourage readers to keep seeking out information on the topics most relevant to the lives of their teens.

Intellectual freedom and the teen librarian

by Heather Booth and Karen Jensen

THE ABILITY TO EXERCISE one's First Amendment rights to read, seek information, and speak freely is a core value of librarianship, and one that those of us working with teens cannot take lightly. As teen advocates, we stand for and with teens, defending not just their right to a space and collection within the library, but their right to read, view, and listen to what they want and need and to be able to find it in our library or to provide access to it elsewhere. It's a heavy responsibility. It's also something that we may not ever spend much time thinking about amid the day-to-day goings-on of the library, but something that most all of us will, at some point in our career, be faced with defending.

Talk to any group of teen librarians and they will share their battle stories.

- "A mom didn't want her daughter reading *ttyl*. She thought it was dirty and ran me through the wringer about it. It was my first day on the job."
- "Someone on my staff wanted a book from the teen collection removed. He had been around a lot longer than me, and I feared for my job. I needed that job."
- "A patron objected to my banned-books display on the grounds that it would encourage people to read banned books. I wanted to just tell her, 'I hope so; that's the point of the display!' but had to follow the procedure instead."
- "My challenge was like going through hell. So many feelings were hurt in the community. So much negativity was created. Even though the book was retained at the end of the process, it was hard to feel victorious."

It is fraught and frustrating but vitally important that we defend the right of teens to access what they want, and the place that these items hold in our collections.

A strong foundation

This may seem easier said than done, but if we set the right groundwork, we make our jobs easier down the road. Every library needs to have a few pieces of groundwork in place. If your library does not have one of the following documents, speaking to the administration about creating the missing piece is really important. If the administration is not interested in moving forward, creating your own set of guidelines or policies by which you work is a decent backup plan. Your library should have the following:

1. A "Materials Selection Policy" or "Collection Development Policy." A policy broad enough to cover the entire collection should suffice because the concepts will be constant across age demographics.
2. An "Intellectual Freedom Policy." This policy should spell out the library's intent to protect the intellectual freedom of its patrons and provide free and open access to the entire collection.
3. A "Materials Challenge Policy" and a "Request for Reconsideration Form." The policy should be informed by the above two documents

and spell out the steps to be taken when a patron initiates a formal challenge and submits a "Request for Reconsideration Form." This form should allow patrons to express their concerns and feelings, should request or require that the patron read or view the material in its entirety before completing the form in hopes of putting the objectionable element in context, should ask the patrons what their desired outcome would be, and should make reference to the "Materials Challenge Policy" to indicate what next steps the library will take.

Once these elements are in place, it's time to begin educating the staff—anyone who interacts with the material and the patrons—on the library's stance on intellectual freedom for teens, why it is important, and how to handle patrons who are upset about material.

Teen advocacy

When a community member challenges the right of a book to be in the library and accessible to teenagers, he or she usually does so out of a belief that children will be changed negatively by exposure to the material. Although librarians are fond of saying that "books change lives," we rarely believe that they change lives in negative ways. Remember that we have this in common with would-be book banners. We both believe that books are powerful tools in the lives of teens. The difference is that advocates of intellectual freedom also acknowledge that there is more of a chance for positive change than negative when the right book lands in the right teen's hands. As advocates for the intellectual freedom of teens, there are some shared acknowledgements that guide us.

- We acknowledge that teens have the right to put the book down when it doesn't suit their needs, interests, values, or morals.

For example, a book about the suicide of a friend may generate painful memories and cut to the bone for a teen who has experienced a similar tragedy.

- We acknowledge that teens are active agents in their own lives and are able to make judgments about their own reading, viewing, and listening material.

Extending the above example, different teens may read the same book and find the experience cathartic and freeing as they come to understand that they are not alone in their feelings. They might find solace in a resolution that reminds teens that their friend's actions were not the fault of anyone else.

- We also acknowledge that parents can and should be involved in the lives of their teens. As such, we acknowledge that not all books are as broadly welcomed in all families, and if parents choose to discourage their own child from reading a book, that is an issue between the parents and the child.

A parent who has had lengthy conversations with her child about the friend's suicide may know much better than a librarian how the teen might react to the book, and we encourage the parent to choose books that suit the emotional needs of the teen.

8

- Finally, we acknowledge that in light of the above point, no other parent or person should be given the power to discourage or limit access of any type of material to the community's teens as a whole.

The whole collection needs to be accessible to every teen so that all readers can find the material they need the most. Every library should have something for everyone, and as the saying goes, every library should also have something to offend everyone. The breadth of interests and preferences in any community is broad, and it is the responsibility of the library to provide access, and the responsibility of the individual, the teen, to make selections that meet needs and interests on an individual basis.

SOURCE: Specially prepared for *The Whole Library Handbook: Teen Services* by Heather Booth, teen services librarian, Thomas Ford Memorial Library, Western Springs, Illinois, and Karen Jensen, teen services librarian, Grand Prairie, Texas.

Evaluating materials for a diverse collection

by Christie Ross Gibrich and Heather Booth

AS WE STRIVE TO INCLUDE more diverse titles in our collections, we can sometimes be steered wrong by incomplete descriptions, inaccurate depictions, and just plain unpopular books. In our effort to add titles that mirror all of the varied and diverse lives our teens lead, we still need to be cognizant of good collection development and management strategies and work to create a collection that is not just diverse, but informative, accurate, and popular.

Once you have located materials to consider purchasing, you might be wondering how best to evaluate these books about people and cultures that may be unfamiliar to you. For the most part, the same criteria you would use for other YA materials still apply, but the following checklist is worth considering:

- Is an underrepresented character the main or a secondary character?
- Is the characterization of underrepresented characters and their culture full of clichés or does it feel accurate?
- How do reviewers, readers, or bloggers of a similar cultural background react to the book? Do they notice inaccuracies or errors? (Social media such as Goodreads or review blogs are especially useful here.)
- Does it present a fresh viewpoint, a new view?
- Are the teens and their relationships, struggles, and solutions believable?
- Does the book preach a lesson?
- Do the characters interact believably with dialogue that feels natural?
- Does it make you want to read more about people like this?
- How are the underrepresented characters treated in the book?
- Do your teens like the book?
- Does the cover art accurately represent the content of the book? Does it do so without reinforcing stereotypes?
- Will it add anything new to your collection?

SOURCE: Specially prepared for *The Whole Library Handbook: Teen Services* by Christie Ross Gibrich, senior librarian, Tony Shotwell Life Center Branch Library, Grand Prairie (Tex.) Public Libraries, and Heather Booth, teen services librarian, Thomas Ford Memorial Library, Western Springs, Illinois.

GLBTQ materials in your teen collection

by Christie Ross Gibrich

BOOKS CAN CHANGE LIVES. Teens seek out books for a variety of reasons: to escape a life that they don't want to be in, for reassurance that there are other places to go and ways to be, for the pure pleasure of dropping into somewhere else and getting into the story, to learn about something, or to make sense of their world when adults either do not or cannot.

This is especially true for teens who are gay, lesbian, bisexual, transsexual or transgender, or questioning (GLBTQ). Although teens generally will read books with GLBTQ content, GLBTQ teens comprise a specialized population that needs our services; yet such teens might not seek those services out. Although mainstream media seems to be popularizing gay characters, GLBTQ teens are at a very fractious point in their lives, and they might not know where they can turn. They might be out, or they might not be. They might know what their sexual preferences are, or they might not. They might not understand why they feel the way they do. They might be dealing with a number of factors that nobody else can ever fully understand, such as harassment and bullying to the point of torture at school, hiding their true selves at home due to fear of rejection, and alienation. Asking an adult in their lives for information, whether a trusted adult or a complete stranger, is likely to be a completely foreign—and frightening—concept.

Research by the Williams Institute in April 2011 indicated that roughly 3.5% of adult Americans identify as gay, lesbian, or bisexual, and 0.3% identify as transgender.

There are no big neon signs that tell you who is GLBTQ and who is not when patrons walk in your library doors, and unless patrons come to you and ask specifically for GLBTQ materials, you may not know that they are seeking them. That is why it is critical to have excellent GLBTQ materials in every teen collection, to have them placed and cataloged with GLBTQ subject headings within the first few subjects, and to be searchable. They must be accessible in order to serve this segment of your population. Although pundits on radio stations and in lecture halls might say that there are none of "these types" in our community, they are wrong. People are GLBTQ, are related to people who are GLBTQ, or know people who are GLBTQ who live everywhere, and they need library services just as much as everybody else. The problem is that if they do not feel welcome, or if you do not have the right materials available or easily locatable, the social stigma around the GLBTQ labels are still so distressing that they may not ask for help; they might just leave. If this person does leave, then you lose a chance to reach out or serve a teen, one who needs the library services desperately, who you never knew you had.

Every library needs a GLBTQ teen collection, no matter how small the library or how small the collection. With your collection, you serve your teens by showing through your collection that there are others out there who are going through the same things that they are going through: the same questions, the

8

same feelings, the same alienation, the same bullying. You can make the library a safe place for GLBTQ teens in many ways. Begin by structuring your collection so that it is easy to find information and by being an adult who can help find more information. Take it to the next level by adding a section on GLBTQ teens and what they go through; offer training materials, making sure your staff know how to interact with these teens and what their special needs are, and how to deal with hard questions that come up, including having ready options for teens who have been kicked out of their homes for coming out. Bring the ethic back to your teens by disallowing homophobic language, bullying, or intimidating behavior in your space or at your programs. You are creating positive experiences with these teens and meeting their needs at the same time, building a bond that can translate into a lasting relationship through adulthood.

Definitions

The terminology of GLBTQ confuses many people. Although the letters often appear in different orders, the meanings are the same.

G stands for *gay*, which primarily refers to guys who are attracted to other guys. It can also be used to refer universally to lesbians and gays.

L stands for *lesbian*, which refers to girls who are attracted to other girls.

B stands for *bisexual*, which refers to people who are attracted to both guys and girls.

T stands for two different things. First, it stands for *transgender*; this refers to people who present themselves in ways that are different from what society accepts as "traditional" for their sex. Second, T stands for *transsexuals*, those who feel that they were born into the wrong body and who may seek to change their outward appearance through medical or cosmetic means in order to match their inward gender identity.

Q can stand for *questioning*, which refers to those who are still searching to figure out who they are. They can end up straight (which refers to people who are attracted to the opposite gender); they can end up lesbian, gay, bisexual, transgender, or transsexual. Most teens will fall into this category at some point because they will have at least one same-sex crush. Q can also stand for *queer*, which refers to anyone who does not fall into the heterosexual (straight) spectrum. The use of this term can be viewed as derogatory, with its historically negative connotations, so GLBTQ teens and young adults are readopting the term for their own purposes.

A final identifier of importance is that of an *ally*. Allies are those people who stand with and support the GLBTQ community.

Finding the materials

In 2011, author Malinda Lo crunched numbers and found that GLBTQ books for teens make up only 0.6% to 1% of all YA publishing, depending on whether or not you count GLBTQ secondary characters. So how do you find these elusive GLBTQ books? More than likely, you have some of them in your collection already. GLBTQ publishing for teens has made some big strides recently, and they have been well-received by the public. Authors like David Levithan, Brent Hartinger, Ellen Hopkins, Laurie Halse Anderson, and Malinda Lo have written wonderful books dealing with GLBTQ characters and themes. Books like *Will Grayson, Will Grayson* and *Beauty Queens* have earned starred reviews from numerous publications and have made YALSA top 10 lists. Furthermore, there are awards and booklists that can help you in your search.

The Rainbow Book List. A joint committee of the American Library Association's Gay, Lesbian, Bisexual, and Transgender Round Table and Social Responsibilities Round Table, the Rainbow Book List committee publishes a recommended booklist every year at the ALA Midwinter Meeting in January. That list consists of recommended titles, fiction and nonfiction, published in the previous 18 months for youth ages birth through 18. The list is aimed at kids, but librarians are more than welcome to use the lists to build their collections. Nominations are posted throughout the year on their blog.

The Stonewall Book Award. Established in 2010, the Stonewall Book Award–Mike Morgan and Larry Romans Children's and Young Adult Literature Award is given to the best children's and young adult book for GLBTQ content. The Stonewall committee publishes not only the award winner but also the runners-up, so you will have a list of the top five books considered. Not all titles are YA, but most that make the top five have been in years past.

Lambda Literary Foundation. The Lambda Literary Foundation "nurtures, celebrates, and preserves LGBT literature through programs that honor excellence, promote visibility, and encourage development of emerging writers." Every year the foundation names the top five for its Children's/Young Adult category, and it names a winner as well.

Library journals and book reviews. Reviews are also helpful, to a point. Reviews will point out the good and bad in a book and will fulfill the requirements that many library systems have for their collection development for one or more positive reviews. Review publications like *Booklist*, *Kirkus*, *VOYA*, and *School Library Journal* routinely release the new and best of YA publications and will include GLBTQ books, especially those by more popular authors.

Reviews for GLBTQ books can be problematic. Often a book review does not point out whether or not the book has GLBTQ content, how much GLBTQ content the book contains, or the quality of the content. For example, there is GLBTQ content in the House of Night series, by P. C. Cast and Kristin Cast, but it involves secondary characters. None of the reviews mention the positive GLBTQ characters of Damien and Jack. Rachel Cohn's *Very LeFreak* has a main character who discovers romance with her same-sex roommate, but reviews in *Kirkus* and *VOYA* do not mention the GLBTQ content at all, while the *Bulletin of the Center for Children's Books*, *Booklist*, and *Horn Book* all mention the content. This is a time when you have to use your judgment in developing your collection.

The hive mind. Electronic discussion lists are also helpful. Many of the young adult librarians on Young Adult Library Services Association–Book discussion list (YALSA-BK) and YALSA Young Adult Advisory Council (YA_YAAC) have good knowledge of the current books that are coming out and can help with requests for new and interesting GLBTQ materials.

Your teens. Talk to your teens. Ask them what they're reading. Their answers might surprise you.

Blogs. Queer YA (daisyporter.org/queerya/) is a blog that focuses solely on GLBTQ books for teens, and Malinda Lo's blog (www.malindalo.com/blog/) has

8

highlighted GLBTQ YA books in publishing as well as her own works. The Rainbow Project (glbtrt.ala.org/rainbowbooks/) posts its nominations without reviews throughout the year. When using blogs as a collection development resource, be sure to check their review policy to ensure that they are credible, meaning that they don't get paid for their reviews, and that they take an honest and critical look at the materials that they write about.

Making the materials available

So you have your materials, and you are ready to put them in your collection. Have you made sure they are accessible? Consider the following pointers:

Are they searchable by GLBTQ subject headings in your catalog? GLBTQ teens may not be willing to talk to your staff about what they need, so they need another way to find the material. If the materials are not properly cataloged and easily searchable, then your patrons are unlikely to find them.

Make sure that your library has a reconsideration (challenge) procedure and that all of your staff members know both the procedures and the steps to follow if a challenge is filed. Although we like to think that our communities are open-minded, there are incidents within libraries every month about GLBTQ books being challenged because of their content, regardless of how many positive reviews or awards they have earned.

Make sure to include your GLBTQ materials on your bibliographies. When you create flyers and bookmarks, think about what books would fit, and add them just as you would any other book. If they fit the theme (such as relationships, scary stories, bullying, sports, and so forth), then include them. Having them listed on your GLBTQ bibliographies is great, but that should not be the only place where they are listed. Treating GLBTQ materials exactly the same as all other subjects is vital.

Include your GLBTQ materials in your programming. Just because you have them on your shelves does not mean that your patrons know that you have them at all. Give booktalks about them at the schools, sell them to your teens, showcase them in your displays, and include them in any programming that you're having. Are you hosting a poetry and coffee night? There is no reason why a book of YA GLBTQ poetry should not be there with the others. Are you talking about relationship safety? Include the books about queer dating. Are you having a college night? Invite a chapter of the Gay-Straight Alliance from the college as well, so its members can talk to the teens, or at least have the alliance's information available for those who might want it.

Conclusion

Books change lives, and nowhere is that more true than with GLBTQ teens. Teens looking for reassurance can pick up a book with positive relationships and know that something is out there for them beyond what they are experiencing, or get answers to their questions. Building a GLBTQ collection is an important part of a teen–young adult services librarian's career, and treating the materials just like any other material in your collection is vital. Just because it's a GLBTQ book doesn't mean it's a good one, but with the tools and tricks outlined above, and the resources below, you have a wonderful base on which to build your start.

You know your population and your teens. The most important advice in young adult services is always this: Trust yourself. Be open to change, and they will start seeking you out for your information.

SOURCE: Specially prepared for *The Whole Library Handbook: Teen Services* by Christie Ross Gibrich, senior librarian, Tony Shotwell Life Center Branch Library, Grande Prairie (Tex.) Public Libraries.

Boys in collection development and library service

by Torrey Maldonado

MY DAD WAS A NONREADER, so was his dad, so were my friends' dads, and so on. If we took a tour of my family and where I'm from, you'll see the number of guys who seem to be nonreaders is so huge that if we all sat on each other's shoulders, our guy-ladder would tower into space. Is it a problem? It may be better if we see it as a rubber-band ball, and each band is an issue regarding guys reading that adds to a mess that is today's massive guy nonreadership. Are so many guys really nonreaders? Well, let's twang some of those rubber-band issues.

First, we're misidentified as nonreaders because a lot of great "guy books" and "reads" that we enjoy are overlooked and aren't promoted in schools. My novel—*Secret Saturdays*—made a few top-10 best-book lists. Guys treat it as if it's a swag item. Yet many won't see it because of old-school purchasing setups, where new, relevant "guy books" rarely blip on radars. There's another rubber-band-issue, where we've all heard people say, "Well, even if I gave [said guy] a great book, he won't read it." That addresses a truth: many guys do dislike reading. I hated to read for the same reasons a lot of guys do— it was tough (at first) and, also, across the United States, a stereotype of manliness is celebrated that paints guys as effeminate if we're avid readers. So guys do what a young me did and chase athleticism or "the bling" while recoiling from literacy. The NBA star Carmelo Anthony is from my hometown; so is a *New York Times* bestselling author. The athlete returned, and hundreds of guys lined up to see him. When the author returned, three guys did. Can we ever untangle all the issues to achieve massive guy readership? Sure! It starts with us shifting our approach to guys and reading. We periodically bring up the topic; however, this problem is enduring so our efforts in fixing it should be enduring.

Allergen-free books for guys

At a signing, a guy proudly told me, "I read your book in a day." That impressed me so I said, "*Wow!* You always read that fast?" He replied, "Nah. I hate books. I'm allergic to books." He saw himself as a nonreader, and others labeled him one, too. He reminded me of the young me and guys I know and others from across our country. That's partly why guys in remote suburbs, rural, and urban areas where I have never visited tell me, "Your book is about my life!" I write what will magnetize the reluctant-reader boy in me, and it seems guys like him get drawn in, too. I also write in *Secret Saturdays* about a theme that plays out in the lives of most guys so there's another point of guy-interest.

8

As a teacher, I'm interested in what hooks guys to books so I've listened to what my "hit guy author" friends say hooked them as young readers, and, interestingly, it's what hooked me, it's what we publish today, and it's what a well-rounded teen collection needs to contain. These elements and categories include fictional characters and dialogue that feels real, books that are cool for guys to be seen carrying, books with chapters as long as the attention spans of today's readership, comics and graphic novels, and thinner books. A myth exists that one "guy's book" is for all guys. With guys, what librarians and educators and my mom tried on me still works, and that's this: "The best salesperson is your peer." Most guys want what their friends have, and, similarly, they want to read what their peers read.

So, my approach is I suggest a "read" almost the way a doctor prescribes medicine: I figure out what issue a guy is struggling with; then I recommend books that similar guys say address his issue.

Positioning the library so guys will listen

My slogan is "GRWGR": "Guys Read What Guys Read." Most guys are into what their friends do. Libraries can branch this seed-idea into tons of ways to link guys to books, starting with bulletin boards. I've seen guys of all ages stop and get engrossed in boards! If a little "me" would've seen a "Top-10 Guys' List" bulletin board with photos of real guys from my school who I admired with their favorite reads, I would've gone straight to the librarian and checked out one of those titles.

Let's have a "Guys Read Fair," where teens "man" tables and their peers tour to see what guys enjoy reading. Recently, I saw a bulletin board that had a banner saying, "Top 25 Most Checked-Out Books." From afar it looked *so cool!* I had to get closer, and when I did, I realized the book I wrote was number one! I was picked over books-to-movies! As much as I loved the "top spot," I wanted to see the students' 24 other picks. I bet guys want to know what their "top-25" favorite male celebrities read. Cue research activities or letter- or email-writing campaigns where guys learn what their favorite celebrities enjoy. Those findings could become a bulletin board. Picture it—"Top 25 Most Read Books by [insert athletes, musicians, actors, etc., here]." These are just some ways we can connect guys and books.

Putting books at center court

Picture a gym full of teen-guy basketball players who just did drills. They're reclining and horsing around. In walks their basketball-program director and a stranger in semiformal attire. One teen barks, "Who's he?!" Another ribs his friend about the stranger: "Why's he dressed for church?" Jokes firework across the crowd about the strange guy. The guy is introduced and starts talking, and soon, all the teens are riveted and sitting up, and they tell the stranger, "Read more!" and they ask, "Where can I get that book?" and "You know other books like that?" That happened this summer; I'm the stranger. The head of a basketball program fell for my book and emailed, saying he had a captive group of guys and hoped I'd come "give them a shot in the arm of literacy." The result: We hooked them to my book and then kept them hooked with follow-ups with similar books.

Going to where guys are works. It is also tough. Do you know how scary it is to stand center court and booktalk in a half-time sports event where athletes just did aerial stunts? But I rely on an approach that serves me. To connect with guys, less is best, and elicit conversation. Since guys have been absent from these talks, once in, let them talk. I see libraries setting up "Teen Centrals" to draw guys in and empower them to make reading lists, inform smarter book purchases, and more. So where to find guys? Social media, after-school visits, town halls, residential facilities, college-camps, jails—really, wherever they are.

Enduring solutions

If we want better men, we must get more guys reading. If my students were here, they'd be able to finish the following quote because I say it so much. "Your attitude will determine your . . ." "*Altitude!*" they'd chant. Not reading builds a small-minded attitude. Not reading is why so many guys' worldview is their zip code. Not reading maintains "the Boy Crisis," the widespread retarding of male development—socially, academically, and professionally—by discouraging males from being academic. I survived "the Boy Crisis"; my father didn't. We both were pressured to follow the crowd, and the crowd felt books equaled school, and school equaled corny or a "girl's thing." My father didn't have a supermom like mine and others to help him get hooked to books. Our different attitudes toward reading made us reach different altitudes, meaning social heights. We both grew up poor. He dropped out of junior high school. I was a welfare kid in a housing project that *Life* magazine in 1988 called the "Crack Capital of the U.S.," and reading helped me cross the tracks to become the first person in my family to attend and graduate from college. I'm now a veteran teacher and book author.

Reading will do wonders for any guy who gets hooked to books. There's a saying: "Where the mind goes, the 'behind' follows." First I read about places, then craved to really see them. Research also proves readers become leaders. I saw a piece where if a guy reads 20 minutes a day, he can add 2 million words to his vocabulary; and in a year, he'll read for 60 school days. If a guy reads 5 minutes a day he'll only read for 12 school days and may gain 300,000 words. If a guy reads 1 minute a day, that equals 180 minutes of reading per school year, and he'll add about 8,000 words. Which guys do you think will be more successful in life—readers or nonreaders?

SOURCE: Specially prepared for *The Whole Library Handbook: Teen Services* by Torrey Maldonado, teacher, New York City.

Collection development mindful of people of color in YA literature
by Debbie Reese

THE AMERICAN LIBRARY ASSOCIATION'S *Core Values of Librarianship* includes this statement: "We value our nation's diversity and strive to reflect that diversity by providing a full spectrum of resources and services to the communities we serve" (ala.org/advocacy/intfreedom/statementspols/corevalues). Striving for that spectrum is not easy for many reasons. Take the title of this section. What does "people of color" mean? Does it mean books by writers who are

8

people of color? Or does it mean books that feature protagonists of color? What if the protagonist is white and one of her friends is African American, American Indian, Asian American, or Latino/Latina American? Does that book count as one about people of color? Does it mean books about people of color and their lives? What if the protagonist happens to be African American but the story has nothing at all to do with African American culture, history, or issues of concern to African Americans or their cultural and political allies? Giving some thought to these questions will help you build a library that can help teens develop into well-rounded citizens who are knowledgeable and respectful of our nation's diversity in a deep—rather than superficial—way.

Purchasing and promoting books about people of color by authors of color provides the opportunity to introduce readers to an author of color and the body of his or her work, but it does more than that. It sends a powerful message to publishers that librarians want books by authors of color. It does not mean librarians do *not* want books told by writers who are outside of a given group, because rejecting a book simply on the identity of its author is never acceptable.

However, books by authors of color do double duty. The story an author of color tells is important, but that author's personal story is equally important, particularly to readers who share that author's identity. Students from minority populations drop out of school in higher numbers than white students, who are more likely to see themselves reflected in books. Providing students of color with books by authors of color provides that reflection for them while also providing them with a model of success. Books by authors of color can also educate readers who carry misinformation or stereotypical ideas about that author's cultural, racial, or national identity.

For example, a great many people do not know that *American Indian* and *Native American* are overly broad terms that obscure the important differences that exist among the more than 500 federally recognized tribal nations in the United States.

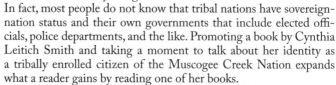

In fact, most people do not know that tribal nations have sovereign-nation status and their own governments that include elected officials, police departments, and the like. Promoting a book by Cynthia Leitich Smith and taking a moment to talk about her identity as a tribally enrolled citizen of the Muscogee Creek Nation expands what a reader gains by reading one of her books.

Since the 1960s, there have been several efforts to provide librarians with critical reviews that point to accurate books about people of color and that point out stereotypes, biases, and errors in books about people of color. The Council on Interracial Books for Children was founded in 1965 and published its *Bulletin* from 1967 through 1985, and it also published an outstanding tool, "Ten Quick Ways to Analyze Children's Books for Racism and Sexism," which librarians can study and apply to their evaluation tool kit. It's available online at readingspark.wordpress .com/adoption-childrens-literature/ten-quick-ways-to-analyze-childrens-books-for-racism-and-sexism/. *Multicultural Review* was published from 1992 though 2008. Though both publications are out of print, they remain a gold mine of information. Consulting them can help you evaluate your existing collection.

Librarian Nancy Larrick wrote "The All White World of Children's Books," *Saturday Review,* September 11, 1965, pp. 63–65, 84–85, in which she said that more than six million "nonwhite children are learning to read and to understand the American way of life in books which either omit them entirely or scarcely mention them." If you find that your shelves are "all white" or perhaps too white, these suggestions may help in your quest to bring your library into alignment with ALA's value statement.

Study the criteria developed by associations whose book awards look critically at people of color, and read books they select for their awards. Incorporate and apply what you learn to your evaluation of other books by and about people of color.

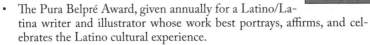

- The American Indian Youth Literature Book Award, given biennially to honor the very best writing and illustration by and about American Indians.
- The Asian/Pacific American Award for Literature, given biennially to books related to the Asian/Pacific American experience in historical or contemporary time periods.
- The Coretta Scott King Book Award, given annually to African American authors and illustrators whose books demonstrate an appreciation of African American culture.
- The Pura Belpré Award, given annually for a Latino/Latina writer and illustrator whose work best portrays, affirms, and celebrates the Latino cultural experience.

Spend time on websites that provide substantive information about multicultural populations:

- At the "Multicultural Literature" web page of the Cooperative Children's Book Center (CCBC) in the School of Education at the University of Wisconsin, you'll find links to "30 Multicultural Books Every Teen Should Know," "Small Presses of Color," "Recommended Websites," and, an outstanding bibliography of professional books about multicultural literature (ccbc.education.wisc.edu/books/multicultural.asp). Take time to look at their annual statistics page, too, where CCBC reports on the numbers of books by and about people of color. If you've found that your shelves are "too white," you might take comfort in knowing that CCBC finds very little is being published. That realization should galvanize you to buy books by and about authors of color, sending that message to publishers that librarians value these books.
- At Cynthia Leitich Smith's website (www.cynthialeitichsmith.com/lit_resources/diversity/multiracial/multi_race_intro.html), you'll find a collection of links to resources on several multicultural populations, including her pages on books with interracial family themes.
- Two of the leading social justice organizations that librarians ought to become familiar with are Rethinking Schools (www.rethinkingschools. org) and Teaching for Change (www.teachingforchange.org). Both provide print and internet resources on people of color.

Subscribe to blogs that focus on books by and about people of color.

- American Indians in Children's Literature (www.americanindiansinchildrensliterature.net).
- The Brown Bookshelf (thebrownbookshelf.com).
- Crazy QuiltEdi (campbele.wordpress.com).
- The Happy Nappy Bookseller (thehappynappybookseller.blogspot.com).
- Imagínense Libros: Celebrating Latino Children's Literature, Literacy, and Libraries (imaginenselibros.blogspot.com).

8

- Paper Tigers (www.papertigers.org/wordpress/).
- Reading In Color (blackteensread2.blogspot.com).

SOURCE: Specially prepared for *The Whole Library Handbook: Teen Services* by Debbie Reese, founder of the Native American House and American Indian studies program at the University of Illinois at Urbana-Champaign.

Reaching reluctant readers, like me

by Kelly Milner Halls

I WAS A ROWDY LITTLE KID, growing up in Texas—a whirlwind, hardly still for a waking moment; a night owl more likely to doze during the day after playing all night. I had a gate on my bedroom door until I started school for just that reason—just so my parents and my sister could rest. But, oh how my mother loved me.

Squirrely as I was, she still took me to the public library, regularly. Once a week, I could check out five different books—a big, fat stack—and for seven days, those books belonged to me. I could build book forts, I could look at the pictures, I could sound out the words, I could "read" them with my mom. It didn't matter to her, as long as I explored each one before I checked out the next five.

With my mom, I was a wild thing, but I was never a reluctant reader. I *loved* books. Then I started school.

In the academic setting, books came with strings attached. At school, I couldn't always choose to read the books that captured my imagination. And at school, my choices were far more limited. At school, I had to read books I was assigned. The cloud descended with dark gray intensity. I became a reluctant reader.

It didn't happen overnight. Even at school, I loved nonfiction books about Abraham Lincoln, mummies, and reptiles. But once those titles were exhausted, once I had to read fiction almost exclusively—even simple fiction like Dick and Jane—I felt lost and alienated. In my mind, there were no books that were meant for me. I came to believe I did not like to read.

So I struggled through 1st grade, 2nd grade, and 3rd grade, convinced reading was a painful duty without a scrap of reward for the effort. Then my 4th-grade teacher performed a miracle. She read *Charlotte's Web,* by E. B. White aloud, and to me she had the voice of an angel. I saw myself in Fern, the little girl who loved animals more than people. I learned that reading could pay off, if you found the right book.

Alas, finding the right book was never easy for me. In fact, the only other book I remember from elementary school is Anna Sewell's masterpiece, *Black Beauty.* I loved looking at life from the stallion's point of view. I loved that he demanded kindness for animals and people alike. But it was the last book that offered me universal connection until I read James Clavell's *Shogun* as a senior in high school.

I couldn't find books that seemed to be written just for me. Librarians then were not the librarians of today.

Fast-forward to my life's work as a full-time children's writer known for writing quirky, weird nonfiction, and you might ask yourself, "How did a reluctant reader grow up to write?" The answer is remarkably simple. I write the books I do today for the child I was half a century ago. I write the books I would have loved but never found. And I see myself in the faces of the kids who embrace them.

I see myself in the boy from New Hampshire who loved *Alien Investigation*. Dressed in camo shorts, snow boots, and a goose-down vest to brave -10° F. temperatures outside, he literally twirled as he left my school-visit presentation, yelling. "Best," twirl. "Day," twirl. "Ever," twirl. Prelude to a gleeful but speedy exit.

I see myself in the boy from Oregon who skipped lunch to talk with me, just a little longer, about *In Search of Sasquatch*.

"Won't your friends miss you at lunch?" I asked him.

"I don't have any friends," he explained, pushing his glasses up the bridge of his nose. "I'm too bright for them to understand me. I'm brighter than 87% of all students my age"—echoes of reassurances from home. "But I am astonished to admit it. You, Kelly Milner Halls, may love facts as much as I do."

I see myself in the bouncy girl from Washington already labeled a troublemaker by her teacher's aide. "Watch out for this one," the aide said to me, as the girl listened. "She's a bad seed. I'll be sure she sits in the back with me so she won't disturb you."

Imagine that aide's surprise when I called the "bad seed" up from exile to be my very high-spirited presentation assistant, and the same girl's smile when I told her I was just like her when I was young.

I see myself in Leo, raised by his grandmother, who never checked out a book until he found *Tales of the Cryptids*. "I never thought the day would come," he told me in a quiet moment.

"What day is that?" I asked him.

"The day when I would meet someone like me," he replied.

I choked back a lump in my throat and answered, "It feels good not to be alone, doesn't it?"

"It does," he whispered. "It really, really does."

I recognize my books may never win the awards created to honor young-reader nonfiction. The unconventional topics that draw my readers to me seem to repel award committee members. And I understand that. As carefully researched and written as they are, they do defy children's book convention. But I am happy.

My accolades are etched on the faces of those reluctant readers who find comfort in the pages of my books—and in the faces of the devoted librarians who skillfully match readers to reads. My trophies are letters anointing me the "best writer ever." My prize is the knowledge that one kid out there feels a little less alone than he used to, because of my books. In that context, I'm a bona fide success. And that context is good enough for me.

SOURCE: Specially prepared for *The Whole Library Handbook: Teen Services* by Kelly Milner Halls, nonfiction writer, Spokane, Washington.

Critical issues in juvenile detention center libraries
by Jeanie Austin

LIBRARIES IN JUVENILE DETENTION CENTERS have increasingly become a focus for research. This article provides a theoretical framework for providing library services to youth housed in juvenile detention centers, deconstructs the idea of "neutrality" in these library services, and establishes librarianship as a locus for social and political change.

8

The public library is often described as politically neutral and serving the democratic role of providing access to all, independent of race, class, sexuality, or ability. But a library is not always neutral. Instead, it can perpetuate practices that continue to privilege white, middle-class, male, heterosexual, and able-bodied populations. Librarians hoping to meet the needs and interests of all potential users must be aware of these issues.

This article derives from my own work with a juvenile detention center library, but it addresses much broader issues in youth advocacy.

At the national scale, there exist large racial and educational disparities between youth in detention centers and their counterparts in the general public. A census taken on February 24, 2010, showed that there were 24,119 youth under age 21 in juvenile detention centers; 17,061 of those youth were identified as races other than white (black, Hispanic, American Indian, Asian, Pacific Islander, and

other). In total, 20,312 were male, and 14,604 of those males were classified as youth of color. An obvious disparity exists for black males, who make up 41% of the juvenile detention center population, compared to 14% of the general population for the same age range. Additionally, youth in detention centers are more likely than youth in the general public to fail to enroll in school or to function at levels beneath their educational level.

This may be due, at least in part, to the "school-to-prison pipeline" described by Johanna Wald and Daniel J. Losen in a special 2003 issue of *New Directions for Youth Development* that concentrated on this topic. Within the pipeline, a disproportionate number of poor and minority youth (mostly male) are likely to encounter disciplinary actions (expulsion and suspension) that, coupled with complicated review processes for readmission, limit their ability to return. School administrators and teachers use such factors as race, dress, friendships, and medical or psychological assessments to establish a level of dangerousness that influence their decisions to expel or suspend. Educators also see youth of color as a threat to their control of the classroom. All of these factors make it more likely that youth will be detained or incarcerated.

The juvenile detention center library can act as a proving ground for deterring experiences that are punitive and isolating for poor and minority youth. Librarians in detention centers can interrupt the flow of youth from schools into prisons by teaching expected behavior, by being culturally competent, and by involving multiple stakeholders.

Disrupting the school-to-prison pipeline is a political goal that defies the notion of library neutrality. In order to work against racial inequalities, juvenile detention center librarians must work with youth to enhance their information literacy skills, explain how and why rules may vary from setting to setting, build the library collection collaboratively, provide culturally competent books that speak to the youth's lived experiences, offer opportunities for transformation and reflection, and determine how youth can contribute to collection development even as they are mediated (consciously or unconsciously) by their setting.

Critical issues

Research on this topic has focused on advocating for libraries in juvenile detention centers, developing best practices, and positioning the library within the juvenile justice system. Other articles examine outreach and programming. Collectively, these works address such critical issues as reading levels, life experiences, interests, physical removal from community resources, and the racial makeup of populations. Youth in the detention center are physically removed from the library and often have limited access to materials. Providing library services to such an underserved population is important in addressing inequalities.

One way to create self-esteem and a positive self-image for children of color is to provide non-Eurocentric representations in picture books. But these representations are often not available. To meet their needs, books must be culture-conscious and reflect the uniqueness and universality of children's experiences.

The same holds true for materials selected for youth in the juvenile detention center. Books that do not include culturally conscious information will, at best, not interest these youth, and at worst may perpetuate power imbalances that deeply affect black male youth. Some books may be culturally competent but fail to link universal experiences to individual experiences. Books that fail to recognize the role of race, racism, and real life in character development may leave youth feeling ostracized.

Relevant reading materials should resonate with youth culture, offer insight into society and politics, contribute to an individual's well-being, discuss collective struggle, provide a model for living, and portray the world realistically.

Life within the detention center is riddled with a different set of stresses and restrictions than those encountered outside. Youth may thus be more inclined to read in the library in order to remain occupied during times of inactivity. Reading serves multiple functions: It enables escapism, transformation, comparison, relationships to characters, and potentially validates or diminishes the reader. This occurs through a process of identity restructuring.

In working toward social transformation, juvenile detention center librarians must be aware of how new knowledge is created, how youth voice and silence can be mediated by context, and how library services can be strengthened by providing programming that supports multiple community resources.

Narratives that surround the juvenile detention center as a setting will shape or limit the types of books that youth express an interest in reading. Narratives of success or failure, reform or recidivism, will influence their choices.

Youth in the center may engage in strategic silences. This can be prompted by a worry that sharing information will affect their sentencing. They may also seek to hide their literacy skills, refuse to fit into specific labels, or resist narratives that involve the detention center setting. Librarians should not assume that youth are always able to freely provide information about their reading preferences.

Interactions with librarians offer youth an opportunity to express their opinions about the library, its organization, and the collection. Librarians can use these conversations to learn more about how youth are using materials and services. Collection development and library organization can then occur in cooperation with youth, rather than a top-down or prescriptive process.

Library services in the detention center take place within a complex institutionalized justice system that may limit or prevent access to certain types of materials, especially audio materials, internet access, and the use of computer databases. If available, computer access can extend the library collection and provide opportunities for librarians and youth to work together to develop such skills as search techniques that will be useful after youth leave the detention center. These

8

skills can be explicitly linked to local organizations that will support youth upon their release, such as public libraries and community centers. Such interactions provide an opportunity to discuss individual learning experiences that counteract the isolation youth may feel in other educational spaces.

Access to specific technologies may involve increased surveillance that limits reflective and transformative thought. To counteract this, librarians can find ways to discuss the content with youth afterwards.

Youth in these centers are physically removed from resources. Library programming can focus on linking youth to relevant community resources that will be available to them upon their release. Public libraries and community centers may prove essential for youth who do not return to formal educational settings.

Conversely, organizations that could be beneficial to youth in detention centers may not be aware of any opportunities to provide services to them. Juvenile detention center librarians can provide outreach services to bridge this gap in awareness by reaching out to appropriate institutions. Outside organizations and individuals can offer fresh suggestions on what materials should be included in the library collection. These relationships can build a critical awareness of the issues surrounding juvenile justice in the larger community.

Conclusion

Many librarians providing services in juvenile detention centers are undoubtedly aware of some or all of these issues. They skillfully navigate setting, collection development, and the complexity of youth voice and community involvement to provide library services in the best interests of youth in the center. From a review of best practices, however, it seems that much of this knowledge is tacitly held and accumulated through experience. Framing the juvenile detention center library as a site for interrupting the school-to-prison pipeline not only validates the knowledge of juvenile detention center librarians, but is also persuasive in conversations that dispute the function of juvenile detention center library services, that label youth in the detention center as unarguably dangerous, and that contest the need for additional library services or staffed libraries.

Librarians are uniquely positioned to provide access to information about the ways in which a variety of institutions have been shaped by issues of oppression, raise public awareness, and facilitate social and political change. Librarians working as advocates, for youth or for all library patrons, will gain invaluable insight through this understanding, and will be better able to address critical issues in their own communities or patron bases. Developing meaningful and diverse collections, incorporating a variety of theoretical approaches into library services, understanding the social and political processes that continue to privilege specific populations, and making available information that describes alternatives to the current distribution of power—these are ways in which librarians can work to ensure that the library serves a role in social and political transformation.

SOURCE: Jeanie Austin, "Critical Issues in Juvenile Detention Libraries," *Journal of Research on Libraries and Young Adults,* July 20, 2012, online at yalsa.ala.org/jrlya/2012/07/critical-issues-in-juvenile-detention-center-libraries/. This paper was originally presented at the ALA 2012 Midwinter Meeting during YALSA's Midwinter Paper Presentation on Trends Impacting Young Adult Services. Jeanie Austin is teen librarian with Oakland (Calif.) Public Library and a PhD student at University of Illinois at Urbana-Champaign GSLIS.

Social media and the Relational Reading Revolution

by Karen Jensen

SOCIAL MEDIA IS CHANGING the book culture. It gives readers a chance to voice their opinions and be heard on a much larger scale. It changes the way we can do things like hosting book clubs, sharing book reviews, and even interacting with authors. In fact, social media is making authors much more accessible than they have ever been before. Several years ago, I jumped on Twitter and realized that a revolution was happening, a Relational Reading Revolution. If I were to diagram how social media is changing book culture, I would draw a triangle, with the three points of the triangle representing author, reader, and librarian.

I began recognizing the first waves of the revolution simply enough: A teen walked in and told me that she loved a certain book, and I tweeted a picture of said teen to the author. Occasionally, the author tweeted back. All of a sudden, I became a superhero with magical powers! I brought teens into contact with authors—people who seemed inaccessible. And with that, I became someone of greater import in the life of the teen. Tweet by tweet, I began building relationships and learning more about their reading interests. And with the influx of book bloggers and tweeters online, I learned more and more about new and related books to recommend to my teen readers.

Counteracting the culture of celebrity

We live in a culture that is overly obsessed with celebrity. We put these people up on a pedestal and give them such importance that we diminish ourselves and those around us because we can never be like *them*. Teens are growing up being told that the best thing they can be, the best goal they can achieve, is to be rich and famous. Not a good person. Not a smart person. Not a good citizen or friend or the person to change the world in meaningful ways. Just rich and famous. But when authors reach out to readers, to teens, they break down that barrier and change the message. They change the goals. By allowing themselves to be more human, more accessible, they show us all that they are just like us—just ordinary people who have the ability to write. What a powerful message this is to our teens. It is so powerful that it can counteract the culture of celebrity that teens grow up in and help them be willing to embrace themselves, no matter who they may be.

Extending the story through relationships

In addition to entering into relationships with readers, authors open the doors of dialogue. The story doesn't have to end when you turn the last page. No, now you can much more easily read how authors research elements of their books, why they choose to write the stories they write, and how you can go about doing it yourself. You can follow authors' progress as they work on current books and share more deeply in their anticipation at the reveal of the cover art and joy when the books are finally released.

8

So how can librarians participate in this Relational Reading Revolution?

1. Talk to your teens honestly about your experiences as a reader. Share what you love, what you don't, and why. Always ask them what they are reading and loving. Of course, you need to read YA books, or graphic novels, or whatever it is your teens are reading, for this first step to even happen.

2. Follow your favorite—and your teens' favorite—authors on Twitter or Facebook, subscribe to their blogs, and bookmark their web pages. Share updates with your teens either personally or on the library's social-media outlets.

3. Help teens make connections. Tweet a message to an author from a teen. Or encourage teens to write a fan letter (most authors have an email on their web pages). Say thank you—and have teens say thank you—when an author does respond. Be sure to remind teens that authors are busy, they have lives and families and tech issues like the rest of us, if they don't respond.

4. Have teens get involved with the story—and authors—by creating artwork based on their favorite books. A lot of authors tweet some of the fan-made artwork they receive (or share them on blogs, Tumblr, etc.), and it enhances the creative journey for us all. Imagine how excited your teens will be to get a response from an author about their artwork.

5. When new books from your teens' favorite authors come out, know who reads what and place holds for them, and give them personalized service. Talk up prereleases when you hear about them. Keep your teens excited about books and reading.

Authors invite readers into the creative process and encourage them to open their eyes and see the layers in the process. There is such an educational richness in this.

This relational readership allows us to feel that we are part of not only the story, but of the author's life. Because teens feel that they have a relationship with authors they like, they have another reason to become dedicated readers. When these favorite authors write a book, teens will read it because they are fans.

The value of time and effort

When authors interact with readers, they are sending a very important message: you are worth the time and effort to engage with; you have value. Teens don't often feel like the adults in this world really value them. One simple act of kindness, sending a 140-character tweet or calling them by name while signing a book, helps them know that they have value. As much as the story in itself is a gift, so are those precious seconds when someone they look up to takes a moment to engage them. We can help our teens build these relationships by using our resources to help them connect with their favorite authors. Follow authors and publishers online so you can find the information and can share it with the teens who follow you.

Different pathways, same goals

Here's the thing about authors and librarians—in some ways, we have a lot in common. We are both trying to get teens reading. One of my best tools is to build a relationship with my teens. As we talk and share books we love, they come to me and ask what I recommend. And I am coming to understand that one of the greatest tools an author has is the same: a relationship. As we share stories, and share our love of stories, we are building a Relational Reading Revolution.

SOURCE: Specially prepared for *The Whole Library Handbook: Teen Services* by Karen Jensen, teen services librarian, Grand Prairie, Texas.

APPENDICES

Appendix A
A sample teen services plan
by Karen Jensen

DEFINITIONS. For the purposes of teen programming and services, the library defines *teens* as anyone entering grade 6 through the completion of grade 12 in accordance with the local school district.

Understanding teen patrons. The teenage years are a time of great change. Teens are trying on a variety of roles and determining their identity; they are behaving in a peer-oriented manner, becoming more independent, and developing a stronger sense of right and wrong. Hormones cause a variety of changes. In addition, research indicates that teenagers use a different part of their brains; they literally think differently than adults do. For information on the teenage brain and how it influences behavior, visit www.nimh.nih.gov/health/publications/the-teen-brain-still-under-construction/index.shtml.

Goals and objectives of teen services

- To create developmentally appropriate and appealing collections, services, and opportunities for teens in our community.
- To meet the developmental, emotional, social, educational, entertainment, and information needs of teens in our community.
- To introduce teens to the library and develop lifelong library users and supporters.
- To provide unique experiences for teens that are developmentally appropriate and provide social opportunities for teens to interact with their peer group. These positive experiences help teens develop positive attitudes about the library.

Programming and contests. Throughout the year we offer a variety of programs and contests. All programs and contests vary to meet the diverse needs and interests of teens grades 6–12. There is a special emphasis on the teen summer reading club each summer and Teen Read Week, which is the third week in October (ala.org/yalsa/).

General notes about programming:

- Hands-on, interactive programs, such as crafts, games, and contests, are more popular than static programs, such as speakers.
- Parents are allowed to stay with their teens during programs. However, younger siblings and adults without teenage children are not permitted to attend to help maintain the safety and enjoyment of teens participating in the program and to maximize the use of limited space.
- Contests are a type of self-directed program that allow teens to work at their own pace while offering them the opportunity to explore library resources, develop research skills, and cultivate their talents.

Registering for programs and turning in written contests:

- Some programs may require registration. This is indicated on the flyers, and all registration takes place at the reference desk. When registering teen patrons, get complete information, including name, grade, telephone number, and information on how they found out about the program.
- Patrons are called the weekend before a program to verify they are still planning to attend.
- If registration is full, up to 10 patrons will be placed on a waiting list. These patrons will be notified the day of the program if space becomes available to them.
- All written contests are turned in at the reference desk. They will not be accepted after closing time on the date indicated on the contest.

Teen coffeehouses. During the school year, we offer a "Teen Coffeehouse" on Tuesdays after school from 3:00 to 4:30 p.m. This has proven to be a popular program in the past. We have an average of 60 teens participate on a weekly basis. Teens are invited to hang out, play games, or work on their homework, and snacks are offered.

Outreach to the schools. We endeavor to reach our target audience during the school year through the public school system. This allows the greatest opportunity to reach a large group of teens with the least amount of cost. Some of the ways we utilize the school system follow:

- Faxing announcements to all schools in the county for upcoming programs, etc.
- Visiting schools.
- Booktalking.
- Working with teachers to produce bibliographies, etc., on specific units or topics of interest to teens or for curriculum support.
- Providing teacher services.

A note about booktalking. A booktalk is a verbal introduction to a book that can last from 30 seconds to several minutes. This dramatic presentation, sometimes including reading from the book itself, introduces teens to a book and gives them just enough information to make them want to check out the book and find out what happened.

- A minimum of three weeks' notice is suggested to schedule a booktalk visit.
- All teachers must talk to the teen services librarian to schedule booktalks.

Teen readers' advisory. Teens today live in a very visual age and utilize technology more than previous generations. It is an increasing struggle to attract teens to the print medium of the book. All reference staff provides basic readers' advisory services to teens. You can utilize the readers' advisory pamphlets provided in the teen area as well as various resources online. When helping teens select books please remember the following:

- Try to provide the teen readers with a couple of choices. Teens who choose books on their own are more likely to read the entire book and enjoy the reading experience.
- Use terminology such as "other teens have enjoyed" and "is popular" to appeal to teen's interest.

Helping teens find and select books:

- Check on the library blog for reading lists on a variety of topics, including inspirational fiction, historical fiction, books for guys, and books for girls, along with books recommended by grade level.
- Read the inside front cover or back cover for a brief synopsis of the book. Pay attention to the topics of the book and the age of the characters. Books with younger teen characters or middle-school settings will deal with situations and subject matters common among this age group. Similarly, books dealing with older teen characters and high school settings will deal with situations and subject matters common among this age group.
- Look up books that interest you in the library's catalog. When you find the title you are looking for, select "details," and you can find subject headings, a brief summary, and sometimes even book excerpts.
- Investigate titles by reading book reviews online. Book reviews can be found online at Amazon or Barnes and Noble. Reviews provided are by professional journals, such as the *School Library Journal*, and other readers, often teens. The online site for *VOYA*, a journal that deals exclusively with book titles of interest to teens, is www.voyamagazine.com.

Teen web page. Teens today are very electronically connected. The teen web page seeks to be a virtual library for teens in our community. We utilize the following technology to help meet the interests of our teen patrons:

- The Teen Web Page—basic program information.
- The Teen Blog—book reviews, basic program information, photos, links, etc.
- The Teen Scene Facebook page—announcements of upcoming programs or books, daily communication.

Teen collection. The teen collection currently focuses on fiction, graphic novels, and audiobooks. There is a small, focused collection of teen nonfiction that covers spirituality, friendship and peer relations, crafts, and so forth. Basic school (academic support) information is interfiled with the adult nonfiction so that teens can find a wide variety of academic resources in one location.

Teens' interests and abilities are as varied as any other age group, and our collection reflects that. The library's policy maintains an adherence to intellectual freedom standards and supports the right of parents to guide their teen's reading selections, as stated in the library's policy. If there are any concerns about materials in the teen area, please follow the library's materials challenge policy.

Merchandising (shelving) in the teen area. Teens are visually oriented and motivated, and we strive to maximize our face-out displays to promote materials and increase circulation.

Miscellaneous information about teen services

- Parents are responsible for helping their teens select appropriate books. The library does not endorse specific titles, nor does it act in loco parentis.
- If you notice that a lot of teens are requesting a book title or asking for specific types of information to complete an assignment, please pass this information along to the teen services librarian. This information is useful to us in collection development, the future development of programs, and the development of research aids such as pathfinders and booklists.

- If a teacher, school, or organization calls inquiring for services we do not currently offer, these requests will be evaluated on a case-by-case scenario depending on time and resources. Please refer these calls to the teen services librarian.

Appendix B
Your teen volunteer plan

by Karen Jensen

THE BASICS of a teen volunteer program:

1. Be sure to have a clearly outlined application in place. Because you are dealing with minors, you'll want to consult with your library's legal consultant while putting your application together. It will include basic information like name, age, and contact information, but you'll also want to include specific guidelines that you want the teens to understand about the agreement they are entering into with the library. I recommend putting a part on your application that clearly outlines the library's expectations of the teen volunteer. It includes things like "You can't wear explicit T-shirts" to "No texting while you are 'on the clock.'" Make sure you have clearly outlined expectations for both staff and your teen volunteers.

2. Get an email address and make this your primary means of communicating with your teens. It's easier to email 54 teens than to try and call them all, and it means you have a "paper" trail should any issues arise.

3. Have periodic training meetings so that teen volunteers can get to know one another, you can make sure everything is running smoothly, and everyone is happy, etc.

4. To keep the program running smoothly, have one primary contact person and one alternate contact person from library staff. I have a backup in case a teen calls off on a day or time that I am not there. Having a primary contact helps minimize confusion, miscommunication, and mixed messages. Also, it allows teens to build those meaningful relationships with library staff that are so essential to the 40 Developmental Assets.

5. Make sure you have clearly outlined staff expectations. A biggie for me is that I want staff to come to me with any problems or concerns and then let me talk to the teens about it. As I am sure you are aware, some staff are better at dealing and interacting with teens than others, and I want to minimize any potential negative interactions. Flagrant and immediate issues would, of course, require staff to intervene ASAP, but other issues can wait for the teen services librarian to handle.

Having a teen volunteer program can be a great way to help manage the busy season of the summer reading program. You can set up a separate sign-up and prize-redemption area that is staffed by trained teen volunteers and continue to let your circulation staff deal with the business of the circulation desk. This also gives teen volunteers a chance to turn around and be role models to the children who come in and see the teens volunteering at the library.

In addition to manning the summer reading program desk, teen volunteers can do things like check award and best-of lists with the catalog, they can assist with children and teen programming, and they can help do all that cutting and folding and copying and stapling that we seem to spend a lot of time doing.

Be sure to create a method that works for you to have your teens sign in and out, and keep track of the number of hours that you work. Many schools will ask for some type of documentation to verify the service hours. Pick a yearly period to have a teen volunteer recognition party to give thanks and hand out certificates.

Although the teens are volunteers, and you definitely want it to be a fun, rewarding experience, remember that this is a great opportunity to start teaching teens about responsibility, professionalism, and the world of work. With a teen volunteer program, you will find a lot of teachable moments to talk about the business of the library, the life of an adult, and the expectations of the world of work.

Sample outline of a teen volunteer program

Objectives of the program: As part of our service to teens, Sample Library provides teens the opportunity to earn community-service hours through volunteer work. Allowing teens the opportunity to volunteer is mutually beneficial to the teen, the community, and the library. Volunteering gives teens the opportunity to acquire a number of the 40 Developmental Assets (www.search-institute.org), which research has demonstrated helps prevent teens from engaging in high-risk behaviors. In addition, teen volunteers help the library accomplish a lot of basic tasks and engage in successful library programming.

Application process: Teens ages 13–17 can sign up to volunteer by filling out the appropriate form. The form requires teens to consent to adhere to the library's confidentiality standards and waive liability. A parent must also sign in order for an application to be valid.

By signing the form, teens affirm that:

- They will follow all policies, rules, and procedures of the library and those set forth in the application contract.
- They will not consume, use, possess, or be under the influence of drugs or alcohol while volunteering.
- They will represent the library in a professional manner.

The "Volunteen" commitment: As part of their teen volunteer service, the librarian and teens should meet as a group quarterly to reward teens for their service, touch base, and make sure that the lines of communication are kept open. Teens wanting to volunteer must be open to being a part of these quarterly meetings, should their schedules permit.

As "Volunteens," our teen volunteers will be asked to assist in children's and teen programming; review books for the library's various online resources; make copies of library paperwork; cut paper, sharpen pencils, and help prepare various craft supplies; and handle other related duties that may arise.

Some specific elements you may want to address in your teen volunteer contract:

- Cell-phone use
- Dress and shoes
- Language while volunteering
- How you want teen volunteers to address patrons who approach them with questions

- Emergency calls
- Visitation from friends and family while volunteering
- Arranging and recording hours, calling in, how you will handle no-call no-shows

Reporting an issue: Make sure that both teen volunteers and staff have a detailed plan for handling any situations that arise. All parties should report the problem to you so that you can handle it. As noted above, flagrant and immediate issues would require staff to intervene immediately and report the incident afterward.

Appendix C
Your teen-driven program plan
by Karen Jensen

GOALS OF GETTING TEENS involved in programming.

- To expand your services to teens in the community
- To provide innovative, creative teen programming by providing a forum for teens to express themselves and share their talents with their peer group
- To meet the developmental needs of teenagers to express themselves proactively and creatively while utilizing the importance of peer influence and recommendation as a great asset in publicity and promotion
- To use teen interests to promote the library collection and services

Plan

Phase 1: Application of teen participants. Set an application period for teens to submit a program idea regarding a hobby, talent, or experiences they would like to share with others. Teens will have to submit a sample for tangible items, such as crafts, hobbies, etc., or a letter of recommendation for talents, such as singing, acting, etc. Or have them audition privately in a meeting with you.
Needs for this phase:

- Application
- Permission form
- Publicity

Phase 2: Programs for teens presented by teens. From these applicants, pick teens to present a program. Meet at least once with all presenters before the program to make sure they have it all together, and go over any ground rules (language, length of time, etc.). In addition, you do all publicity and support materials.
Needs for this phase:

- Individual program flyers
- An individual meeting time for each presenter (approximately 30 minutes)
- Program/presentation checklist for each presenter

Appendix D
Marketing resources:
A guide with annotations
by Heather Booth and Karen Jensen

Basic Marketing. www.BasicMarketingIdeas.com.

This resource is for all aspects of marketing for small-business owners, who, like librarians, don't have a lot of extra time and are likely not trained marketing professionals.

Dempsey, Kathy. *The Accidental Library Marketer*. Medford, N.J.: Information Today, 2009. themwordblog.blogspot.com.

Just as many of us may be accidental teen librarians, assigned the task without much or any prior training or experience, most teen librarians will, at some point, be tasked with marketing responsibilities. Dempsey understands that this happens and walks readers through the process of becoming familiar with marketing tasks, in addition to the why and how of it all, focusing specifically on library marketing. Dempsey also blogs at themwordblog.blogspot.com, a useful companion and online resource.

Handmadeology—The Science of Handmade. www.handmadeology.com.

Like a small home craft business, teen librarians' success is due, in a large part, to word-of-mouth marketing through our target audience, so we can share many of the same tips. Aimed at those who make and sell items online, Handmadeology includes lots of useful tips on marketing through social media.

Hoff, Brian. "10 Common Typography Mistakes." The Design Cubicle. www .thedesigncubicle.com/2008/12/10-common-typography-mistakes.

In a brief online article, Hoff points out common errors of typography. Although many of them seem basic, this article is a useful reminder to look at our documents and publications with fresh eyes before sending them on to our teens.

I Love Typography. ilovetypography.com.

This is an excellent glimpse into the diverse world of typography for those of us who have not studied design and marketing. Typography decisions are all around us, and this blog points that out in, as one would expect, a clear, visually appealing format.

Krause, Jim. *Design Basics Index*. Cincinnati, Ohio: How Design Books, 2004.

Jim Krause is the author of several useful books in this index series on layout, type, color, and design basics. Anyone looking for a more detailed understanding of how these components work together would be well served by his books, in particular *Design Basics*.

The Library Marketing Toolkit. www.librarymarketingtoolkit.com.

Collaboratively run, with contributors with both library and marketing backgrounds, this blog provides practical resources.

Marketing the Library. www.olc.org/marketing.

The Ohio Library Council's project is as described. This is a training tool for librarians and a marketing resource specifically for libraries.

Smallwood, Carol, et al. *Marketing Your Library: Tips and Tools That Work.* Jefferson, N.C.: McFarland, 2012.

Focusing on case studies, this is a handy guide as you begin to create or expand on your teen library marketing efforts.

South Jersey Regional Library Cooperative, Trading Spaces: Reinventing the Library Environment. www.sjrlc.org/tradingspaces/.

Particularly informative on issues of organizing space and addressing issues of merchandising.

Typography Daily. typography-daily.com.

Visit Typography Daily, another typography-focused blog, for musings and reflections on design decisions as well as lots of inspiration and font suggestions.

Vasile, Christian. "Graphic Design Basics: Parts 1, 2, and 3." 1st Web Designer. www.1stwebdesigner.com/design/graphic-design-basics-elements/
www.1stwebdesigner.com/design/graphic-design-basics-design-principles/
www.1stwebdesigner.com/design/graphic-design-basics-part-3-composition/

A useful primer, this three-part article walks the reader through understanding design elements, how the various elements work together, and how to use them effectively. Visual examples clearly illustrate his points, and the articles should be read in order for the best effect.

Contributors

Amy Alessio has enjoyed the advice of teens in programs for more than 17 years in her work as an award-winning librarian at the Schaumburg (Ill.) Township Library. She has a degree in criminology from the University of Illinois and an MLIS from Dominican University. She reviews teen mysteries for Teenreads .com and *Crimespree Magazine* as well as adult mysteries and romances for *Booklist*. She wrote *Mind-Bending Mysteries and Thrillers for Teens* (ALA Editions, 2014) and coauthored *A Year of Programs for Teens 2* (ALA Editions, 2013) with Kim Patton. Information on her presentations on vintage crafts and cookbooks as well as readers' advisory topics can be found at www.amyalessio.com.

Jeanie Austin received an MLIS from the Graduate School of Library and Information Science at the University of Illinois at Urbana-Champaign. Jeanie's research interests include the power of and access to information and information sharing in radical political movements, and she provided library services for a juvenile detention center from 2009 until 2013. Jeanie was the previous project coordinator for Mix IT Up!, an IMLS-funded project that recruits traditionally underrepresented students to work with underserved youth in a variety of settings (mixituplis.wordpress.com). Jeanie is currently a teen librarian with Oakland (Calif.) Public Library and a PhD student at UIUC.

Naomi Bates is a teacher librarian at Northwest High School in Justin, Texas. She is an active blogger and tweeter as well as a state and national presenter for libraries, both school and public. She believes that relationships are the foundation to any library and librarian and believes it is the strongest connector of books for teens. She was chosen as one of five librarians for the *SLJ*/Gale Cengage Library Leader program in 2010. She was the recipient of the Texas Computer Educator's Association Library Media Specialist of the Year award 2011 and served as the chair of the Texas Association of School Librarians for the Texas Library Association in 2012. She remains active in her state associations and in promoting national library associations. If you can't find her online, she will be behind a book feeding her other passion.

Erinn Batykefer is cofounder and managing editor of the Library as Incubator Project (www.libraryasincubatorproject.org), a website and social-media network that focuses on libraries as incubators for creativity and the arts. She earned both her MFA in writing and her MLIS from the University of Wisconsin–Madison. Her first poetry collection, *Allegheny, Monongahela* (Red Hen Press, 2009), won the Benjamin Saltman Poetry Award, and the poem "Pittsburgh as Self-Portrait" was featured on the Pennsylvania Center for the Book's Public Poetry Project broadsides, which were displayed in coffee shops, libraries, and public transit around the state. Erinn's work focuses on social media, community programming and engagement, and library "makerspaces." She was named a 2014 *Library Journal* Mover and Shaker.

Joni Richards Bodart, internationally known as the leading expert on book-talking, is an associate professor at San Jose State University SLIS, where she is in charge of the Youth Librarianship curriculum. Her first booktalking series from H. W. Wilson, the Booktalk! series, is considered to be the standard in the field. She is also the author of *Radical Reads: 101 Edgy Books for Young Adults* and

Radical Reads 2: Working with the Newest Edgy Novels for Teens, both published by Scarecrow Press. She was awarded the 2010 Scholastic Library Publishing Award (formerly the Grolier Award) for lifetime achievement and excellence in youth librarianship, and her most recent book, *They Suck, They Bite, They Eat, They Kill: The Psychological Meaning of Supernatural Monsters in Young Adult Fiction* (Lanham, Md.: Scarecrow, 2012), analyzes the meaning and uses of supernatural monsters in young adult literature. She is currently working on a companion title, *They Scar, They Hurt, They Hate, They Kill,* on the importance of human monsters (toxic adults or teens) in young adult literature.

Erin Bush has worked with youth as a writing tutor, an alternative school instructor, a school librarian, and currently as a library associate at District of Columbia Public Library in Washington, D.C. Readers' advisory (and especially recommending under-the-radar titles) is her passion, which she shares with readers of YALSA's teen literature blog, The Hub, in the occasional column "Best Books You're Not Reading." In addition to books and libraries, she is interested in alternative learning and can be found on Twitter as @wholenewedu.

Eric Devine is the young adult fiction author of *Dare Me, Tap Out,* and *This Side of Normal.* He is also a high school English teacher and education consultant. Eric married his high school sweetheart, and together they are raising two daughters in upstate New York. He is represented by Kate McKean, of the Howard Morhaim Literary Agency. He can be found on Twitter @eric_devine, facebook. com/ericdevineauthor, and at ericdevine.org.

Christie Ross Gibrich has worked with teens since 2001. She holds a BA from the University of Illinois at Urbana–Champaign and earned her MLS from Texas Woman's University (whose football team is *still* undefeated). She is the senior librarian of the Tony Shotwell Life Center Branch Library, in Grand Prairie, Texas, where she is dedicated to making the library a community center and second home to the tweens, teens, and families in the area. She has been on several committees for YALSA, chaired the Amelia Bloomer Project and the Rainbow List, and has presented at both the Texas Library Association Conference and at the American Library Association Annual Conference. She blogs about anything and everything tween and teen at the Teen Librarian Toolbox.

Francisca Goldsmith has been a librarian for more than 30 years and a book critic for most of that time. She has worked as a reference librarian, teen services coordinator, collection manager, and director of branch services in a variety of library systems, and she has been teaching staff development through the Infopeople Project for more than 10 years. In YALSA, she has served on the inaugural Odyssey Award Committee, the Printz Award Committee, and the Margaret Edwards Award Committee, as well as through two board tenures. She is a frequent contributor to *Booklist* and *School Library Journal,* and she also writes for various other professional journals.

Kelly Milner Halls has spent the past two decades crafting high-interest, well-researched nonfiction for reluctant readers. Tackling topics including dinosaurs, sasquatch, mummies, aliens, ghosts, and others, she has offered credibility and a healthy dose of skepticism to themes popular but mysterious to her target populations. Her books *Albino Animals, Tales of the Cryptids,* and *In Search of Sas-*

quatch have all been named YALSA Quick Picks for Reluctant Readers. *Albino Animals* and *Wild Dogs* were both Orbis Pictus recommended books. She makes her home in Spokane, Washington, with two daughters, two dogs, two cats, and a five-foot rock iguana named Gigantor.

Justin Hoenke is a teen librarian and video-gaming enthusiast who has written about these subjects for publications such as *Library Journal* and *VOYA* and is a regular contributor for the blog Tame the Web. Justin was a member of the 2010 ALA Emerging Leaders class and was named a *Library Journal* Mover and Shaker in March 2013. Justin is currently the teen librarian at the Chattanooga Public Library in Chattanooga, Tennessee. His professional interests include video gaming in libraries, engaging in teen librarianship, creating local collections, and community building. Follow Justin on Twitter at @justinlibrarian, and read his blog at www.justinthelibrarian.com.

Allison Jenkins has worked with teens since 2005. She holds a degree in English literature from the University of North Texas and earned her MLS from Texas Woman's University. For the past five years, she served as the teen services librarian for the Irving (Tex.) Public Library, where she focused on fostering relationships between teens and young adult authors through author visits and teen programs. She recently became a stay-at-home mom to her son, Chase.

Abby Johnson is the children's manager at the New Albany–Floyd County (Ind.) Public Library, where she has worked since 2009. She has written several articles for the *American Libraries* "Youth Matters" column and contributes monthly to the ALSC Blog. You can find her on the web at abbythelibrarian.com, where she has blogged since 2007.

Gretchen Kolderup is a library evangelist, teen advocate, and self-appointed ambassador for YA literature. She received her bachelor's degree in mathematics from Purdue University and her MLS from Indiana University, was the first teen services librarian at the New Canaan (Conn.) Library, and is now the manager of Young Adult Education and Engagement at the New York Public Library. She was the winner of the 2013 YALSA Volunteer of the Year Award and the 2013 YALSA/ABC-CLIO/Greenwood Service to Young Adults Achievement Award. She blogs at www.librarified.net.

Torrey Maldonado is a veteran New York City teacher. Previously, he trained schools to implement mediation programs through the U.S.'s largest victim-services agency. He earned degrees from Vassar and Baruch in sociology and educational administration. Picturing a *Tweens and Teens Conflict-Resolution Manual*, he instead penned a cross-cataloged middle-grade and YA title, *Secret Saturdays*, that the ALA put on its "Quick Picks" and 2013 "Attracting Reluctant Male Readers" book lists. *Secret Saturdays* also was voted the "National Night Out against Violence" book and showcased at New York City librarian conferences for its Common Core State Standards alignment. Learn more about Torrey's efforts in education and literacy at www.torreymaldonado.com.

Casey Rawson is currently a doctoral student in the School of Information and Library Science at the University of North Carolina at Chapel Hill, where she earned an MSLS in 2011. She also holds an MAT in middle-grades education from the University of Louisville and is a former 6th- and 7th-grade science teacher. Her research interests focus on how school librarians can collaborate effectively with teachers in STEM content areas. She has also worked on projects related to diversity in young adult literature, the literacy needs of African American male youth, portrayals of scientists in children's picture books, and gender schemas and IT career choices.

Margaret Redrup-May is a professional librarian with more than 25 years' experience working in a variety of libraries, including school, technical and further education, academic, and public libraries. Margaret's real love in the profession is the public library, where variety is the spice of life, with an interesting mix of customers, resources, and programming. She holds a number of degrees, in education, librarianship, religions, and human-resource management, which either makes her an interesting pub conversationalist or a great singer. Margaret is currently the outreach programs coordinator at Blacktown City Libraries in New South Wales, Australia, serving a very large local government area (where 1 in 70 Australians live). Her team is responsible for children, youth, multicultural, adult, and promotional services within the library service.

Debbie Reese has a doctorate in education from the University of Illinois and is completing an MLIS at San Jose State University. A founder of the Native American House and American Indian studies program at the University of Illinois, she taught American Indian teens at two American Indian boarding schools and is the editor and publisher of the web-based resource, *American Indians in Children's Literature* (americanindiansinchildrensliterature.net). Her chapters and articles have appeared in books and journals used in education and library science. She is tribally enrolled at Nambé Pueblo, New Mexico.

Maggie Hommel Thomann is the reader services manager at the Park Ridge (Ill.) Public Library, where she previously served as young adult librarian. She has worked with youth in various roles, including as a librarian, workshop leader, and instructor at Northwestern University's Center for Talent Development. She is especially interested in teaching teens about new media and technology that they can use in creative ways. She received her MLIS from the University of Illinois at Urbana-Champaign and has written for the *Bulletin of the Center for Children's Books*, *VOYA*, and *School Library Monthly*.

Allison Tran is the teen services librarian for the Mission Viejo Library, in Orange County, California. She is passionate about connecting teens with good books and empowering them with information literacy, technology, and social-media skills. An active YALSA member, she currently manages YALSA's young adult literature blog, The Hub. She also reviews books and apps for *School Library Journal*. Follow Allison on Twitter at @alli_librarian.

Kristin Treviño is a teen services librarian at the Irving (Tex.) Public Library, coordinating YA collection development, programming, and author visits. She received her bachelor's in history from the University of Texas at Arlington and an MLS from the University of North Texas. If you can manage to peek past the massive stacks of books, journals, notebooks, and papers on her desk, you will usually find Kristin designing a new teen book list or bookmark while plotting yet another author visit.

Katherine Trouern-Trend is a youth services librarian at the Hartford (Conn.) Public Library. She is a 2010 graduate of Simmons College GSLIS, in Boston. Katherine's areas of expertise are teen services, family literacy, information literacy, open learning, digital media, and community engagement. Katherine is the current chair of the ALA Ethnic and Multicultural Information Exchange Round Table (EMIERT). She is also a member of YALSA's National Guidelines Oversight Committee and recently chaired YALSA's National Teen Space Guidelines Task Force. Katherine has presented at local and national conferences about digital media and teen services. Follow Katherine on Twitter at @kttrend.

Stacy Vandever Wells earned her MLS from the University of North Texas in 2006 with an emphasis in youth services. She's active in YALSA, sitting on committees and task forces, and serves on the committee for the Young Adult Keller Festival (a teen book festival). She is a book lover at heart and can be found on her blog at girlsinthestacks.com.

Melissa Wheelock-Diedrichs has been a teen librarian since 2003. She received her MLS from Indiana University–Purdue University Indianapolis, and currently works at the Kokomo–Howard County (Ind.) Public Library, where she specializes in teen collection development. She is a member of ALA and the Indiana Library Federation, and she currently serves on the Eliot Rosewater Indiana High School Book Award Committee. In her spare time, she reviews books on her blog, Mel's Books and Info, at bookgirl-mel.blogspot.com.

Index